Oxford
School
Atlas

Editorial Adviser
Dr Patrick Wiegand

OXFORD
UNIVERSITY PRESS

Great Clarendon Street, Oxford OX2 6DP
Oxford University Press is a department of the University of Oxford.
It furthers the University's objective of excellence in research, scholarship,
and education by publishing worldwide in

Oxford   New York
Auckland   Cape Town   Dar es Salaam   Hong Kong   Karachi
Kuala Lumpur   Madrid   Melbourne   Mexico City   Nairobi
New Delhi   Shanghai   Taipei   Toronto

With offices in

Argentina   Austria   Brazil   Chile   Czech Republic   France   Greece
Guatemala   Hungary   Italy   Japan   Poland   Portugal   Singapore
South Korea   Switzerland   Thailand   Turkey   Ukraine   Vietnam

Oxford is a registered trade mark of Oxford University Press
in the UK and in certain other countries

© Oxford University Press 2012

First published 2006
Second edition 2007
Third edition 2012

© Maps copyright Oxford University Press

ISBN 978 0 19 913701 5 (hardback)

ISBN 978 0 19 913702 2 (paperback)

7 9 10 8 6

Printed in Singapore by KHL Printing Co. Pte Ltd

Paper used in the production of this book is a natural, recyclable product
made from wood grown in sustainable forests. The manufacturing process
conforms to the environmental regulations of the country of origin.

Acknowledgements

Illustrations by:
Mark Duffin **p.5** (satellite), **p.7** (compass), **p.72**, **p.73**; Tracey Learoyd **p.78**, **p.79**; Tracey Learoyd and
Adrian Smith **p.10** *and thereafter* (landscape pictograms); ODI **p.27**, **p.86**, **p.87** (population figures)

The publishers would also like to thank the following for permission to reproduce the
following photographs:
p.18 top to bottom: Robert Harding World Imagery/Alamy; The Photolibrary Wales/Alamy;
Geogphotos film/Alamy; Worldwide Picture Library/Alamy; Science Photo Library; **p.19 top to bottom**:
Sinclair Stammers/Science Photo Library; Ric Ergenbright/Corbis; **p.24 top to bottom**: Roger
Antrobus/Corbis; Jon Arnold Images Ltd/Alamy; Denny Rowland/Alamy; Robert Harding Picture Library
Ltd/Alamy; **p.25l**: Daniel Goodings/Shutterstock.com; **p.25 top to bottom**: Back Page Images/Rex
Features; Getty Images; **25bl**: Robert Harding World Imagery/Alamy; **p.30tl**: Sipa Press/Rex Features;
p.30ml: Chuck Pefley/Alamy; **p.30 left to right**: David Young-Wolff/Alamy; N. Cameron/Alamy; Honey
Salvadori/Alamy; allOver photography/Alamy; Robert Harding Picture Library Ltd/Alamy; Ana & Jenny/
Alamy; **p.31 left to right**: Jon Arnold Images Ltd/Alamy; Richard Naude/Alamy; Christian Aslund/Getty;
AFP/Getty Images; **p.37 clockwise from top left**: Lonely Planet Images; Todd Gipstein/Corbis;
Foodfolio/Alamy; Mimmo Frassineti/Rex Features; Getty Images; Spaceborne Imaging Radar-C/X-band
Synthetic Aperture Radar/NASA/Corbis; Bernhard Edmaier/Science Photo Library; Vittoriano Rastelli/
Corbis; **p.42**: NASA/TRMM; MODIS Rapid Response Team at NASA GSFC; **p.43**: A.Piatanesi/Instituto
Nazionale di Geofisica e Vulcanologia, Italy; Digital Globe/Eurimage/Science Photo Library; **p.46**: CNES,
1989 Distribution Spot Image/Science Photo Library; Planetary Visions Ltd/Science Photo Library;
p.47: Lonely Planet Images; X.Zhen -UNEP/Still Pictures; B. Cruickshank/Alamy; Robert Fried/Alamy;
Getty Images; AFP/Getty Images; NASA/GSFC/METI/ERSDAC/JAROS, and U.S./Japan ASTER Science Team;
p.49: DOD Photo/Alamy; Robert Harding Picture Library Ltd/Alamy; Chad Ehlers/Alamy; PhotoLink/
Getty; Lonely Planet Images; Yoshikazu Tsuno/AFP/Getty Images; Korekazu Yashiro/Hard Rain Picture
Library; **p.53**: Chris P./Shutterstock; Ben Radford/Corbis; Hector Conesa/Shutterstock; Pascal Deloche/
Godong/Godong/Corbis; **p.54 top row**: Roger De La Harpe/Gallo Images/Corbis; Lonely Planet Images;

p.54 bottom row: Lonely Planet Images; Still Pictures; Lonely Planet Images; **p.55 top to bottom**: Still
Pictures; Lonely Planet Images; Thomas Mukoya/Reuters/Corbis; Chinch Gryniewicz/Ecoscene/Corbis;
p.60: Ed Young/Corbis; Ed Young/Agstockusa/Science Photo Library; Richard Cummins/Corbis; Lonely
Planet Images; Alamy; Buzz Pictures/Alamy; David Parker/Science Photo Library; Jim Sugar/Corbis;
p.61: Noaa/Science Photo Library; Digital Globe, Eurimage/Science Photo Library; **p.64 top to bottom**:
Lonely Planet Images; Wolfgang Kaehler/Corbis; Sue Cunningham Photographic/Alamy; Anders
Gunnartz/Lineair/Still Pictures; **p.65**: Wolfgang Kaehler/Corbis; Fernando Bueno/Getty; Alamy; Robert
Harding Picture Library Ltd/Alamy; Mireille Vautier/Alamy; Jacques Jangoux/Getty; Mike Goldwater/
Alamy; Paulo Fridman/Alamy; Nasa/Science Photo Library; **p.68**: Nasa/Science Photo Library; G.
Rowell/Corbis; Robert Harding World Imagery; Images Courtesy Ted Scambos, National Snow And Ice
Data Center, University Of Colorado, Boulder, Based On Data From MODIS; **p.69**: Robert Harding
World Imagery; US Geological Survey/Science Photo Library; **p.72**: Worldwide Picture Library/Alamy;
Ken Welsh/Alamy; **p.73**: John Van Hasselt/Corbis; Wildcountry/Corbis; **p.76 top row l-r**: Mediacolor's/
Alamy; Andrew Woodacre/Alamy; Horst Mahr/Photolibrary.com; **p.76 bottom row l-r**: Dave G.
Houser/Corbis; Charles & Josette Lenars/Corbis; **p.77 top row l-r**: David Litschel/Alamy; Jim Steinberg/
Photolibrary.com; **p.77 bottom row l-r**: Staffan Widstrand/Corbis; Egmont Strigl/Photolibrary.com;
Simon Fraser/Science Photo Library; **p.78**: Worldwide Picture Library/Alamy; **p.79**: FLPA/Alamy; David
Parker/Science Photo Library; Lonely Planet Images; **p.81**: PCL/Alamy; SUNNYphotography.com/Alamy;
p.82 top to bottom: Joel Sartore/Getty; Ron Giling/Lineair/Still Pictures; Gordon Wiltsie/Getty;
p.83: Still Pictures; **p.84 top to bottom**: Adrian Arbib/Alamy; Fred Prouser/Reuters/Corbis; H. Tin/Still
Pictures; **p.85**: Richard Cooke/Alamy; AFP/Getty Images

The photographs and illustrations were sourced by Pictureresearch.co.uk

The page design is by Adrian Smith

The publishers are grateful to the following colleagues in geography education for their helpful
comments and advice during the development stages of this atlas: Kirsty Cook,
Karen Elliot, Donna Forrester, Mel Gibson, Geoff Gilbert, Robin Robson, John Ziltener.

2 Contents

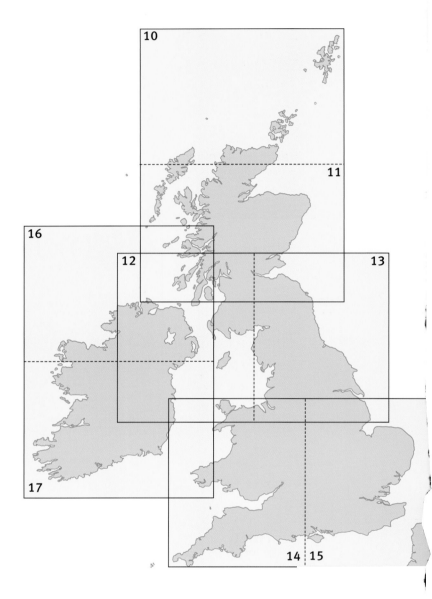

Contents 3

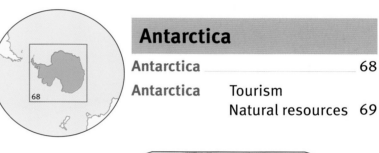

Atlas literacy

Map language

Title —
names the map area

Sub-title —
describes what the map shows

Key (also called a legend)
explains the symbols
used on the map

Scale —
shows how large
the map is.

Scale information
can be shown
- as a statement
- as a ratio (also called
  a representative
  fraction)
- as a scale line

Information panel —
provides extra information,
often about extremes
or records

Map locator
shows where the map
area is on a smaller
scale map

Globe locator
shows where the map
area is on the globe

Comparitor
shows how large the
map area is compared
to the British Isles

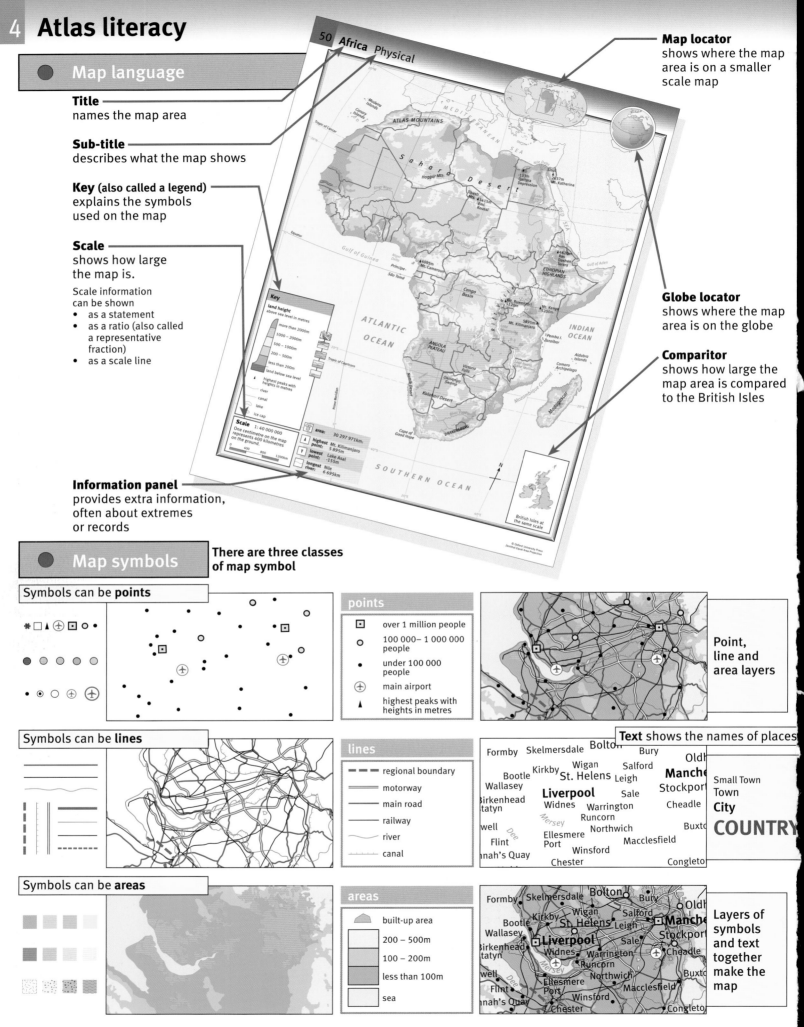

Map symbols

**There are three classes
of map symbol**

Symbols can be **points**

points

⊡	over 1 million people
○	100 000– 1 000 000 people
•	under 100 000 people
⊕	main airport
▲	highest peaks with heights in metres

Point,
line and
area layers

Symbols can be **lines**

lines

- - -	regional boundary
══	motorway
——	main road
——	railway
～	river
╫	canal

Text shows the names of places

Small Town
Town
City
COUNTRY

Symbols can be **areas**

areas

	built-up area
	200 – 500m
	100 – 200m
	less than 100m
	sea

Layers of
symbols
and text
together
make the
map

© Oxford University Press

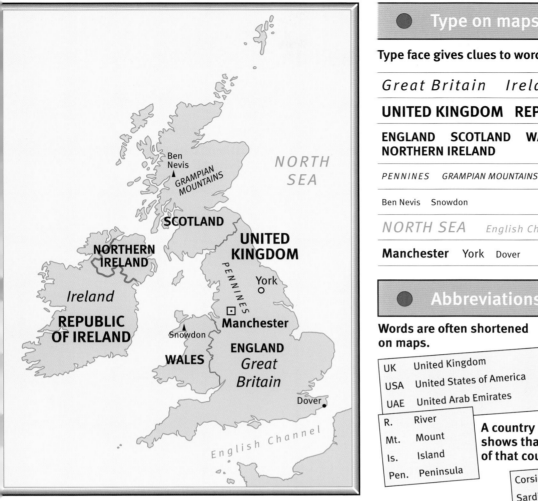

Type on maps

Type face gives clues to word meaning.

Great Britain Ireland	islands
UNITED KINGDOM REPUBLIC OF IRELAND	countries
ENGLAND SCOTLAND WALES NORTHERN IRELAND	parts of the United Kingdom
PENNINES GRAMPIAN MOUNTAINS	physical features
Ben Nevis Snowdon	mountain peaks
NORTH SEA English Channel	sea areas
Manchester York Dover	settlements

Abbreviations and brackets

Words are often shortened on maps.

UK	United Kingdom
USA	United States of America
UAE	United Arab Emirates

R.	River
Mt.	Mount
Is.	Island
Pen.	Peninsula

A country name in brackets shows that a place is part of that country.

Corsica is part of France.

Sardinia is part of Italy.

Satellite images and map styles

Satellite images show radiation from different types of land use on the Earth as colours.

These colours are often very different from those that would be seen on an aerial photograph.

Key

orange	rough pasture
red	forest and woodland
dark blue	urban areas

Topographic maps show the main features of the physical landscape as well as settlements, communications and boundaries.

Key

	land between 200m and 500m
	motorway
⊕	main airport

Thematic maps show information about themes such as geology, climate, tourism and sport.

This map shows population.

Key

	areas with over 250 people per square kilometre
○	cities with between 400 000 and 1 000 000 people
•	towns with between 25 000 and 100 000 people

The Earth is a sphere*.

Two sets of imaginary lines help us describe where places are on the Earth.

All the lines are numbered and some have special names.

* It is actually slightly flattened at the north and south poles.

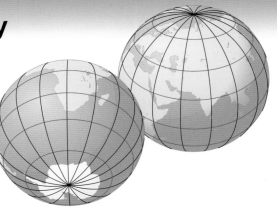

● Longitude

Lines of longitude measure distance east or west. These lines are called **meridians**.

The **Prime Meridian** (also called the Greenwich Meridian) is at longitude 0°.

The **International Date Line** (on the other side of the Earth) is based on longitude 180°.

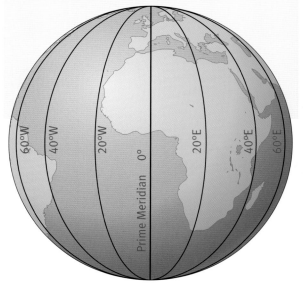

● Latitude

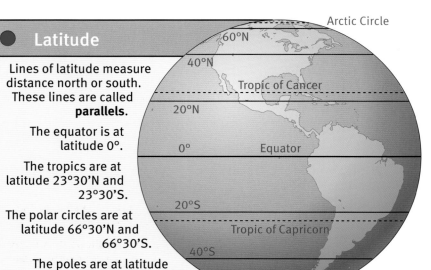

Lines of latitude measure distance north or south. These lines are called **parallels**.

The equator is at latitude 0°.

The tropics are at latitude 23°30'N and 23°30'S.

The polar circles are at latitude 66°30'N and 66°30'S.

The poles are at latitude 90°N and 90°S.

● Map projections

There are many ways of showing the spherical surface of the Earth on a flat map.

Most world maps in this atlas use the Eckert IV projection.

This shows land masses at their correct size in relation to each other but there is some distortion in shape.

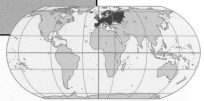

World map used in the United Kingdom.

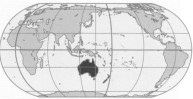

World map used in Australia.

This world map (called an Oblique Aitoff) allows a good view of the northern hemisphere.

● Grid codes

In this atlas, the lines of latitude and longitude are used to make a grid.

The columns of the grid have letters.

The rows of the grid have numbers.

Numbers and letters together make a grid code that can be used to describe where places are on the Earth.

Abuja is in B4   Durban is in C2

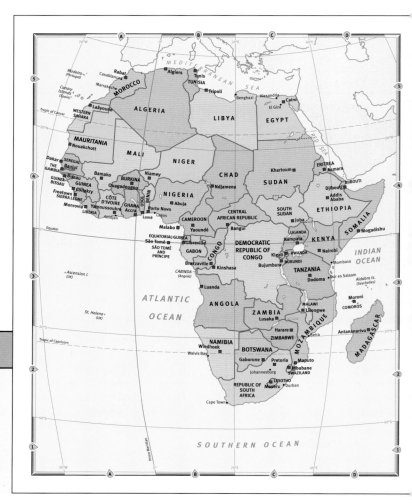

Direction

A compass is used for finding direction.

The needle of a compass always points to magnetic north.

North on atlas maps follows the lines of longitude.

The Earth rotates around an axis that passes through the geographic North and South Poles.

Magnetic North (2005)

ARCTIC OCEAN

North Pole

CANADA

USA (ALASKA)

RUSSIAN FEDERATION (RUSSIA)

GREENLAND

Arctic Circle

ICELAND

NORWAY

SWEDEN

FINLAND

Scale

Maps are much, much smaller than the areas they show. A few centimetres on the map stand for very many kilometres on the ground.

This map has a ratio (or representative fraction) of 1: 55 000 000. The map is 55 million times smaller than the area it shows.

Scale 1: 55 000 000

Thar Desert

HIMALAYA 8848m

River Indus

River Ganges

The Gulf

ARABIAN SEA

Deccan

Bay of Bengal

Socotra

Laccadive Islands

Mouths of the Ganges

Each division on the scale line is one centimetre.

The scale line shows how many kilometres are represented by one centimetre.

| 0 | 550 | 1100 | 1650km |

0 1 2 3 4 5 6
CENTIMETRES

GRAMPIAN MOUNTAINS

Pitlochry

Ben Lawers 1214m

Crieff

Perth

Sidlaw Hills

Dundee

Ben Lomond 974m

Glenrothes

Stirling

Dunfermline

Kirkintilloch

Glasgow

Edinburgh

Loch Earn

Loch Lomond

Firth of Forth

Tay

Scale One centimetre on the map represents **25 kilometres** on the ground.

0 25 50 75km

The distance between Glenrothes and Dunfermline is about 25km

NORTHWEST HIGHLANDS

Inverness

Loch Ness

Cairngorms

Spey

Dee

Aberdeen

1344m Ben Nevis

GRAMPIAN MOUNTAINS

Perth

Dundee

Tay

Loch Lomond

Glasgow

Edinburgh

Firth of Forth

Firth of Clyde

Clyde

SOUTHERN UPLANDS

Scale One centimetre on the map represents **50 kilometres** on the ground.

0 50 100 150km

The distance between Perth and Edinburgh is about 50km

Orkney Islands

Cape Wrath

Outer Hebrides

NORTHWEST HIGHLANDS

Spey

Dee

GRAMPIAN MOUNTAINS

Dundee

Firth of Forth

Glasgow

Edinburgh

SOUTHERN UPLANDS

North Channel

Belfast

Isle of Man

Lake District

PENNINES

Tees

UNITED KINGDOM

Scale One centimetre on the map represents **100 kilometres** on the ground.

0 100 200 300km

The distance between Glasgow and Dundee is about 100km

Larger scale smaller area more detail

Smaller scale larger area less detail

HONDURAS
Tegucigalpa
NICARAGUA
Managua
San José
COSTA RICA
PANAMA
Panama City

ST. VINCENT AND THE GRENADINES
ST. LUCIA
BARBADOS
GRENADA
TRINIDAD AND TOBAGO

Caracas

VENEZUELA
Georgetown
GUYANA
SURINAME
Paramaribo
Cayenne
French Guiana (France)

Bogotá

COLOMBIA

Equator

Quito

ECUADOR

PERU
Lima

BRAZIL

La Paz
BOLIVIA
Brasília

PARAGUAY
Asunción

Santiago
CHILE
Buenos Aires
ARGENTINA
URUGUAY
Montevideo

Falkland Islands (UK)

On world maps the scale is only true along the equator.

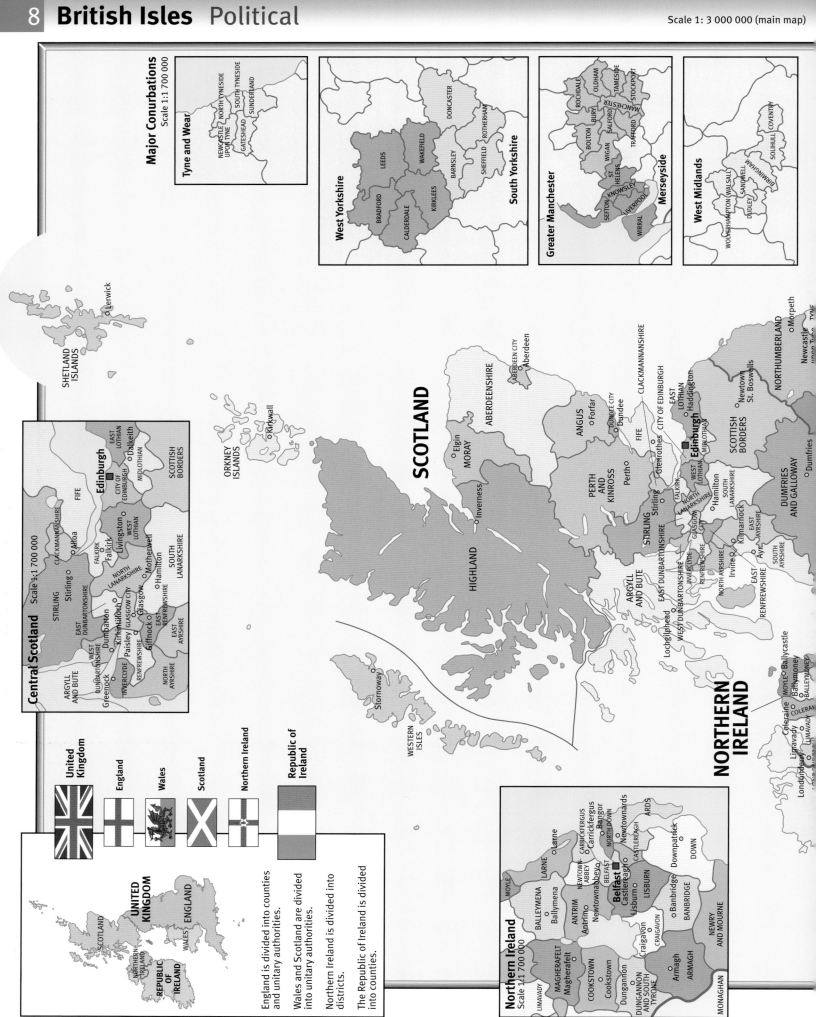

Major Conurbations
Scale 1:1 700 000

Tyne and Wear

NEWCASTLE UPON TYNE · NORTH TYNESIDE · SOUTH TYNESIDE · GATESHEAD · SUNDERLAND

West Yorkshire

LEEDS · WAKEFIELD · BRADFORD · CALDERDALE · KIRKLEES · DONCASTER · BARNSLEY · SHEFFIELD · ROTHERHAM

South Yorkshire

Greater Manchester

ROCHDALE · OLDHAM · BURY · MANCHESTER · TAMESIDE · STOCKPORT · BOLTON · SALFORD · TRAFFORD · WIGAN · ST HELENS · KNOWSLEY · SEFTON · LIVERPOOL · WIRRAL

Merseyside

West Midlands

WOLVERHAMPTON (WALSALL) · SANDWELL · DUDLEY · BIRMINGHAM · SOLIHULL · COVENTRY

Central Scotland Scale 1:1 700 000

Edinburgh · EAST LOTHIAN · Dalkeith · CITY OF EDINBURGH · MIDLOTHIAN · SCOTTISH BORDERS · FIFE · CLACKMANNANSHIRE · Alloa · FALKIRK · Falkirk · WEST LOTHIAN · Livingston · Motherwell · NORTH LANARKSHIRE · Hamilton · SOUTH LANARKSHIRE · STIRLING · Stirling · EAST DUNBARTONSHIRE · Dumbarton · Kirkintilloch · Paisley · Glasgow · GLASGOW CITY · EAST RENFREWSHIRE · Giffnock · EAST AYRSHIRE · ARGYLL AND BUTE · WEST DUNBARTONSHIRE · Greenock · INVERCLYDE · RENFREWSHIRE · NORTH AYRSHIRE

Lerwick

SHETLAND ISLANDS

Kirkwall

ORKNEY ISLANDS

ABERDEEN CITY · Aberdeen

ABERDEENSHIRE

SCOTLAND

Elgin · MORAY

ANGUS · Forfar

DUNDEE CITY · Dundee

FIFE · CITY OF EDINBURGH

PERTH AND KINROSS · Perth

Glenrothes

Edinburgh · EAST LOTHIAN · Haddington

WEST LOTHIAN · MIDLOTHIAN

SCOTTISH BORDERS

Newtown St. Boswells

NORTHUMBERLAND · Morpeth

Newcastle upon Tyne · TYNE

Inverness

HIGHLAND

STIRLING · Stirling · FALKIRK · Falkirk · NORTH LANARKSHIRE · Hamilton · SOUTH LANARKSHIRE

GLASGOW CITY · Hamilton

ARGYLL AND BUTE · EAST DUNBARTONSHIRE · WEST DUNBARTONSHIRE · Lochgilphead · INVERCLYDE · Irvine · Kilmarnock · EAST AYRSHIRE · Ayr · SOUTH AYRSHIRE · NORTH AYRSHIRE · RENFREWSHIRE · EAST RENFREWSHIRE

DUMFRIES AND GALLOWAY · Dumfries

Stornoway

WESTERN ISLES

NORTHERN IRELAND

Coleraine · MOYLE · Ballycastle · Ballymoney · BALLYMONEY

Limavady · COLERAINE

LIMAVADY

Londonderry

United Kingdom

England

Wales

Scotland

Northern Ireland

Republic of Ireland

England is divided into counties and unitary authorities.

Wales and Scotland are divided into unitary authorities.

Northern Ireland is divided into districts.

The Republic of Ireland is divided into counties.

United Kingdom

SCOTLAND

NORTHERN IRELAND

WALES

ENGLAND

REPUBLIC OF IRELAND

Northern Ireland Scale 1:1 700 000

Larne · LARNE · CARRICKFERGUS · Carrickfergus · Bangor · NORTH DOWN · Newtownards · ARDS

MOYLE

BALLYMENA · Ballymena · ANTRIM · Antrim · NEWTOWN-ABBEY · Newtownabbey · NEWTOWNARDS · CASTLEREAGH · Castlereagh · Belfast · BELFAST · Lisburn · LISBURN · Downpatrick · DOWN · Banbridge · BANBRIDGE

MAGHERAFELT · Magherafelt · COOKSTOWN · Cookstown · Dungannon · DUNGANNON AND SOUTH TYRONE · Craigavon · CRAIGAVON · Armagh · ARMAGH · NEWRY AND MOURNE

LIMAVADY · MONAGHAN

© Oxford University Press

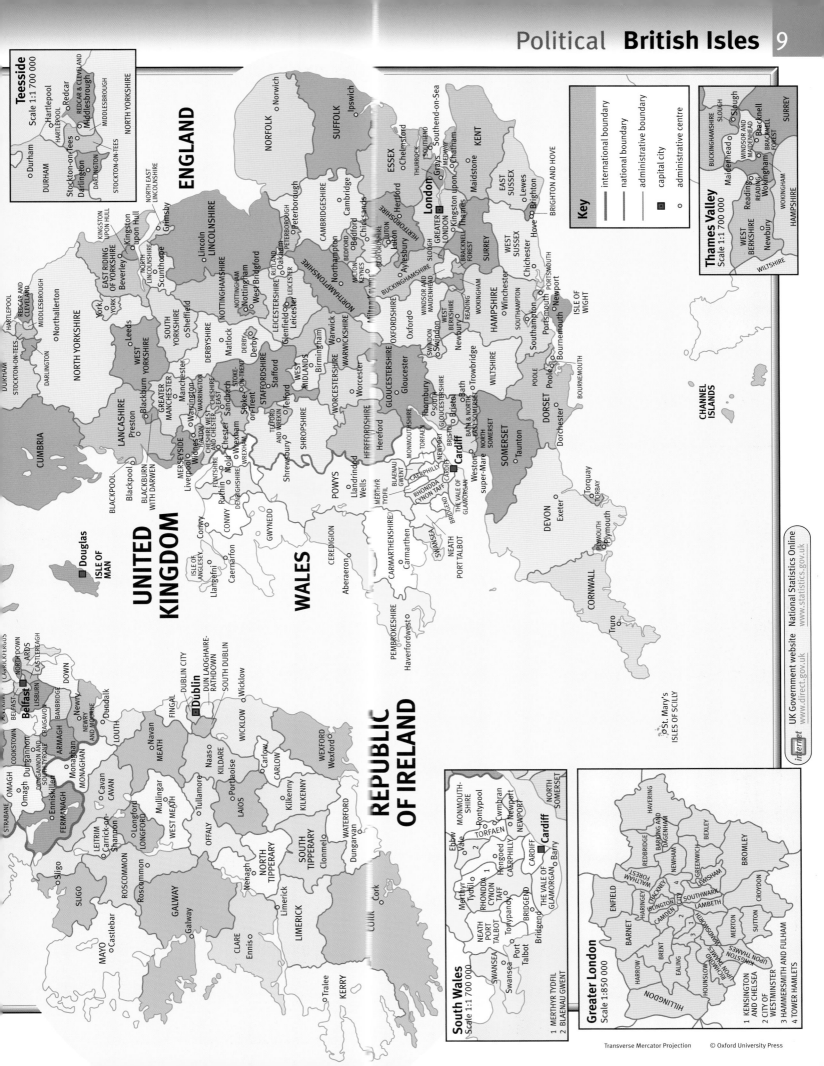

Teesside Scale 1:1 700 000

- Hartlepool / HARTLEPOOL
- Stockton-on-Tees
- Durham / DURHAM
- Darlington / DARLINGTON / STOCKTON-ON-TEES
- Redcar / REDCAR & CLEVELAND
- Middlesbrough / MIDDLESBROUGH
- NORTH YORKSHIRE

Thames Valley Scale 1:1 700 000

- BUCKINGHAMSHIRE
- Maidenhead / Slough / SLOUGH
- WINDSOR AND MAIDENHEAD
- Bracknell / BRACKNELL FOREST / WOKINGHAM
- SURREY
- Reading / READING / Wokingham
- WEST BERKSHIRE / Newbury
- HAMPSHIRE
- WILTSHIRE

Key
- international boundary
- national boundary
- administrative boundary
- ■ capital city
- ○ administrative centre

ENGLAND

NORFOLK ○ Norwich
SUFFOLK ○ Ipswich
○ Southend-on-Sea
ESSEX ○ Chelmsford
THURROCK
Grays ○ Chatham / MEDWAY
London ■ Maidstone
GREATER LONDON
Kingston upon Thames KENT
CAMBRIDGESHIRE
Cambridge ○
Hertford ○ HERTFORDSHIRE
EAST SUSSEX ○ Lewes
○ Brighton / BRIGHTON AND HOVE
WEST SUSSEX ○ Chichester
Chichester

NORTH EAST LINCOLNSHIRE
NORTH LINCOLNSHIRE
Scunthorpe ○
Grimsby
Kingston upon Hull / KINGSTON UPON HULL
Beverley ○ EAST RIDING OF YORKSHIRE
○ Lincoln / LINCOLNSHIRE
PETERBOROUGH ○ Peterborough
○ Oakham / RUTLAND
NORTHAMPTONSHIRE ○ Northampton
BEDFORD ○ Bedford
MILTON KEYNES
Luton / LUTON
Aylesbury ○ BUCKINGHAMSHIRE
OXFORDSHIRE ○ Oxford
WINDSOR AND MAIDENHEAD
WEST BERKSHIRE ○ Reading / READING
WOKINGHAM
HAMPSHIRE ○ Winchester
SURREY
○ Southampton / SOUTHAMPTON
Portsmouth / PORTSMOUTH
Newport ○ ISLE OF WIGHT

NORTH YORKSHIRE
York ○ YORK
Leeds ○ WEST YORKSHIRE
SOUTH YORKSHIRE ○ Sheffield
Nottingham ○ NOTTINGHAMSHIRE
○ Nottingham
DERBYSHIRE
Matlock ○ ○ Derby / DERBY
LEICESTERSHIRE
Glenfield ○ ○ Leicester / LEICESTER
○ West Bridgford

CUMBRIA
LANCASHIRE
Preston ○
BLACKBURN WITH DARWEN
Blackburn ○
Blackpool ○ BLACKPOOL
GREATER MANCHESTER
Manchester ○
MERSEYSIDE
Liverpool ○
HALTON Widnes ○ Warrington / WARRINGTON
CHESHIRE WEST AND CHESTER / CHESHIRE EAST
Chester ○
Sandbach
Stoke-on-Trent / STOKE-ON-TRENT
STAFFORDSHIRE ○ Stafford
Telford / TELFORD AND WREKIN
SHROPSHIRE ○ Shrewsbury
WEST MIDLANDS ○ Birmingham
WARWICKSHIRE ○ Warwick
WORCESTERSHIRE ○ Worcester
○ Hereford / HEREFORDSHIRE
GLOUCESTERSHIRE ○ Gloucester
Thornbury
SOUTH GLOUCESTERSHIRE
Bristol ○ BRISTOL
BATH & NORTH EAST SOMERSET ○ Bath
NORTH SOMERSET
Weston-super-Mare ○
SOMERSET ○ Taunton
DEVON
Exeter ○
Torquay ○ TORBAY
PLYMOUTH
Plymouth ○
CORNWALL
Truro ○

WILTSHIRE
SWINDON ○ Swindon
Newbury
WEST BERKSHIRE
POOLE
Poole ○
Bournemouth ○ BOURNEMOUTH
DORSET ○ Dorchester

WALES
ISLE OF ANGLESEY
Llangefni ○
Caernarfon ○ GWYNEDD
CONWY ○ Conwy
DENBIGHSHIRE ○ Ruthin
FLINTSHIRE ○ Mold
WREXHAM ○ Wrexham
CEREDIGION ○ Aberaeron
POWYS ○ Llandrindod Wells
CARMARTHENSHIRE ○ Carmarthen
PEMBROKESHIRE ○ Haverfordwest
SWANSEA ○ Swansea
NEATH PORT TALBOT
BLAENAU GWENT
MERTHYR TYDFIL
RHONDDA CYNON TAFF
CAERPHILLY ○
TORFAEN
MONMOUTHSHIRE
Newport / NEWPORT
Cardiff ■ CARDIFF
BRIDGEND ○ Bridgend
THE VALE OF GLAMORGAN

UNITED KINGDOM

■ Douglas
ISLE OF MAN

NORTHERN IRELAND / Belfast area labels:
STRABANE
OMAGH ○ Omagh
FERMANAGH ○ Enniskillen
COOKSTOWN ○ Cookstown
DUNGANNON AND SOUTH TYRONE
MAGHERAFELT
ARMAGH ○ Armagh
CRAIGAVON
BANBRIDGE ○ Banbridge
NEWRY AND MOURNE ○ Newry
DOWN
ANTRIM
BALLYMENA
LARNE
CARRICKFERGUS
NEWTOWNABBEY
NORTH DOWN
ARDS
CASTLEREAGH
LISBURN
BELFAST ■ Belfast

REPUBLIC OF IRELAND

MAYO ○ Castlebar
SLIGO ○ Sligo
LEITRIM ○ Carrick-on-Shannon
ROSCOMMON ○ Roscommon
LONGFORD ○ Longford
CAVAN ○ Cavan
MONAGHAN ○ Monaghan
LOUTH ○ Dundalk
MEATH ○ Navan
FINGAL
DUBLIN CITY ■ Dublin
DUN LAOGHAIRE-RATHDOWN
SOUTH DUBLIN
WICKLOW ○ Wicklow
KILDARE ○ Naas
WEST MEATH ○ Mullingar
OFFALY ○ Tullamore
LAOIS ○ Portlaoise
CARLOW ○ Carlow
KILKENNY ○ Kilkenny
WEXFORD ○ Wexford
GALWAY ○ Galway
CLARE ○ Ennis
LIMERICK ○ Limerick
NORTH TIPPERARY ○ Nenagh
SOUTH TIPPERARY ○ Clonmel
WATERFORD ○ Dungarvan
KERRY ○ Tralee
CORK ○ Cork

CHANNEL ISLANDS

St. Mary's
ISLES OF SCILLY

South Wales Scale 1:1 700 000

- Merthyr Tydfil
- RHONDDA CYNON TAFF
- MONMOUTHSHIRE
- Pontypool
- EBBW VALE
- Cwmbran
- TORFAEN
- Hengoed
- CAERPHILLY
- Newport / NEWPORT
- NORTH SOMERSET
- NEATH PORT TALBOT
- Swansea / SWANSEA
- Port Talbot
- Torpyandy
- BRIDGEND
- Bridgend
- CARDIFF
- Cardiff ■
- THE VALE OF GLAMORGAN
- Barry ○

1 MERTHYR TYDFIL
2 BLAENAU GWENT

Greater London Scale 1:850 000

- ENFIELD
- BARNET
- HARINGEY
- WALTHAM FOREST
- REDBRIDGE
- HAVERING
- BARKING AND DAGENHAM
- NEWHAM
- HACKNEY
- ISLINGTON
- CAMDEN
- BRENT
- HARROW
- HILLINGDON
- EALING
- HOUNSLOW
- RICHMOND UPON THAMES
- KINGSTON UPON THAMES
- MERTON
- WANDSWORTH
- LAMBETH
- SOUTHWARK
- TOWER HAMLETS
- GREENWICH
- LEWISHAM
- BEXLEY
- BROMLEY
- CROYDON
- SUTTON

1 KENSINGTON AND CHELSEA
2 CITY OF WESTMINSTER
3 HAMMERSMITH AND FULHAM
4 TOWER HAMLETS

Transverse Mercator Projection   © Oxford University Press

UK Government website   National Statistics Online
www.direct.gov.uk   www.statistics.gov.uk
internet

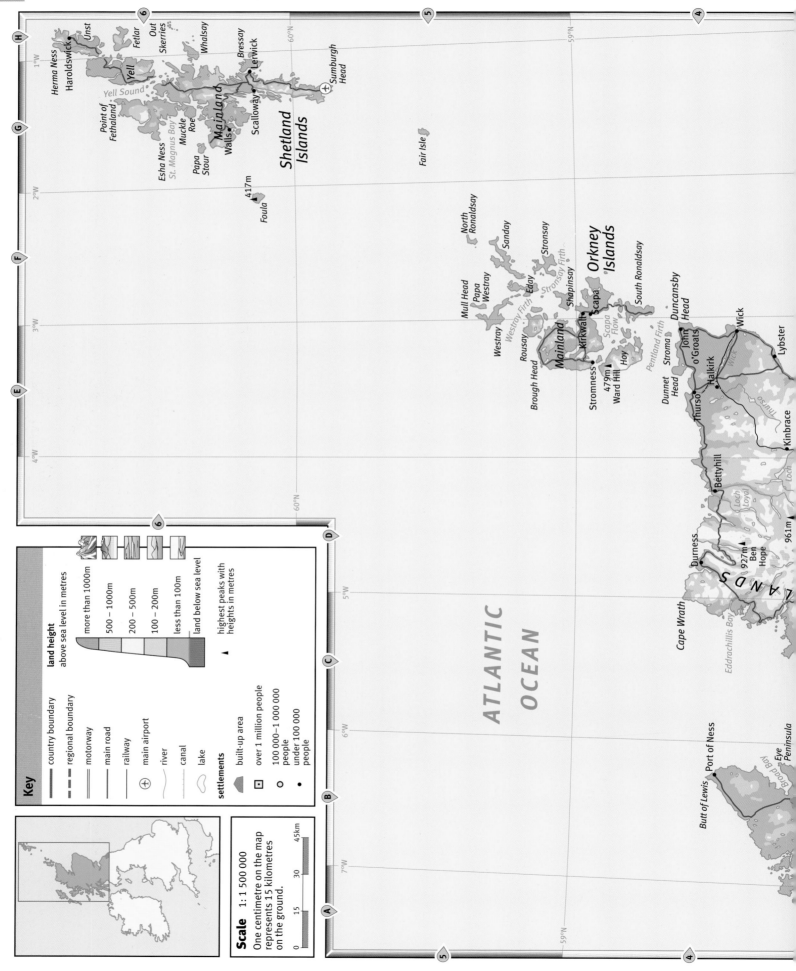

Herma Ness
Unst
Fetlar
Out Skerries
Haroldswick
Whalsay
Bressay
Yell
Lerwick
Yell Sound
Scalloway
Point of Fethaland
Mainland
Muckle Roe
Walls
Esha Ness
St. Magnus Bay
Papa Stour
Shetland Islands
Sumburgh Head

417m
Foula

Fair Isle

North Ronaldsay
Sanday
Stronsay
Mull Head
Papa Westray
Eday
Shapinsay
Stronsay Firth
Orkney Islands
Westray
Westray Firth
Rousay
Shapinsay
Scapa
South Ronaldsay
Kirkwall
Brough Head
Mainland
Scapa Flow
Duncansby Head
Wick
Stromness
479m
Ward Hill
Hoy
Pentland Firth
Stroma
John o'Groats
Lybster
Dunnet Head
Halkirk
Wick
Thurso
Kinbrace
Bettyhill
Loch Naver
961m
Durness
927m
Ben Hope
Loch Loyal
LANDS
Cape Wrath
Eddrachillis Bay

ATLANTIC OCEAN

Butt of Lewis
Port of Ness
Broad Bay
Eye Peninsula

Key

land height
above sea level in metres

more than 1000m
500 – 1000m
200 – 500m
100 – 200m
less than 100m
land below sea level

▲ highest peaks with heights in metres

country boundary
regional boundary
motorway
main road
railway
⊕ main airport
river
canal
lake

settlements

■ built-up area
▣ over 1 million people
○ 100 000–1 000 000 people
• under 100 000 people

Scale 1 : 1 500 000

One centimetre on the map represents 15 kilometres on the ground.

0   15   30   45km

Transverse Mercator Projection
© Oxford University Press

NORTH SEA

ENGLAND

© Oxford University Press

Key

─────── country boundary
- - - - - regional boundary
━━━━━━━ motorway
─────── main road
─────── railway
⊕ main airport
river
canal
lake

settlements

built-up area
▣ over 1 million people
○ 100 000–1 000 000 people
• under 100 000 people

land height
above sea level in metres

more than 1000m
500 – 1000m
200 – 500m
100 – 200m
less than 100m
land below sea level
▲ highest peaks with heights in metres

Scale 1: 1 500 000
One centimetre on the map represents 15 kilometres on the ground.

0   15   30   45km

Transverse Mercator Projection
© Oxford University Press

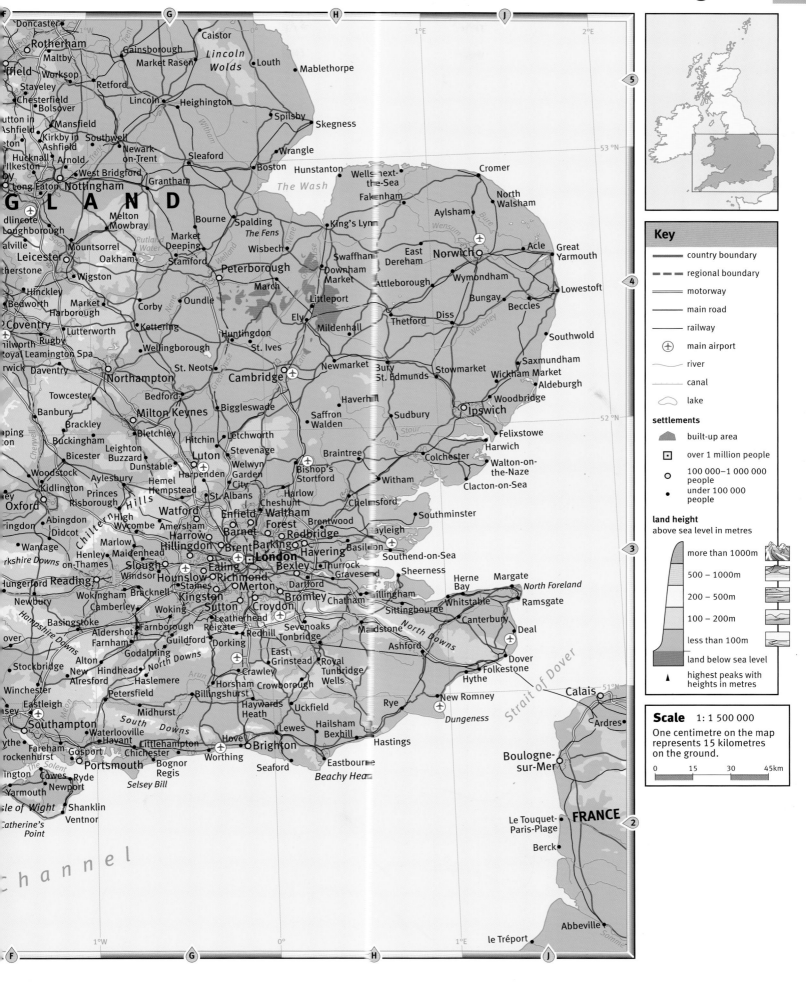

Doncaster
Rotherham
Maltby
ffield Worksop Gainsborough
Staveley Retford Market Rasen
Chesterfield Bolsover Lincoln Heighington
tton in Mansfield Southwell
Ashfield Kirkby in Ashfield
Hucknall Arnold Newark-on-Trent
by Ilkeston West Bridgford
Long Eaton Nottingham Grantham
E N G L A N D Melton Bourne
dlincote Mowbray
alville Loughborough Market Deeping
Leicester Mountsorrel Oakham
herstone Wigston
Hinckley
Bedworth Market Corby
Coventry Harborough Kettering
hilworth Lutterworth Wellingborough
Royal Leamington Spa Daventry Northampton
rwick Towcester Bedford
Banbury Brackley Milton Keynes Biggleswade
ping Buckingham Bletchley
on Bicester Leighton Buzzard Hitchin
Woodstock Aylesbury Dunstable Luton
Kidlington Princes Risborough Harpenden
Oxford High Wycombe Hemel Hempstead Welwyn Garden City
ngdon Abingdon Amersham St. Albans
Didcot Watford
Wantage Marlow Harrow
rkshire Downs Henley on-Thames Maidenhead Hillingdon Brent
Hungerford Reading Slough Ealing London
Newbury Windsor Hounslow Richmond
Wokingham Bracknell Staines Kingston Merton
Basingstoke Camberley Woking Sutton Croydon
over Aldershot Farnborough Leatherhead
Farnham Guildford Reigate Redhill
Alton Godalming Dorking
Stockbridge New Hindhead North Downs East Grinstead
Alresford Haslemere Crawley
Winchester Petersfield Horsham Crowborough Royal Tunbridge Wells
Eastleigh Midhurst Billingshurst
sey South Downs Haywards Heath Uckfield
ythe Waterlooville Havant Lewes
Fareham Littlehampton Hove Hailsham
Gosport Chichester Worthing Brighton Bexhill
rockenhurst Bognor Regis Seaford Eastbourne
The Solent Portsmouth Hastings
ington Cowes Ryde Beachy Head
Yarmouth Newport
sle of Wight Shanklin
Catherine's Ventnor
Point

Caistor
Lincoln Wolds Louth Mablethorpe
Spilsby
Skegness
Wrangle
Boston Hunstanton Wells-next-the-Sea Cromer
Sleaford The Wash North Walsham
Fakenham Aylsham
The Fens Spalding King's Lynn Norwich Acle Great Yarmouth
Wisbech Swaffham East Dereham Wymondham Lowestoft
Rutland Water Stamford Peterborough Downham Market Attleborough Bungay Beccles
March Littleport Thetford Diss Southwold
Oundle Ely Mildenhall
St. Ives Huntingdon Bury St. Edmunds Stowmarket Saxmundham
St. Neots Newmarket Wickham Market Aldeburgh
Cambridge Haverh Woodbridge
Saffron Walden Sudbury Ipswich
Letchworth Stevenage Braintree Felixstowe
Bishop's Stortford Colchester Harwich
Harlow Witham Walton-on-the-Naze
Cheshunt Chelmsford Clacton-on-Sea
Enfield Waltham Forest Brentwood
Barnet Redbridge Southminster
Barking ayleigh Southend-on-Sea
Havering Basildon
Bexley Thurrock
Bromley Gravesend Sheerness Herne Bay Margate
Dartford North Foreland
Chatham Whitstable Ramsgate
illingham Sittingbourne Canterbury
Maidstone North Downs Deal
Sevenoaks Ashford Dover
Tonbridge Folkestone
Hythe
New Romney
Rye
Dungeness Calais
Ardres
Strait of Dover
Boulogne-sur-Mer
FRANCE
Le Touquet-Paris-Plage
Berck
le Trépot
Abbeville

Channel

Key

———	country boundary
– – –	regional boundary
═══	motorway
———	main road
———	railway
⊕	main airport
~~	river
———	canal
⌂	lake

settlements

◢	built-up area
⊡	over 1 million people
○	100 000–1 000 000 people
•	under 100 000 people

land height
above sea level in metres

more than 1000m	
500 – 1000m	
200 – 500m	
100 – 200m	
less than 100m	
land below sea level	
▲	highest peaks with heights in metres

Scale   1: 1 500 000

One centimetre on the map represents 15 kilometres on the ground.

0   15   30   45km

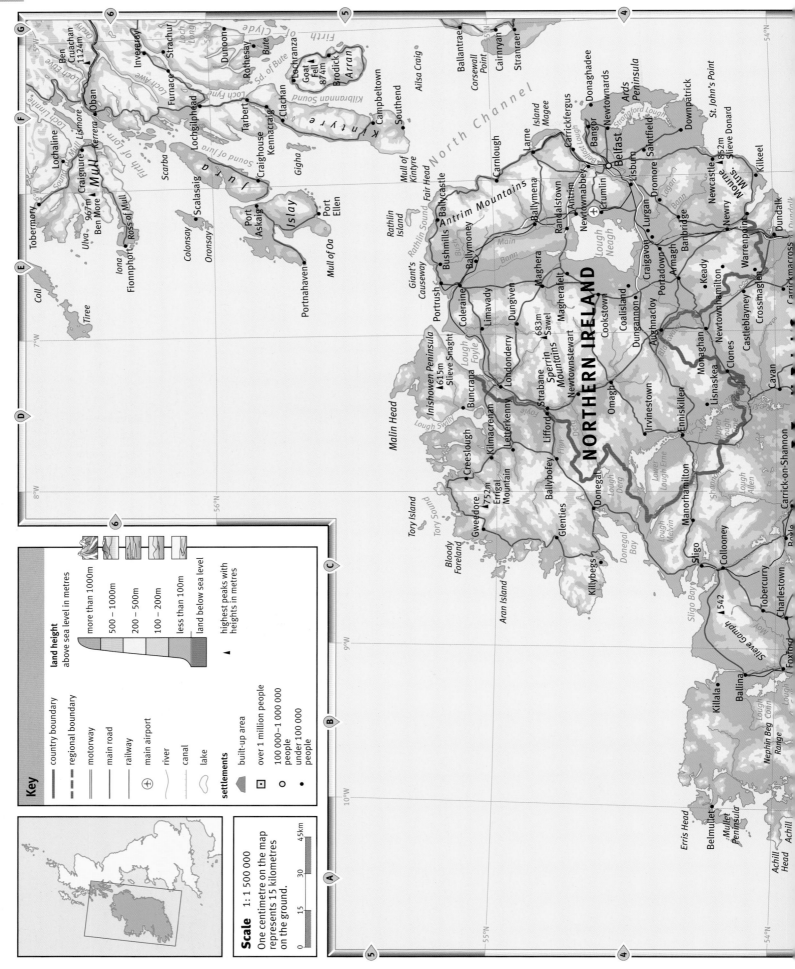

Key

land height
above sea level in metres

- more than 1000m
- 500 – 1000m
- 200 – 500m
- 100 – 200m
- less than 100m
- land below sea level

▲ highest peaks with heights in metres

- country boundary
- regional boundary
- motorway
- main road
- railway
- ⊕ main airport
- river
- canal
- lake

settlements

- built-up area
- ▣ over 1 million people
- ○ 100 000 – 1 000 000 people
- • under 100 000 people

Scale 1 : 1 500 000

One centimetre on the map represents 15 kilometres on the ground.

0   15   30   45km

Transverse Mercator Projection
© Oxford University Press

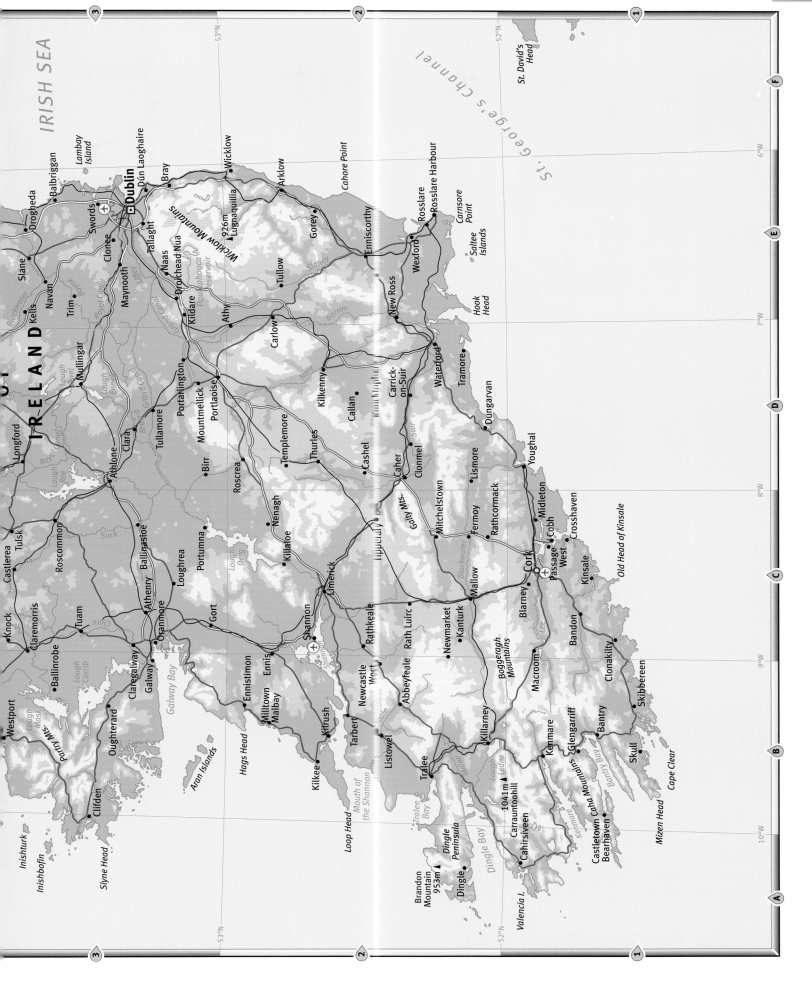

IRISH SEA

St. David's Head

St. George's Channel

IRELAND

Inishturk
Inishbofin
Slyne Head
Clifden
Westport
Patry Mts.
Oughterard
Ballinrobe
Knock
Claremorris
Tuam
Claregalway
Galway
Galway Bay
Aran Islands
Hags Head
Kilkee
Loop Head
Mouth of the Shannon
Kilrush
Milltown Malbay
Ennistimon
Ennis
Shannon
Gort
Oranmore
Athenry
Ballinasloe
Loughrea
Portumna
Lough Derg
Killaloe
Nenagh
Limerick
Rathkeale
Newcastle West
Tarbert
Listowel
Tralee
Tralee Bay
Dingle Peninsula
Brandon Mountain 953m
Dingle
Dingle Bay
Valencia I.
Carrauntoohill 1041m
Cahirsiveen
Carravntooohill
Kenmare
Castletown Bearhaven
Caha Mountains
Glengarriff
Bantry
Bantry Bay
Skull
Cape Clear
Mizen Head
Skibbereen
Clonakilty
Bandon
Kinsale
Old Head of Kinsale
Crosshaven
Cobh
Passage West
Cork
Blarney
Macroom
Killarney
Boggeragh Mountains
Newmarket
Kanturk
Mallow
Rath Luirc
Abbeyfeale
Mitchelstown
Fermoy
Rathcormack
Midleton
Youghal
Lismore
Dungarvan
Tramore
Waterford
Clonmel
Caher
Galty Mts.
Tipperary
Cashel
Callan
Thurles
Templemore
Roscrea
Birr
Athlone
Clara
Tullamore
Mountmellick
Portlaoise
Portarlington
Roscommon
Castlerea
Tulsk
Longford
Lough Ree
Mullingar
Lough Ennell
Lough Owel
Kells
Navan
Trim
Kildare
Athy
Carlow
Kilkenny
Carrick-on-Suir
New Ross
Enniscorthy
Wexford
Rosslare
Rosslare Harbour
Carnsore Point
Saltee Islands
Hook Head
Cahore Point
Gorey
Arklow
Tullow
Wicklow
Wicklow Mountains
Lugnaquillia 926m
Poulaphouca Reservoir
Naas
Droichead Nua
Maynooth
Tallaght
Dublin
Dún Laoghaire
Bray
Clonee
Swords
Slane
Drogheda
Balbriggan
Lambay Island
Slaney
Barrow
Nore
Suir
Blackwater
Lee
Maine
Lough Leane
Kenmare
Grand Canal
Royal Canal
Liffey
Boyne
Blackwater
Suck
Clare
Lough Corrib
Lough Mask

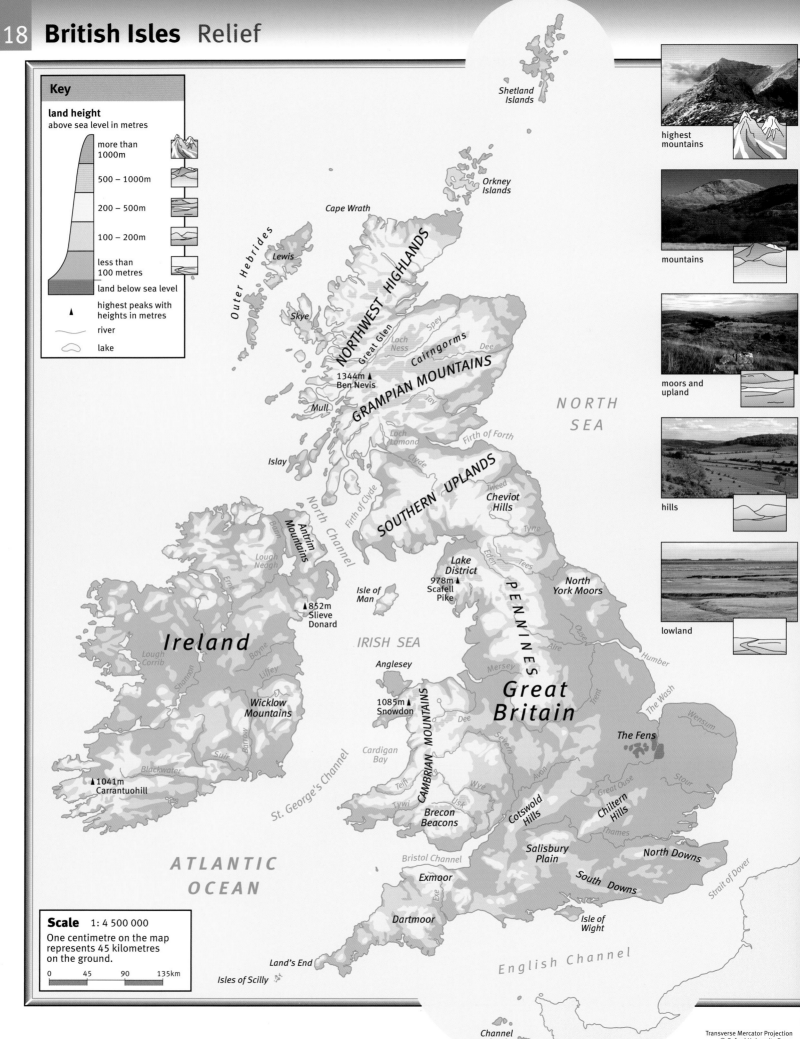

Key

land height
above sea level in metres

more than 1000m

500 – 1000m

200 – 500m

100 – 200m

less than 100 metres

land below sea level

▲ highest peaks with heights in metres

river

lake

highest mountains

mountains

moors and upland

hills

lowland

Shetland Islands

Orkney Islands

Cape Wrath

Outer Hebrides

Lewis

Skye

NORTHWEST HIGHLANDS

Great Glen

Loch Ness

Spey

Cairngorms

Dee

1344m ▲ Ben Nevis

GRAMPIAN MOUNTAINS

Mull

Tay

Islay

Loch Lomond

Firth of Forth

Clyde

Firth of Clyde

SOUTHERN UPLANDS

Tweed

Cheviot Hills

NORTH SEA

North Channel

Antrim Mountains

Bann

Lough Neagh

Erne

Tyne

Eden

Tees

Lake District

978m ▲ Scafell Pike

North York Moors

PENNINES

Isle of Man

▲852m Slieve Donard

Ouse

Aire

Humber

Ireland

Lough Corrib

Shannon

Boyne

Liffey

IRISH SEA

Anglesey

Mersey

Trent

The Wash

Wensum

Wicklow Mountains

Barrow

Suir

Blackwater

1085m ▲ Snowdon

CAMBRIAN MOUNTAINS

Dee

Severn

Great Britain

The Fens

Stour

▲1041m Carrantuohill

St. George's Channel

Cardigan Bay

Teifi

Wye

Usk

Avon

Great Ouse

Chiltern Hills

Tywi

Brecon Beacons

Cotswold Hills

Thames

Salisbury Plain

North Downs

ATLANTIC OCEAN

Bristol Channel

Exmoor

Exe

South Downs

Strait of Dover

Dartmoor

Isle of Wight

Land's End

English Channel

Isles of Scilly

Channel Islands

Scale 1: 4 500 000
One centimetre on the map represents 45 kilometres on the ground.

0   45   90   135km

Transverse Mercator Projection
© Oxford University Press

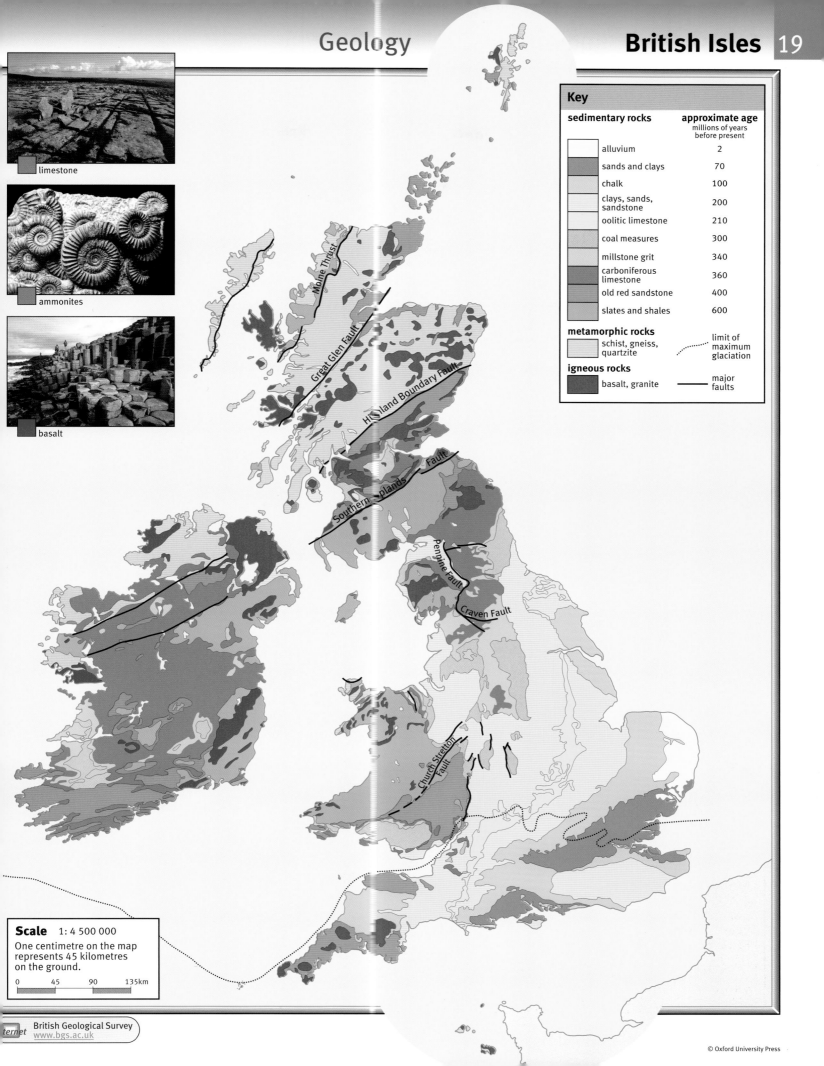

limestone

ammonites

basalt

Key

| sedimentary rocks | | approximate age
millions of years
before present |
|---|---|---|
| | alluvium | 2 |
| | sands and clays | 70 |
| | chalk | 100 |
| | clays, sands, sandstone | 200 |
| | oolitic limestone | 210 |
| | coal measures | 300 |
| | millstone grit | 340 |
| | carboniferous limestone | 360 |
| | old red sandstone | 400 |
| | slates and shales | 600 |

metamorphic rocks

schist, gneiss, quartzite

······ limit of maximum glaciation

igneous rocks

basalt, granite

——— major faults

Moine Thrust

Great Glen Fault

Highland Boundary Fault

Southern Uplands Fault

Pennine Fault

Craven Fault

Church Stretton Fault

Scale   1: 4 500 000
One centimetre on the map
represents 45 kilometres
on the ground.

0   45   90   135km

British Geological Survey
www.bgs.ac.uk

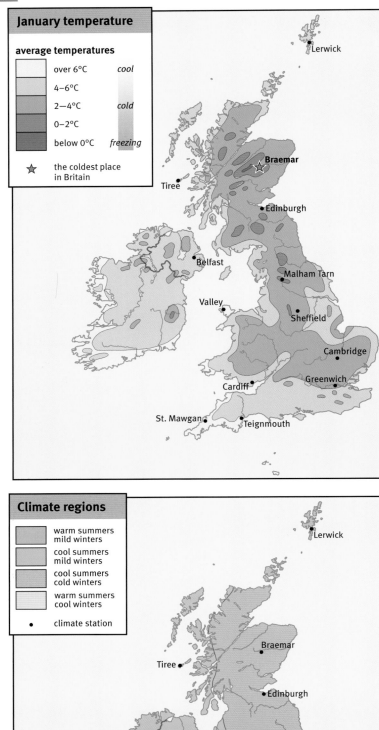

January temperature

average temperatures

over 6°C	*cool*
4–6°C	
2–4°C	*cold*
0–2°C	
below 0°C	*freezing*

★ the coldest place in Britain

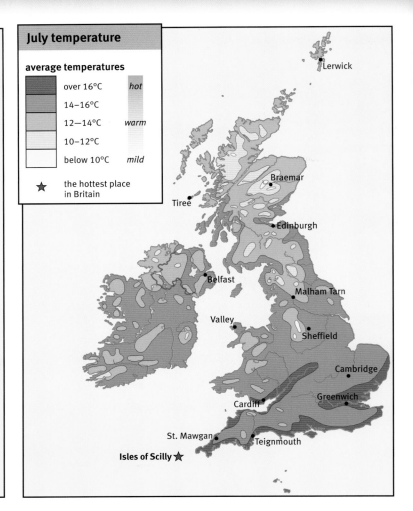

July temperature

average temperatures

over 16°C	*hot*
14–16°C	
12–14°C	*warm*
10–12°C	
below 10°C	*mild*

★ the hottest place in Britain

Isles of Scilly ★

Climate regions

	warm summers mild winters
	cool summers mild winters
	cool summers cold winters
	warm summers cool winters
•	climate station

Climate graphs

for selected British climate stations

average monthly rainfall in milimetres

average monthly temperature in °C

9m height above sea level

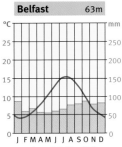

Belfast   63m

annual precipitation 862mm

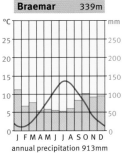

Braemar   339m

annual precipitation 913mm

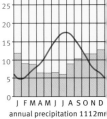

Cambridge   26m

annual precipitation 1112mm

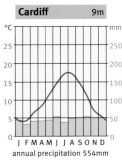

Cardiff   9m

annual precipitation 554mm

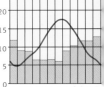

Edinburgh   61m

annual precipitation 676mm

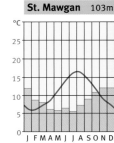

St. Mawgan   103m

annual precipitation 1043cm

internet Met Office
www.metoffice.gov.uk

BBC Weather
www.bbc.co.uk/weather

Transverse Mercator Projection   © Oxford University Press

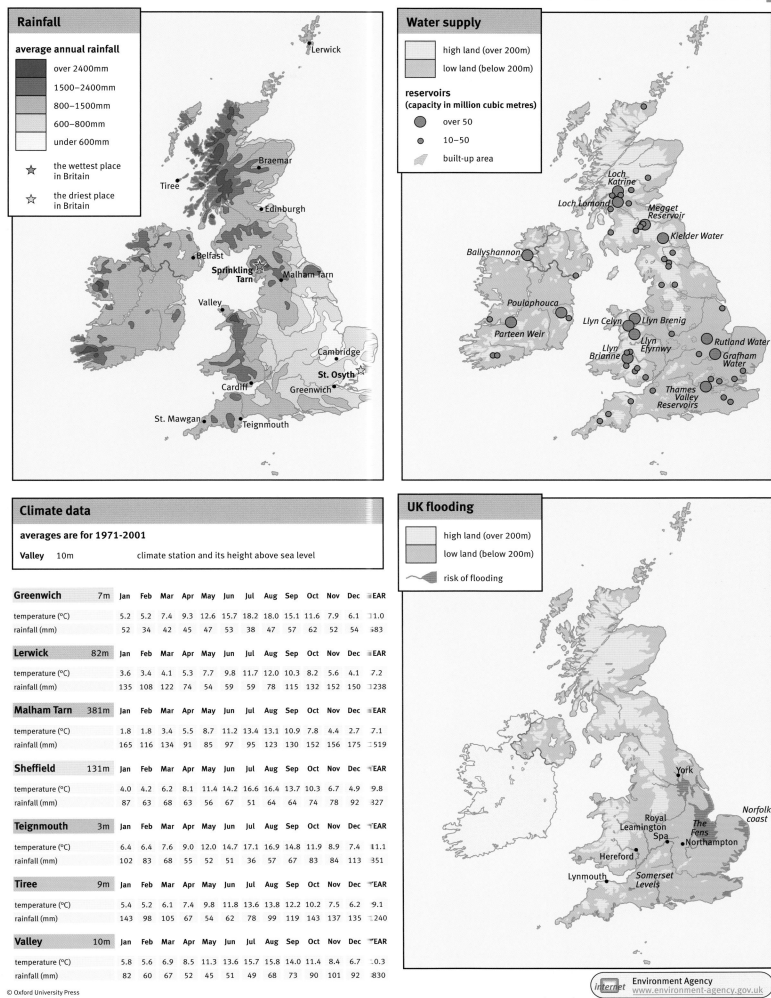

Rainfall

average annual rainfall

- over 2400mm
- 1500–2400mm
- 800–1500mm
- 600–800mm
- under 600mm
- ★ the wettest place in Britain
- ☆ the driest place in Britain

Labels: Lerwick, Braemar, Tiree, Edinburgh, Belfast, Sprinkling Tarn, Malham Tarn, Valley, Cambridge, St. Osyth, Cardiff, Greenwich, St. Mawgan, Teignmouth

Water supply

- high land (over 200m)
- low land (below 200m)

reservoirs (capacity in million cubic metres)

- ● over 50
- ● 10–50
- built-up area

Labels: Loch Katrine, Loch Lomond, Megget Reservoir, Kielder Water, Ballyshannon, Poulaphouca, Parteen Weir, Llyn Celyn, Llyn Brenig, Llyn Brianne, Llyn Efyrnwy, Rutland Water, Grafham Water, Thames Valley Reservoirs

Climate data

averages are for 1971-2001

Valley	10m	climate station and its height above sea level

Greenwich	7m	Jan	Feb	Mar	Apr	May	Jun	Jul	Aug	Sep	Oct	Nov	Dec	YEAR
temperature (°C)		5.2	5.2	7.4	9.3	12.6	15.7	18.2	18.0	15.1	11.6	7.9	6.1	11.0
rainfall (mm)		52	34	42	45	47	53	38	47	57	62	52	54	583

Lerwick	82m	Jan	Feb	Mar	Apr	May	Jun	Jul	Aug	Sep	Oct	Nov	Dec	YEAR
temperature (°C)		3.6	3.4	4.1	5.3	7.7	9.8	11.7	12.0	10.3	8.2	5.6	4.1	7.2
rainfall (mm)		135	108	122	74	54	59	59	78	115	132	152	150	1238

Malham Tarn	381m	Jan	Feb	Mar	Apr	May	Jun	Jul	Aug	Sep	Oct	Nov	Dec	YEAR
temperature (°C)		1.8	1.8	3.4	5.5	8.7	11.2	13.4	13.1	10.9	7.8	4.4	2.7	7.1
rainfall (mm)		165	116	134	91	85	97	95	123	130	152	156	175	1519

Sheffield	131m	Jan	Feb	Mar	Apr	May	Jun	Jul	Aug	Sep	Oct	Nov	Dec	YEAR
temperature (°C)		4.0	4.2	6.2	8.1	11.4	14.2	16.6	16.4	13.7	10.3	6.7	4.9	9.8
rainfall (mm)		87	63	68	63	56	67	51	64	64	74	78	92	827

Teignmouth	3m	Jan	Feb	Mar	Apr	May	Jun	Jul	Aug	Sep	Oct	Nov	Dec	YEAR
temperature (°C)		6.4	6.4	7.6	9.0	12.0	14.7	17.1	16.9	14.8	11.9	8.9	7.4	11.1
rainfall (mm)		102	83	68	55	52	51	36	57	67	83	84	113	851

Tiree	9m	Jan	Feb	Mar	Apr	May	Jun	Jul	Aug	Sep	Oct	Nov	Dec	YEAR
temperature (°C)		5.4	5.2	6.1	7.4	9.8	11.8	13.6	13.8	12.2	10.2	7.5	6.2	9.1
rainfall (mm)		143	98	105	67	54	62	78	99	119	143	137	135	1240

Valley	10m	Jan	Feb	Mar	Apr	May	Jun	Jul	Aug	Sep	Oct	Nov	Dec	YEAR
temperature (°C)		5.8	5.6	6.9	8.5	11.3	13.6	15.7	15.8	14.0	11.4	8.4	6.7	10.3
rainfall (mm)		82	60	67	52	45	51	49	68	73	90	101	92	830

UK flooding

- high land (over 200m)
- low land (below 200m)
- risk of flooding

Labels: York, Royal Leamington Spa, The Fens, Northampton, Norfolk coast, Hereford, Somerset Levels, Lynmouth

internet **Environment Agency** www.environment-agency.gov.uk

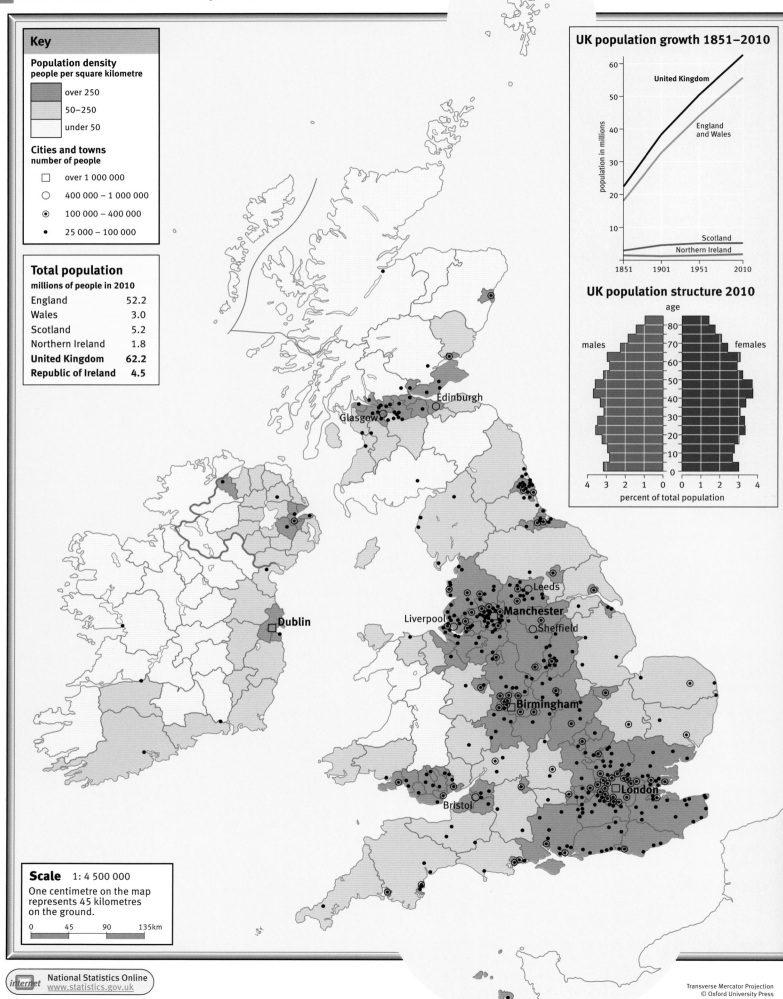

Key

Population density
people per square kilometre

	over 250
	50–250
	under 50

Cities and towns
number of people

□	over 1 000 000
○	400 000 – 1 000 000
◉	100 000 – 400 000
•	25 000 – 100 000

Total population
millions of people in 2010

England	52.2
Wales	3.0
Scotland	5.2
Northern Ireland	1.8
United Kingdom	**62.2**
Republic of Ireland	**4.5**

UK population growth 1851–2010

United Kingdom
England and Wales
Scotland
Northern Ireland

population in millions

1851 1901 1951 2010

UK population structure 2010

age

males   females

percent of total population

Edinburgh
Glasgow

Dublin

Leeds
Liverpool Manchester
Sheffield

Birmingham

Bristol

London

Scale   1: 4 500 000

One centimetre on the map
represents 45 kilometres
on the ground.

0   45   90   135km

National Statistics Online
www.statistics.gov.uk

Transverse Mercator Projection
© Oxford University Press

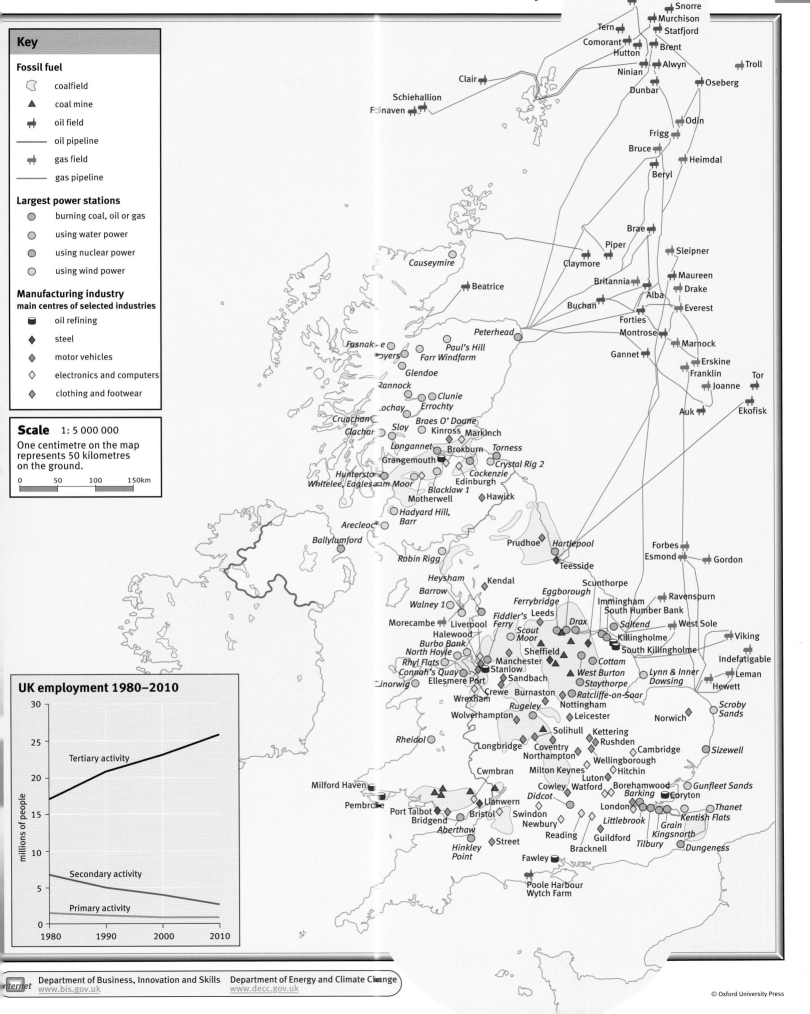

Department of Business, Innovation and Skills www.bis.gov.uk   Department of Energy and Climate Change www.decc.gov.uk

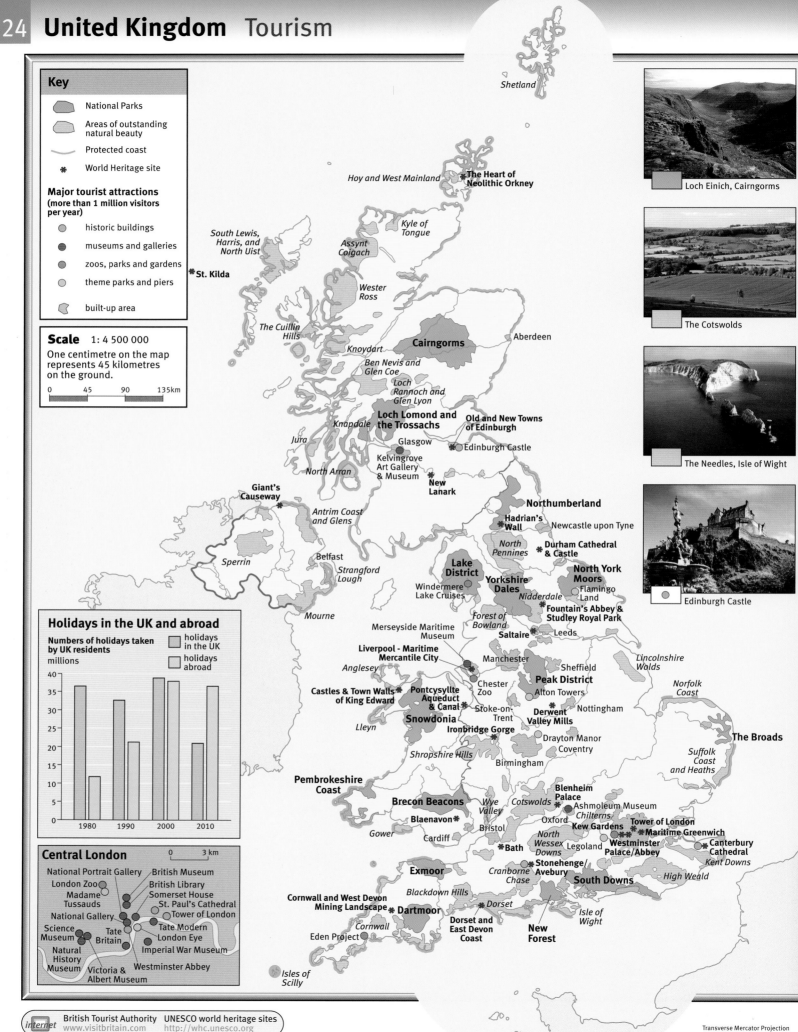

Key

- National Parks
- Areas of outstanding natural beauty
- Protected coast
- World Heritage site

Major tourist attractions
(more than 1 million visitors per year)

- historic buildings
- museums and galleries
- zoos, parks and gardens
- theme parks and piers
- built-up area

Scale 1: 4 500 000

One centimetre on the map represents 45 kilometres on the ground.

0   45   90   135km

Holidays in the UK and abroad

Numbers of holidays taken by UK residents
millions

- holidays in the UK
- holidays abroad

40
35
30
25
20
15
10
5
0
1980 1990 2000 2010

Central London

0   3 km

- National Portrait Gallery
- London Zoo
- Madame Tussauds
- National Gallery
- Science Museum
- Natural History Museum
- Victoria & Albert Museum
- British Museum
- British Library
- Somerset House
- St. Paul's Cathedral
- Tower of London
- Tate Modern
- London Eye
- Imperial War Museum
- Tate Britain
- Westminster Abbey

Map labels

Shetland

Hoy and West Mainland
The Heart of Neolithic Orkney

Kyle of Tongue

South Lewis, Harris, and North Ust

Assynt Coigach

St. Kilda

Wester Ross

The Cuillin Hills

Knoydart

Cairngorms

Aberdeen

Ben Nevis and Glen Coe

Loch Rannoch and Glen Lyon

Loch Lomond and the Trossachs

Old and New Towns of Edinburgh

Jura

Glasgow

Kelvingrove Art Gallery & Museum

Edinburgh Castle

North Arran

Knapdale

New Lanark

Giant's Causeway

Antrim Coast and Glens

Northumberland

Hadrian's Wall

Newcastle upon Tyne

Belfast

Sperrin

North Pennines

Durham Cathedral & Castle

Strangford Lough

Lake District

Yorkshire Dales

North York Moors

Flamingo Land

Mourne

Windermere Lake Cruises

Nidderdale

Fountain's Abbey & Studley Royal Park

Forest of Bowland

Saltaire

Leeds

Merseyside Maritime Museum

Liverpool - Maritime Mercantile City

Manchester

Sheffield

Lincolnshire Wolds

Anglesey

Chester Zoo

Peak District

Norfolk Coast

Castles & Town Walls of King Edward

Pontcysyllte Aqueduct & Canal

Alton Towers

Stoke-on-Trent

Nottingham

Snowdonia

Derwent Valley Mills

Lleyn

Ironbridge Gorge

Drayton Manor

Coventry

Suffolk Coast and Heaths

Shropshire Hills

Birmingham

The Broads

Pembrokeshire Coast

Blenheim Palace

Brecon Beacons

Wye Valley

Cotswolds

Chilterns

Ashmolean Museum

Blaenavon

Oxford

Kew Gardens

Tower of London

Gower

Bristol

North Wessex Downs

Legoland

Maritime Greenwich

Cardiff

Bath

Westminster Palace/Abbey

Canterbury Cathedral

Kent Downs

Stonehenge/ Avebury

South Downs

High Weald

Exmoor

Cranborne Chase

Blackdown Hills

Dorset

Isle of Wight

Cornwall and West Devon Mining Landscape

Dartmoor

Cornwall

Dorset and East Devon Coast

New Forest

Eden Project

Isles of Scilly

Photo captions

Loch Einich, Cairngorms

The Cotswolds

The Needles, Isle of Wight

Edinburgh Castle

Sports venues 2011

major clubs or grounds

- Association Football
- Rugby Union
- Rugby League
- Cricket
- major sports stadium or centre

Scale 1 : 4 500 000

One centimetre on the map represents 45 kilometres on the ground.

| 0 | 45 | 90 | 135km |

Anfield
6 January 2012

Galpharm Stadium
23 September 2011

Franklin's Gardens
5 September 2010

Grace Road
15 September 2011

Wembley Stadium

SCOTLAND

Inverness Caledonian Thistle
Aberdeen
Dundee United
St. Johnstone
Dunfermline
Celtic
Murrayfield
Glasgow Warriors
St. Mirren
Hibernian
Hearts
Rangers
Edinburgh
Hampden Park
Kilmarnock
Motherwell

UNITED KINGDOM

NORTHERN IRELAND
Ulster
Windsor Park

REPUBLIC OF IRELAND
Connacht
Leinster
Landsdowne Road
Munster

Newcastle Falcons
Newcastle United
Sunderland
Durham
Riverside Ground

Manchester United
Salford City Reds
Blackburn Rovers
Bolton Wanderers
Wigan Athletic
Wigan Warriors
Everton
Liverpool
St. Helens
Crusaders
Warrington Wolves

Bradford Bulls
Leeds Rhinos
Yorkshire Headingley
Castleford Tigers
Hull Kingston Rovers
Hull FC
Wakefield Wildcats
Huddersfield Giants
Manchester City
Sale Sharks
Lancashire Old Trafford
Stoke City
Nottinghamshire Trent Bridge
Derbyshire
Leicester Tigers
Leicestershire

Norwich City

ENGLAND

Wolverhampton Wanderers
Aston Villa
West Bromwich Albion
Warwickshire Edgbaston
Worcestershire

Worcester Warriors
Northamptonshire
Northampton Saints
Wembley Stadium
Tottenham Hotspur
Arsenal
Saracens
London Wasps
Essex
Middlesex Lords
QPR
Chelsea
Kent
Surrey The Oval
Fulham
Sussex

WALES
Newport-Gwent Dragons
Gloucester Rugby
Ospreys
Scarlets
Glamorgan
Swansea
Gloucestershire
Cardiff Blues
Millennium Stadium
Bath Rugby
Somerset
Harlequins
London Irish
London Broncos
Twickenham
Hampshire
Exeter Chiefs

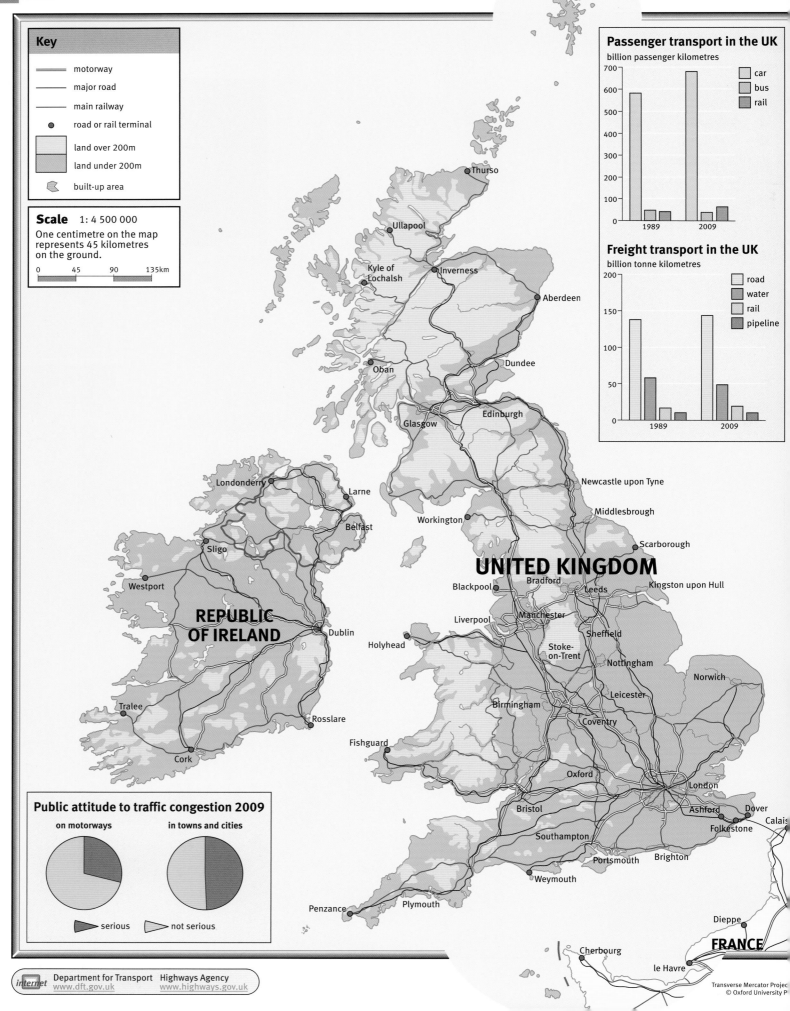

Key

motorway
major road
main railway
● road or rail terminal
land over 200m
land under 200m
built-up area

Scale 1: 4 500 000

One centimetre on the map represents 45 kilometres on the ground.

0 45 90 135km

Passenger transport in the UK
billion passenger kilometres

- car
- bus
- rail

1989   2009

Freight transport in the UK
billion tonne kilometres

- road
- water
- rail
- pipeline

1989   2009

Public attitude to traffic congestion 2009

on motorways   in towns and cities

serious   not serious

Thurso
Ullapool
Kyle of Lochalsh
Inverness
Aberdeen
Dundee
Oban
Edinburgh
Glasgow

Londonderry
Larne
Belfast
Workington
Newcastle upon Tyne
Middlesbrough
Scarborough
Sligo
Kingston upon Hull

UNITED KINGDOM

Westport
Blackpool   Bradford   Leeds
Liverpool   Manchester
REPUBLIC OF IRELAND
Sheffield
Dublin
Holyhead   Stoke-on-Trent   Nottingham
Norwich
Leicester
Tralee   Birmingham
Rosslare   Coventry
Fishguard
Cork
Oxford
London
Bristol   Ashford   Dover
Calais
Folkestone
Southampton
Portsmouth   Brighton
Weymouth
Penzance   Plymouth
Dieppe
FRANCE
Cherbourg
le Havre

Department for Transport   Highways Agency
www.dft.gov.uk   www.highways.gov.uk

Transverse Mercator Projec
© Oxford University P

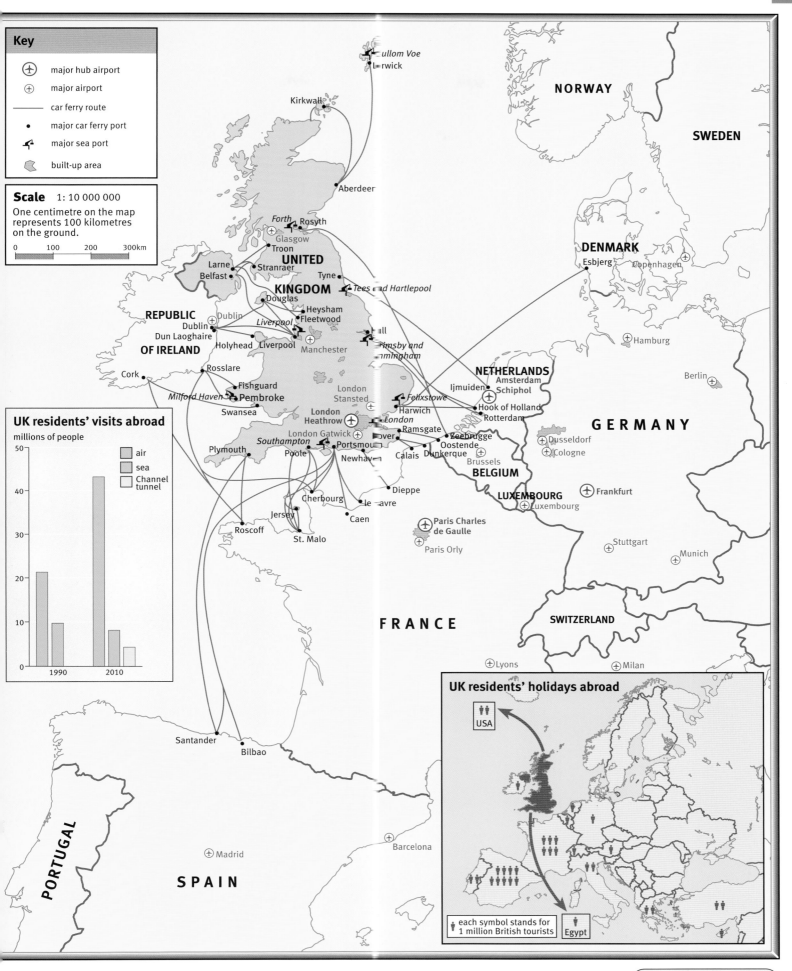

Key

- ✈ major hub airport
- ⊕ major airport
- — car ferry route
- • major car ferry port
- ⚓ major sea port
- ▨ built-up area

Scale 1: 10 000 000
One centimetre on the map represents 100 kilometres on the ground.

0   100   200   300km

UK residents' visits abroad

millions of people

- ▨ air
- ▨ sea
- ▨ Channel tunnel

50
40
30
20
10
0

1990   2010

UK residents' holidays abroad

each symbol stands for 1 million British tourists

USA

Egypt

NORWAY

SWEDEN

DENMARK

GERMANY

NETHERLANDS

BELGIUM

LUXEMBOURG

SWITZERLAND

FRANCE

SPAIN

PORTUGAL

UNITED KINGDOM

REPUBLIC OF IRELAND

Sullom Voe
Lerwick
Kirkwall
Aberdeen
Forth
Rosyth
Glasgow
Troon
Larne
Belfast
Stranraer
Tyne
Tees and Hartlepool
Douglas
Heysham
Fleetwood
Dublin
Liverpool
Liverpool
Manchester
Holyhead
Dun Laoghaire
Rosslare
Hull
Grimsby and Immingham
Cork
Fishguard
Milford Haven
Pembroke
Swansea
London Stansted
Felixstowe
Harwich
London Heathrow
London
Ramsgate
London Gatwick
Dover
Plymouth
Southampton
Portsmouth
Poole
Newhaven
Calais
Dunkerque
Oostende
Zeebrugge
Brussels
Cherbourg
le Havre
Caen
Dieppe
Jersey
St. Malo
Roscoff
Santander
Bilbao
Madrid
Barcelona
Esbjerg
Copenhagen
Hamburg
Berlin
Amsterdam
Schiphol
Ijmuiden
Hook of Holland
Rotterdam
Dusseldorf
Cologne
Frankfurt
Luxembourg
Stuttgart
Munich
Lyons
Milan
Paris Charles de Gaulle
Paris Orly

internet National Statistics Online www.statistics.gov.uk

ARCTIC CIRCLE

GREENLAND SEA

Iceland
▲ 1491m Mount Hekla

N

ATLANTIC OCEAN

Faroe Islands

Shetland Islands

Orkney Islands

Ireland

Great Britain

NORTH SEA

Friesian Islands

English Channel

Thames

Seine

Loire

Bay of Biscay

Cape Finisterre

Cantabrian Mts.

Duero

Ebro

Pyrénées

Tagus

Cape St. Vincent

Str. of Gibraltar

Massif Central

Jura

Mont Blanc 4807m

A L P S

Rhône

Po

Corsica

Balearic Islands

Menorca

Mallorca

Ibiza

Sardinia

A P P E N N I N E S

TYRRHENIAN SEA

Mt. Etna 3323m ▲

Sicily

Malta

M E D I T E R R A N E A N   S E A

Lofoten Islands

S c a n d i n a v i a

Lappland

Gulf of Bothnia

Lake Vänern

Lake Vättern

Gotland

Jylland

Bornholm

BALTIC SEA

Elbe

Oder

Rhine

Vistula

North European Plain

Danube

Hungarian Basin

2548m ▲

Dinaric Alps

ADRIATIC SEA

Pindos Mountains

2917m ▲ Mt. Olympus

Peloponnese

IONIAN SEA

AEGEAN SEA

Crete

Rhodes

Kola Peninsula

WHITE SEA

North Dvina

Lake Onega

Lake Ladoga

Lake Peipus

Rybinsk Reservoir

Central Russian Uplands

Dniepr

Dniester

Don

Donets

C A R P A T H I A N S

BLACK SEA

SEA OF AZOV

CAUCASUS

5642m ▲ Mt. Elbrus

CASPIAN SEA

5123m ▲ Mt. Ararat

Lake Van

Anatolian Plateau

Taurus Mountains

Cyprus

U R A L   M O U N T A I N S

Ob

Pechora

Volga

TROPIC OF CANCER

Conical Orthomorphic Projection
© Oxford University Press

Key

land height
above sea level in metres

- more than 2000m
- 1000 – 2000m
- 500 – 1000m
- 200 – 500m
- less than 200m
- land below sea level

▲ highest peaks with heights in metres

‿ river

⋯ canal

◠ lake

ice cap

area:		10 214 392km²
▲ **highest point:**	Mt. Elbrus	5 642m
▽ **lowest point:**	Caspian Sea	-28m
longest river:	Volga	3 688km

Scale 1: 24 000 000

0   240   480   720km

ICELAND
Reykjavik

ATLANTIC OCEAN

Arctic Circle
Prime Meridian

N O R W A Y
S W E D E N
FINLAND
Oslo
Stockholm
Helsinki
St. Petersburg

RUSSIAN FEDERATION (RUSSIA)

Nizhniy-Novgorod
Moscow

Tallinn
ESTONIA
LATVIA
Riga
LITHUANIA
KALININGRAD (Russia)
Vilnius
Minsk
BELARUS

NORTH SEA
Edinburgh
Belfast
REPUBLIC OF IRELAND
Dublin
UNITED KINGDOM
Manchester
Birmingham
London
NETHERLANDS
Hamburg
Rotterdam
Amsterdam
BELGIUM
Brussels
Düsseldorf
GERMANY
Berlin
POLAND
Warsaw
Kiev
Kharkov
Volgograd
Donets'k
Rostov-on-Don
U K R A I N E

LUXEMBOURG
Luxembourg
Paris
Prague
CZECH REP.
Krakow
SLOVAKIA
Bratislava
MOLDOVA
Chisinau
Odessa

FRANCE
Bern
Munich
Vienna
AUSTRIA
Budapest
HUNGARY
ROMANIA
Bucharest

Bordeaux
Lyons
SWITZERLAND
LIECHTENSTEIN
Ljubljana
SLOVENIA
Milan
Zagreb
CROATIA
BOSNIA-HERZEGOVINA
Sarajevo
Belgrade
SERBIA
MONTENEGRO
Podgorica
KOSOVO
Pristina
Sofia
BULGARIA
BLACK SEA
GEORGIA
T'bilisi

Oporto
PORTUGAL
Lisbon
SPAIN
Madrid
ANDORRA
MONACO
SAN MARINO
I T A L Y
Rome
Naples
Skopje
FYRO MACEDONIA
Tiranë
ALBANIA
GREECE
Istanbul
Ankara
Izmir
Adana
T U R K E Y

Marseilles
Barcelona
Valencia
Seville
Gibraltar (UK)
Ceuta (Sp.)
Melilla (Sp.)

M E D I T E R R A N E A N   S E A

Valletta
MALTA

Athens
Nicosia
CYPRUS

BALTIC SEA
DENMARK
Copenhagen
Göteborg

European Union

SWEDEN
FINLAND
REPUBLIC OF IRELAND
UNITED KINGDOM
DENMARK
ESTONIA
LATVIA
LITHUANIA
NETHERLANDS
BELGIUM
LUXEMBOURG
GERMANY
POLAND
CZECH REP.
SLOVAKIA
AUSTRIA
HUNGARY
SLOVENIA
ROMANIA
FRANCE
PORTUGAL
SPAIN
I T A L Y
BULGARIA
GREECE
MALTA
CYPRUS

Tropic of Cancer

population:
655 884 785 *

largest country: Ukraine 603 698km²

country with most people:
Germany 82 689 000

largest city: Istanbul, Turkey
9 946 000

* does not include Russian Federation

Key

colours show countries

SPAIN country names are shown like this

■ capital city

• other major city

Scale 1: 24 000 000
0   240   480   720km

internet European Union Gateway
http://europa.eu/index_en.htm

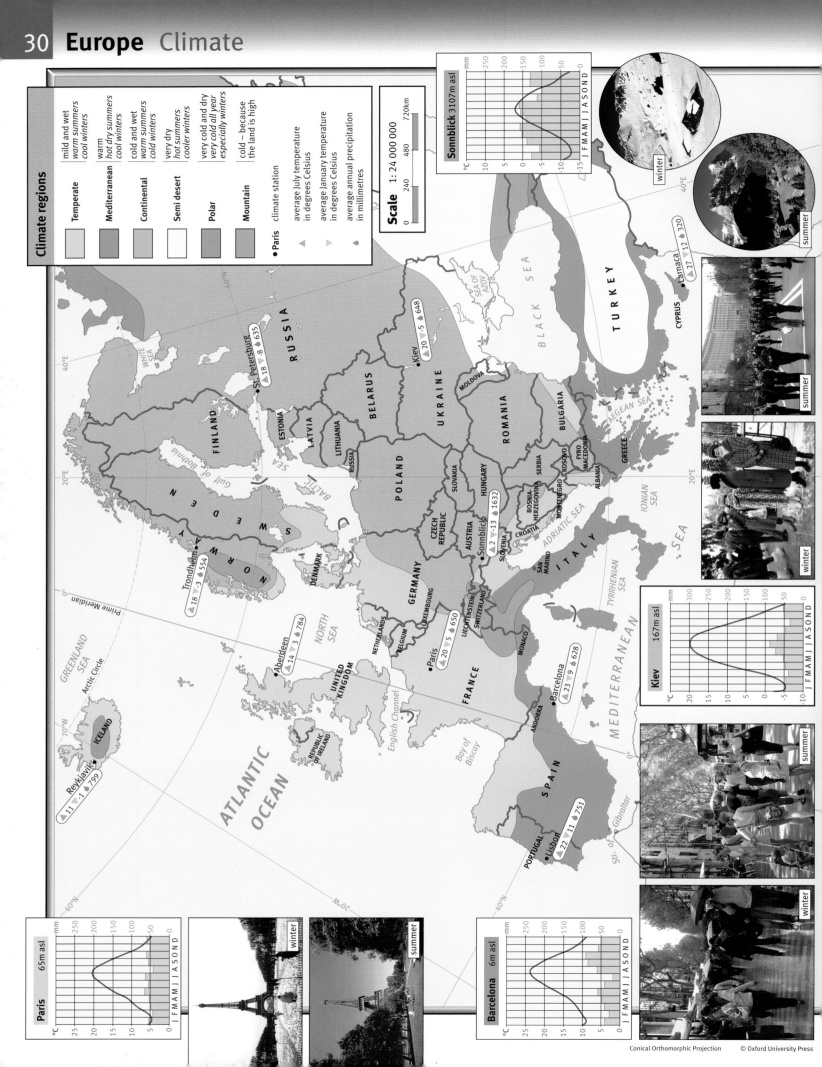

Climate regions

Temperate	mild and wet	*warm summers* *cool winters*
Mediterranean	warm	*hot dry summers* *cool winters*
Continental	cold and wet	*warm summers* *cold winters*
Semi desert	very dry	*hot summers* *cooler winters*
Polar	very cold and dry	*very cold all year* *especially winters*
Mountain	cold – because	*the land is high*

- Paris   climate station

◄ average July temperature in degrees Celsius

► average January temperature in degrees Celsius

● average annual precipitation in millimetres

Scale 1 : 24 000 000

0   240   480   720km

Sonnblick 3107m asl

Paris

ATLANTIC OCEAN

GREENLAND SEA

Arctic Circle

ICELAND

Reykjavik ◄11 ▼-1 ●799

Prime Meridian

NORTH SEA

Aberdeen ◄14 ►3 ●784

UNITED KINGDOM

REPUBLIC OF IRELAND

English Channel

Bay of Biscay

FRANCE

Paris ◄20 ►5 ●650

NETHERLANDS

BELGIUM

LUXEMBOURG

GERMANY

DENMARK

NORWAY

Trondheim ◄18 ►-3 ●554

SWEDEN

FINLAND

Gulf of Bothnia

WHITE SEA

St. Petersburg ◄18 ►-8 ●635

RUSSIA

BALTIC SEA

ESTONIA

LATVIA

LITHUANIA

RUSSIA

BELARUS

POLAND

UKRAINE

Kiev ◄20 ►-5 ●648

MOLDOVA

CZECH REPUBLIC

SLOVAKIA

AUSTRIA

Sonnblick ◄2 ▼-13 ●1632

HUNGARY

LIECHTENSTEIN

SWITZERLAND

SLOVENIA

CROATIA

BOSNIA-HERZEGOVINA

SERBIA

MONTENEGRO

KOSOVO

FYRO MACEDONIA

ALBANIA

ROMANIA

BULGARIA

GREECE

ADRIATIC SEA

IONIAN SEA

ITALY

SAN MARINO

MONACO

ANDORRA

SPAIN

Barcelona ◄23 ►9 ●628

Lisbon ◄22 ▼11 ●751

PORTUGAL

Str. of Gibraltar

MEDITERRANEAN SEA

TYRRHENIAN SEA

AEGEAN SEA

BLACK SEA

SEA OF AZOV

TURKEY

CYPRUS

Larnaca ◄27 ▼12 ●320

Kiev 167m asl

Paris 65m asl

winter

summer

Barcelona 6m asl

summer

winter

winter

summer

summer

winter

Conical Orthomorphic Projection   © Oxford University Press

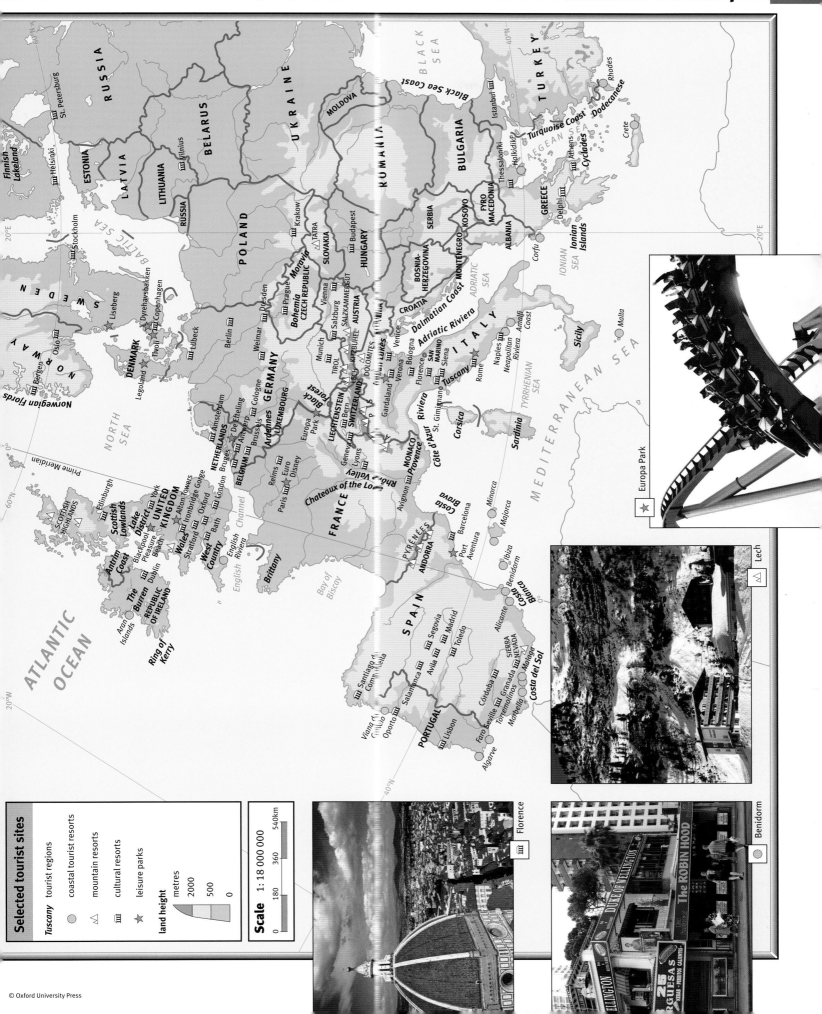

Selected tourist sites

Tuscany tourist regions

⬤ coastal tourist resorts

△ mountain resorts

🏛 cultural resorts

★ leisure parks

land height

metres
2000
500
0

Scale 1:18 000 000

0   180   360   540km

Europa Park

Lech

Florence

Benidorm

30°W · Arctic Circle

A · 20°W · B · 70°N · 10°W · C · Prime Meridian · D · 0° · 10°E · E

ICELAND

Ísafjördut

Reykjavík

Akureyri

Mount Hekla
1491

Höfn

NORWEGIAN
SEA

Vesterålen Is.
Lofoten Is.

Bodø

N
O
R
W
A
Y

Na

Scandinavia

60°N

Faroe
Islands
(Den.)

Trondheim

Galdhøpiggen
2470m

S
W
E
D
E
N

Glåma

Indals

ATLANTIC

OCEAN

Shetland
Islands

Outer
Hebrides

Orkney
Islands

Bergen

Stavanger

Oslo

Uppsa

Lake
Vänern

Stockhol

50°N

1344m
Ben Nevis

Inverness

Aberdeen

Dundee

Glasgow

Edinburgh

Galway

Belfast

Newcastle
upon Tyne

Skagerrak

NORTH
SEA

Lake
Vättern

Jönköping

Göteborg

Ålborg

Öl

Kattegat

DENMARK

Århus

Copenhagen

Malmö

**REPUBLIC
OF IRELAND**

Dublin

Manchester
Liverpool

UNITED

Leeds

KINGDOM

Odense

Bornholm

Cork

Birmingham

Cardiff

Norwich

Kiel

Rostock

Plymouth

Bristol

London

The Hague

Amsterdam

Frisian Is.

Hamburg

Bremen

Szczecin

NETHERLANDS

Elbe

Land's End
Isles of
Scilly

Southampton

Strait of Dover

Rotterdam

Essen

Hannover

Berlin

Pozna

English Channel

Calais

Antwerp

BELGIUM

Düsseldorf

Leipzig

Oder

Wrocław

Channel
Islands

Brest

le Havre

Lille

Brussels

Cologne

Bonn

GERMANY

Dresden

Rennes

le Mans

Rouen

Paris

Reims

LUXEMBOURG
Luxembourg

**Frankfurt-
am-Main**

Prague

CZECH RE

Orléans

Nancy

Seine

Nuremberg

Brno

Nantes

Tours

Strasbourg

Rhine

Stuttgart

Linz

Bratisla

FRANCE

Djon

Basel

Danube

Munich

Salzburg

Saône

Loire

Bay of Biscay

SWITZERLAND
Bern

Zürich

LIECHTENSTEIN

Innsbruck

AUSTRIA

Vienna

10°W

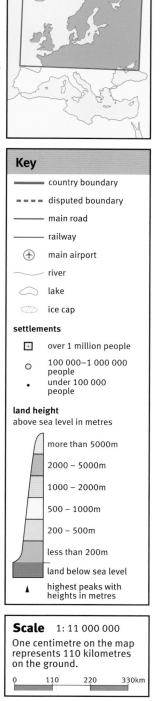

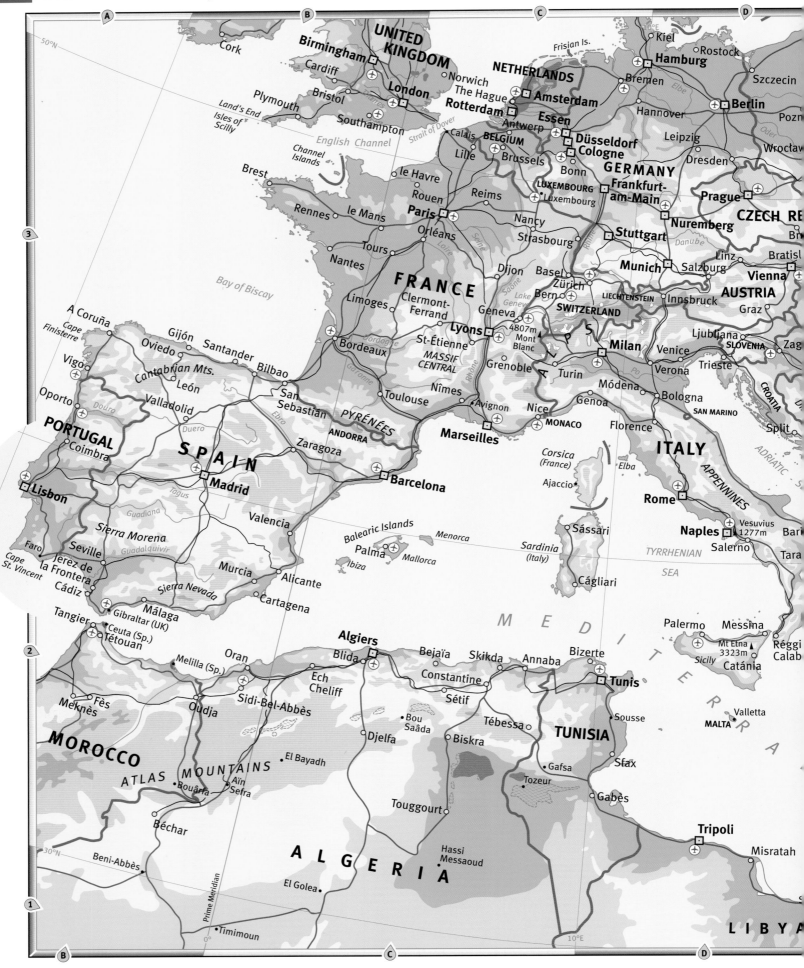

Cork

Birmingham

UNITED
KINGDOM

Frisian Is.

Kiel

Rostock

Hamburg

Szczecin

Cardiff

Norwich

NETHERLANDS

Bremen

50°N

Plymouth

Bristol

London

The Hague

Amsterdam

Hannover

Berlin

Pozn

Southampton

Calais

Rotterdam

Antwerp

Essen

Leipzig

Dresden

Wrocła

Land's End
Isles of
Scilly

Channel
Islands

English Channel

Strait of Dover

Lille

BELGIUM

Brussels

Düsseldorf
Cologne

Bonn

GERMANY

Prague

CZECH RE

Brest

le Havre

Rouen

Reims

LUXEMBOURG

Luxembourg

Frankfurt-
am-Main

Br

Rennes

le Mans

Paris

Orléans

Nancy

Strasbourg

Stuttgart

Nuremberg

Linz

Bratisl

Tours

FRANCE

Dijon

Basel

Munich

Salzburg

Vienna

Nantes

Limoges

Clermont-
Ferrand

Geneva

Bern

Zürich

Innsbruck

AUSTRIA

A Coruña

Bay of Biscay

Cape
Finisterre

Vigo

Gijón

Oviedo

Santander

Bordeaux

St-Étienne

Lyons

MASSIF
CENTRAL

4807m
Mont
Blanc

SWITZERLAND

LIECHTENSTEIN

A L P S

Graz

Ljubljana

Zag

Oporto

Cantabrian Mts.

León

Bilbao

San
Sebastián

Grenoble

Turin

Milan

Venice

SLOVENIA

Trieste

Douro

Valladolid

Duero

Ebro

Nîmes

Módena

Verona

Po

CROATIA

PORTUGAL

Coimbra

SPAIN

Zaragoza

Toulouse

PYRÉNÉES

ANDORRA

Avignon

Marseilles

Nice

MONACO

Genoa

Bologna

Florence

SAN MARINO

ITALY

ADRIATIC

Split

Lisbon

Madrid

Valencia

Corsica
(France)

Elba

APPENNINES

Tagus

Guadiana

Sierra Morena

Rome

Faro

Seville

Murcia

Alicante

Balearic Islands

Menorca

Ajaccio

Sássari

Naples

Vesuvius
1277m

Bari

Cape
St. Vincent

Jerez de
la Frontera

Cádiz

Guadalquivir

Sierra Nevada

Cartagena

Palma

Ibiza

Mallorca

Sardinia
(Italy)

Salerno

Tara

TYRRHENIAN

Málaga

Gibraltar (UK)

SEA

Cágliari

M E D I T E R

Tangier

Ceuta (Sp.)

Tétouan

Melilla (Sp.)

Oran

Algiers

Blida

Bejaïa

Skikda

Annaba

Bizerte

Palermo

Messina

Fès

Meknès

Sidi-Bel-Abbès

Ech
Cheliff

Constantine

Sétif

Tunis

Mt Etna
3323m

Sicily

Catánia

Réggi
Calab

Oudja

Bou
Saâda

Tébessa

Sousse

Valletta

MOROCCO

El Bayadh

Djelfa

Biskra

TUNISIA

MALTA

Melilla

ATLAS MOUNTAINS

Bouârfa

Aïn
Sefra

Gafsa

Sfax

Béchar

Tozeur

Gabès

Beni-Abbès

30°N

Touggourt

Tripoli

ALGERIA

Hassi
Messaoud

Misratah

Prime Meridian

0°

El Golea

Timimoun

10°E

L I B Y A

RUSSIA
Kaliningrad
North European Plain
Gdansk
Bydgoszcz
Białystok

BELARUS

Mahilyow
Homyel'
Bryans'k
Orel
Voronezh

RUSSIAN FEDERATION (RUSSIA)

Minsk
Kursk

POLAND
Brest
Dnieper
Pripet

Warsaw
Lodz
Lublin

Katowice
Krakow
rava

Zhytomyr
Vinnytsya
L'viv

Kiev

UKRAINE

Kharkiv

Donets'k
Shakhty
Rostov-on-Don

Dnipropetrovsk
Zaporizhzhya
Mariupol
Kryvyy Rih

SLOVAKIA

Chernivtsi
Dniester

CARPATHIANS

Miskolc

Budapest
Debrecen

HUNGARY

Cluj-Napoca

MOLDOVA
Chişinău

ROMANIA

Galaţi
Braşov
Brăila

Odessa
Kherson

Krasnodar

SEA OF AZOV
Kerch'
Crimea
Simferopol
Sevastopol
Sochi

Timişoara

Ploieşti
Belgrade

BOSNIA–HERZEGOVINA
Sarajevo

Niš
Bucharest
Danube

Varna

BLACK SEA

Constanta

Sofia
BULGARIA
Plovdiv
Burgas

SERBIA

MONTENEGRO
Priština
KOSOVO
dgorica
Skopje
FYRO MACEDONIA

Tiranë
ALBANIA

Rhodope Mountains

Samsun

Zonguldak

Istanbul

Ankara

Sivas

T U R K E Y

Kayseri

Thessaloníki

▲Mt. Olympus 2917m

Pindus Mts.

GREECE
Lárisa

Corfu

Bursa
Eskişehir

Balikesir

AEGEAN SEA

Évoia

İzmir

Konya

Taurus Mountains
Adana
Gaziantep

Mersin

Aleppo

Patras Piraeus
Athens

Peloponnese
Cyclades

Antalya

CYPRUS
Nicosia
Limassol

Latakia

Tripoli
LEBANON
Beirut

IONIAN SEA

Rhodes

Iraklión
Khania
Crete

Haifa
ISRAEL
Tel Aviv-Yafo
Jerusalem

Port Said

Alexandria

Suez

E G Y P T

El Giza **Cairo**

Sinai

Al Bayda
Darnah
Tubruq

Benghazi

EAN SEA

Key

—— country boundary
- - - disputed boundary
—— main road
—— railway
⊕ main airport
〜 river
◠ lake
⬭ ice cap
▨ seasonal lake
≈ marsh

settlements

▢ over 1 million people
○ 100 000–1 000 000 people
• under 100 000 people

land height
above sea level in metres

more than 5000m
2000 – 5000m
1000 – 2000m
500 – 1000m
200 – 500m
less than 200m
land below sea level
▲ highest peaks with heights in metres

Scale   1: 11 000 000

One centimetre on the map represents 110 kilometres on the ground.

0   110   220   330km

Key

— country boundary
— regional boundary
— main road
— railway
⊕ main airport
∿ river
◡ lake
ice cap

settlements
⊡ over 1 million people
○ 100 000–1 000 000 people
• under 100 000 people

land height
above sea level in metres

more than 5000m
2000 – 5000m
1000 – 2000m
500 – 1000m
200 – 500m
less than 200m
land below sea level
▲ highest peaks with heights in metres

SWITZERLAND
Lausanne
Montreux
Geneva
Annecy
Lake Geneva
Rhône
JURA
ALPS
Chur
St. Moritz
Jungfrau 4158m
Matterhorn 4477m
Mont Blanc 4807m
VALLE D'AOSTA
Aosta
Novara
Como
Lake Maggiore
Lake Como
Lake Garda
Bernina Pass
Brenner Pass
3798m Gross Glockner
AUSTRIA
Leoben
Graz
Klagenfurt
Villach
TRENTINO-ALTO ADIGE
Bolzano
Trento
Dolomites
FRIULI VENEZIA GIULIA
Udine
Kranj
Maribor
Varazdin
Ljubljana
SLOVENIA
Zagreb
FRANCE
Briançon
3841m Mt. Viso
PIEMONTE
Cuneo
Turin
Alessándria
Po
LOMBARDIA
Monza
Milan
Bérgamo
Brescia
Verona
Vicenza
Padua
VENETO
Treviso
Venice
Trieste
Rijeka
Karlovac
CROATIA
Senj
Zadar
Nice
Antibes
Cannes
Fréjus
St-Tropez
MONACO
Côte d'Azur
Genoa
La Spézia
Reggio nell'Emilia
Parma
Piacenza
Cremona
Módena
Ferrara
Bologna
EMILIA-ROMAGNA
Forlí
Ravenna
Rimini
San Marino
SAN MARINO
Ancona
Po
LIGURIAN SEA
Livorno
Pisa
Prato
Florence
TOSCANA
Arezzo
Siena
Lake Trasimeno
Elba
APPENNINES
Cape Corse
Bastia
Monte Cinto 2710m
Ponte Leccia
Corsica (France)
Ajaccio
Bonifacio
Olbia
Sassari
Nuoro
Sardinia (Italy)
Oristano
SARDEGNA
Cágliari
Iglesias
Cape Carbonara
Cape Bon
Pantelleria (Italy)
Perugia
UMBRIA
Assisi
ITALY
Terni
Lake Bolsena
Viterbo
Civitavecchia
MARCHE
Pescara
L'Aquila
2487m Mt. Velino
ABRUZZO
Termoli
MOLISE
Campobasso
Tivoli
Rome
LAZIO
Latina
Cassino
Fóggia
CAMPANIA
Vesuvius 1277m
Naples
Salerno
Capri
Potenza
BASILICATA
Mt. Pollino 2248m
Bari
Monopoli
PUGLIA
Táranto
Gulf of Táranto
Bríndisi
Lecce
Gallipoli
Otranto
Cape Santa Maria of Leuca
Cosenza
CALABRIA
Catanzaro
Reggio di Calabria
Messina
Lipari Islands
Nebrodi Mts. 3323m Mt. Etna
Palermo
Trápani
Marsala
Sicily
SICILIA
Agrigento
Caltanissetta
Catania
Siracusa
Cape Passero
Cape Spartivento
ADRIATIC SEA
TYRRHENIAN SEA
MEDITERRANEAN SEA
IONIAN SEA
'Annaba
Bizerte
Tunis
TUNISIA
Sousse
Medjerda
MALTA
Valletta

Scale 1 : 5 000 000
0   50   100   150km

Conical Orthomorphic Projection
© Oxford University Press

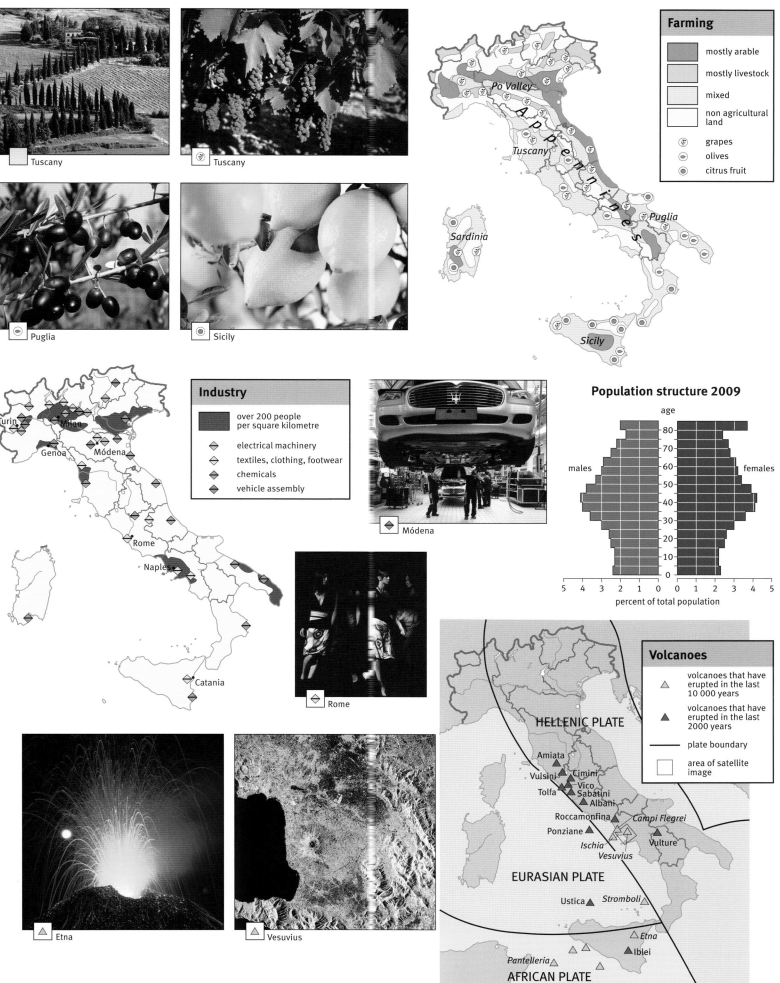

Tuscany

Tuscany

Puglia

Sicily

Farming

- mostly arable
- mostly livestock
- mixed
- non agricultural land
- grapes
- olives
- citrus fruit

Po Valley

Appennines

Tuscany

Sardinia

Puglia

Sicily

Industry

- over 200 people per square kilometre
- electrical machinery
- textiles, clothing, footwear
- chemicals
- vehicle assembly

Turin

Milan

Genoa

Módena

Rome

Naples

Catania

Módena

Rome

Population structure 2009

age

males

females

percent of total population

Volcanoes

- volcanoes that have erupted in the last 10 000 years
- volcanoes that have erupted in the last 2000 years
- plate boundary
- area of satellite image

HELLENIC PLATE

Amiata

Vulsini

Cimini

Tolfa

Vico

Sabatini

Albani

Roccamonfina

Campi Flegrei

Ponziane

Vulture

Ischia

Vesuvius

EURASIAN PLATE

Ustica

Stromboli

Etna

Iblei

Pantelleria

AFRICAN PLATE

Linosa

Etna

Vesuvius

ARCTIC OCEAN

North Pole

Ⓙ Ⓗ Ⓖ

Ⓐ Ⓑ Ⓒ Ⓓ Ⓔ Ⓕ

Bering Strait

BARENTS SEA

BERING SEA

Prime Meridian

Arctic Circle

Central Siberian Plateau

Siberian Lowland

Kamchatka

SEA OF OKHOTSK

Sakhalin

Kuril Islands

URAL MOUNTAINS

Lake Ladoga
Lake Onega
Volga
Ob
Yenisey
Angara
Lena
Lake Baykal
Amur (Heilong Jiang)

Hokkaido

Mt. Elbrus 5642m
CAUCASUS
Mt. Ararat 5123m
Anatolian Plateau
BLACK SEA
Caspian Sea
Kazakh Upland
Lake Balkhash
Aral Sea
Irtysh
ALTAI MOUNTAINS
Gobi Desert

SEA OF JAPAN

H o n s h u
Mt. Fuji 3776m

MEDITERRANEAN SEA
Elburz Mts.
ZAGROS MTS.
Dead Sea
Euphrates
Tigris

TIEN SHAN
Qullai Garmo 7495m
Tarim Basin
Turpan Depression −154m
KUNLUN SHAN
Huang He

YELLOW SEA
Kyushu
Ryukyu Islands
EAST CHINA SEA

RED SEA
Arabian Peninsula
The Gulf
Hindu Kush
8611m K2
Plateau of Tibet
Mt. Everest 8848m
HIMALAYA
Brahmaputra
Chang Jiang (Yangtze)

Taiwan

PACIFIC OCEAN

Gulf of Aden
Socotra
60°E
Indus
Thar Desert
Ganges
Deccan
Mouths of the Ganges
Irrawaddy
Salween
Mekong

SOUTH CHINA SEA
Luzon
Mindoro
Mindanao

ARABIAN SEA
Bay of Bengal
Laccadive Islands
Andaman Islands
ANDAMAN SEA
Nicobar Islands
Gulf of Thailand
Malay Peninsula
Mt. Kinabalu 4094m
CELEBES SEA

Maldive Archipelago
Equator 0°
Sumatra
Borneo
Sulawesi
New Guinea

INDIAN OCEAN
JAVA SEA
Java
Bali
Timor
TIMOR SEA
ARAFURA SEA

Tropic of Cancer
Tropic of Capricorn

N

Key

land height
above sea level in metres

more than 5000m	
2000 – 5000m	
1000 – 2000m	
500 – 1000m	
200 – 500m	
less than 200m	
land below sea level	
▲	highest peaks with heights in metres
	river
	canal
	lake
	ice cap

Scale 1: 55 000 000

0   550   1100   1650km

🐾	**area:**	44 534 173km²
▲	**highest point:**	Mt. Everest 8 848m
▽	**lowest point:**	Dead Sea shore −395m
▭	**longest river:**	Chang Jiang 6 380km

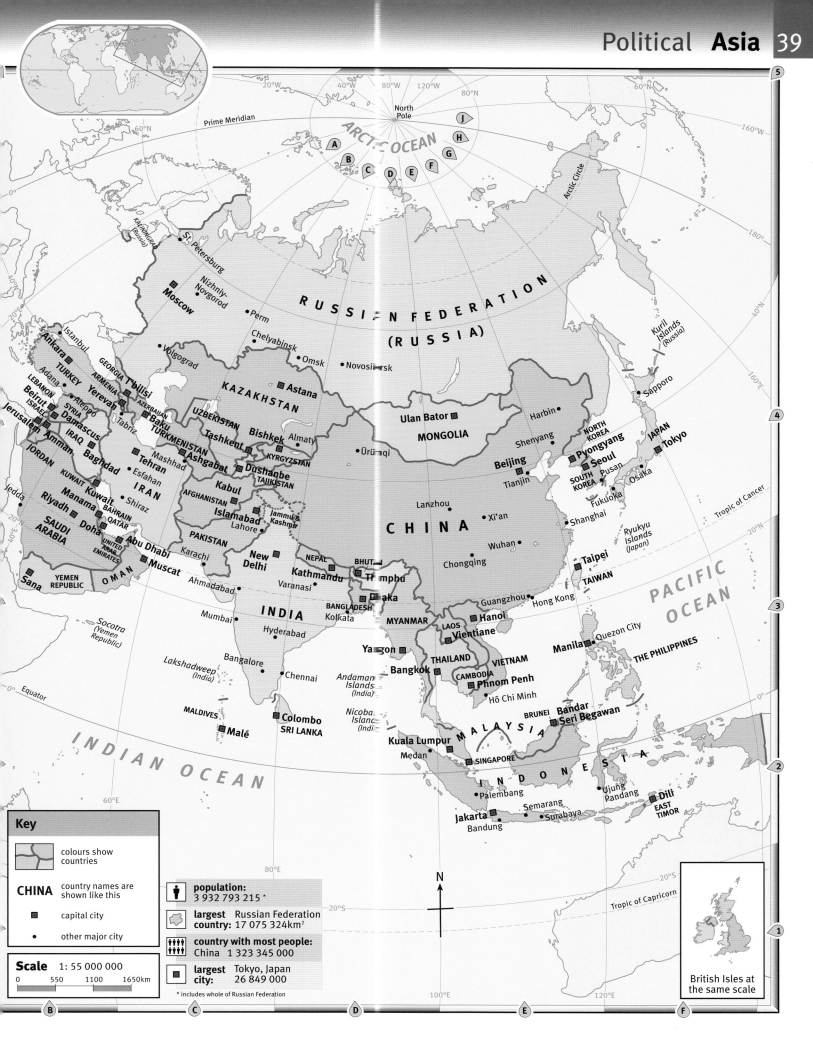

North Pole

ARCTIC OCEAN

Ⓙ
Ⓗ
Ⓐ
Ⓖ
Ⓑ
Ⓒ
Ⓓ Ⓔ Ⓕ

Prime Meridian

20°W   40°W   80°W   120°W   80°N   160°W

60°N

Arctic Circle

KALININGRAD
(Russia)

• St. Petersburg

■ Moscow

Nizhniy-
Novgorod

• Perm

• Chelyabinsk

• Volgograd

• Omsk

• Novosibirsk

R U S S I A N   F E D E R A T I O N

(R U S S I A)

60°E

40°N

160°E

Kuril
Islands
(Russia)

• Sapporo

• Istanbul
■ Ankara
TURKEY
GEORGIA ■ T'bilisi
Adana   ARMENIA ■ Yerevan
LEBANON ■ Aleppo
SYRIA   AZERBAIJAN ■ Baku
■ Beirut ■ Damascus   Tabriz
ISRAEL
Jerusalem ■ IRAQ   TURKMENISTAN
■ Amman ■ Baghdad
JORDAN   ■ Tehran
KUWAIT   Mashhad •
• Jedda   ■ Kuwait   Esfahan •
Riyadh ■ ■ Manama IRAN
SAUDI   BAHRAIN   ■ Shiraz
ARABIA   ■ Doha QATAR
■ ■ Abu Dhabi
UNITED
ARAB
EMIRATES
■ Muscat
■ Sana   OMAN
YEMEN
REPUBLIC

■ Astana

KAZAKHSTAN

UZBEKISTAN

■ Tashkent   ■ Bishkek

■ Ashgabat   ■ Dushanbe   • Almaty
TAJIKISTAN   KYRGYZSTAN

■ Kabul

AFGHANISTAN

■ Islamabad
Lahore •   Jammu &
Kashmir

PAKISTAN

• Karachi

• Ahmadabad

• Ürümqi

• Lanzhou

■ Ulan Bator

MONGOLIA

C H I N A

• Xi'an

• Harbin

• Shenyang

■ Beijing
• Tianjin

NORTH
KOREA
■ Pyongyang
■ Seoul
SOUTH   Pusan •
KOREA

JAPAN
■ Tokyo

• Fukuoka
• Osaka

• Shanghai

Ryukyu
Islands
(Japan)

Tropic of Cancer

20°N

PACIFIC
OCEAN

• Wuhan

• Chongqing

• Guangzhou

• Hong Kong

■ Taipei

TAIWAN

■ New
Delhi

NEPAL
■ Kathmandu
BHUTAN
■ Thimphu

• Varanasi

• Mumbai

I N D I A

• Hyderabad

• Bangalore

Lakshadweep
(India)

• Chennai

BANGLADESH
■ Dhaka

MYANMAR

■ Yangon

Andaman
Islands
(India)

■ Hanoi
LAOS
■ Vientiane

THAILAND   VIETNAM

■ Bangkok   CAMBODIA
■ Phnom Penh
• Hô Chi Minh

■ Manila   • Quezon City

THE PHILIPPINES

0°

MALDIVES

■ Malé

■ Colombo
SRI LANKA

Nicobar
Islands
(India)

BRUNEI ■ Bandar
Seri Begawan

I N D I A N   O C E A N

Equator

60°E

Socotra
(Yemen
Republic)

■ Kuala Lumpur
• Medan

M A L A Y S I A

■ SINGAPORE

I N D O N E S I A

• Palembang

• Ujung
Pandang

■ Dili
EAST
TIMOR

0°

2

80°E

• Semarang
■ Jakarta   • Surabaya
• Bandung

N

20°S

Tropic of Capricorn

20°S

100°E

120°E

Key

colours show
countries

CHINA   country names are
shown like this

■   capital city

•   other major city

Scale   1 : 55 000 000

0   550   1100   1650km

👤 **population:**
3 932 793 215 *

🗺 **largest**   Russian Federation
country: 17 075 324km²

👥 **country with most people:**
China   1 323 345 000

■ **largest**   Tokyo, Japan
city: 26 849 000

* includes whole of Russian Federation

British Isles at
the same scale

Ⓑ   Ⓒ   Ⓓ   Ⓔ   Ⓕ

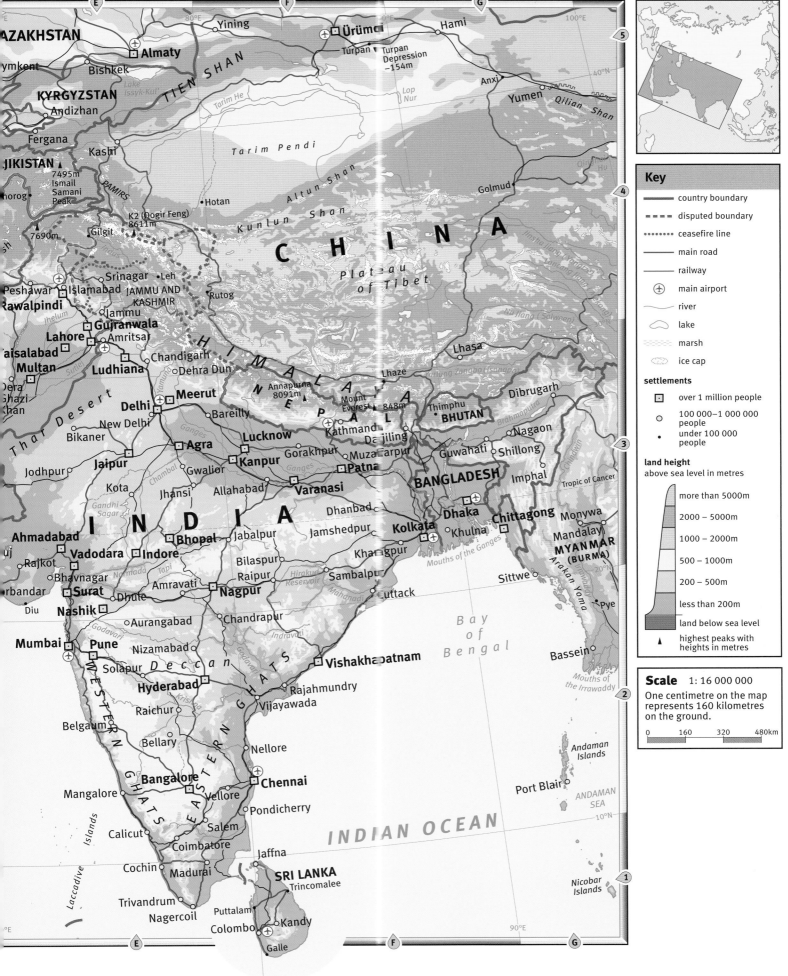

AZAKHSTAN

Yining

Ürümc

Hami

Almaty

ymkent

Bishkek

Turpan

Turpan
Depression
−154m

Anxi

KYRGYZSTAN

TIEN SHAN

Lake
Issyk-Kul

Lop
Nur

Yumen

Qilian Shan

Andizhan

Tarim He

Fergana

JIKISTAN

Kashi

Tarim Pendi

Golmud

7495m
Ismail
Samani
horog Peak

Hotan

Altun Shan

K2 (Dogir Feng)
8611m

Kunlun Shan

CHINA

7690m

Gilgit

Plateau
of Tibet

Srinagar • Leh

Rutog

Peshawar

Islamabad

JAMMU AND
KASHMIR

Rawalpindi

Jammu

Lhasa

aisalabad Gujranwala

Amritsar

HIMALAYA

Lhaze

Lahore

Dibrugarh

Chandigarh

Dehra Dun

Mount
Everest 848m

Thimphu

Dera
ghazi
han Multan

Ludhiana

NEPAL

Annapurna
8091m

BHUTAN

Nagaon

Meerut

Bareilly

Kathmand

Da iling

Shillong

Delhi

Ganges

Lucknow

Gorakhpur

Muza arpur

Guwahati

New Delhi

Bikaner

Thar Desert

Patna

BANGLADESH

Imphal

Jaipur

Agra

Kanpur

Ganges

Varanasi

Jodhpur

Gwalior

Jhansi

Allahabad

Kota

Chambal

Dhanbad

Dhaka

Chittagong

Monywa

Gandhi
Sagar

INDIA

Jabalpur

Jamshedpur

Kolkata

Khulna

Mandalay

Ahmadabad

Bhopal

Kha gpur

MYANMAR
(BURMA)

uj Vadodara

Indore

Bilaspur

Mouths of the Ganges

Rajkot

Narmada

Tapi

Raipur

Hirakud
Reservoir

Sambalp

Arakan Yoma

rbandar Bhavnagar

Surat

Amravati

Nagpur

Mahanadi

Sittwe

Diu Dhule

Nashik

Chandrapur

Cuttack

Pye

Godavari

Aurangabad

Indravati

Mumbai Pune

Nizamabad

Bay
of
Bengal

Bassein

Deccan

Godavari

Solapur

WESTERN GHATS

Hyderabad

Vishakha atnam

Mouths of
the Irrawaddy

Raichur

Krishna

Rajahmundry

Belgaum

Vijayawada

EASTERN GHATS

Bellary

Nellore

Andaman
Islands

Bangalore

Chennai

Mangalore

Vellore

ANDAMAN
SEA

Calicut

Pondicherry

Port Blair

Salem

Coimbatore

Laccadive
Islands

Cochin

Jaffna

INDIAN OCEAN

Madurai

SRI LANKA

Nicobar
Islands

Trivandrum

Trincomalee

Nagercoil

Puttalam

Colombo Kandy

Galle

Key

———	country boundary
- - -	disputed boundary
·······	ceasefire line
———	main road
———	railway
⊕	main airport
～～	river
⬯	lake
░░	marsh
⬭	ice cap

settlements

☐	over 1 million people
○	100 000–1 000 000 people
•	under 100 000 people

land height
above sea level in metres

more than 5000m

2000 – 5000m

1000 – 2000m

500 – 1000m

200 – 500m

less than 200m

land below sea level

▲ highest peaks with heights in metres

Scale 1: 16 000 000

One centimetre on the map
represents 160 kilometres
on the ground.

0   160   320   480km

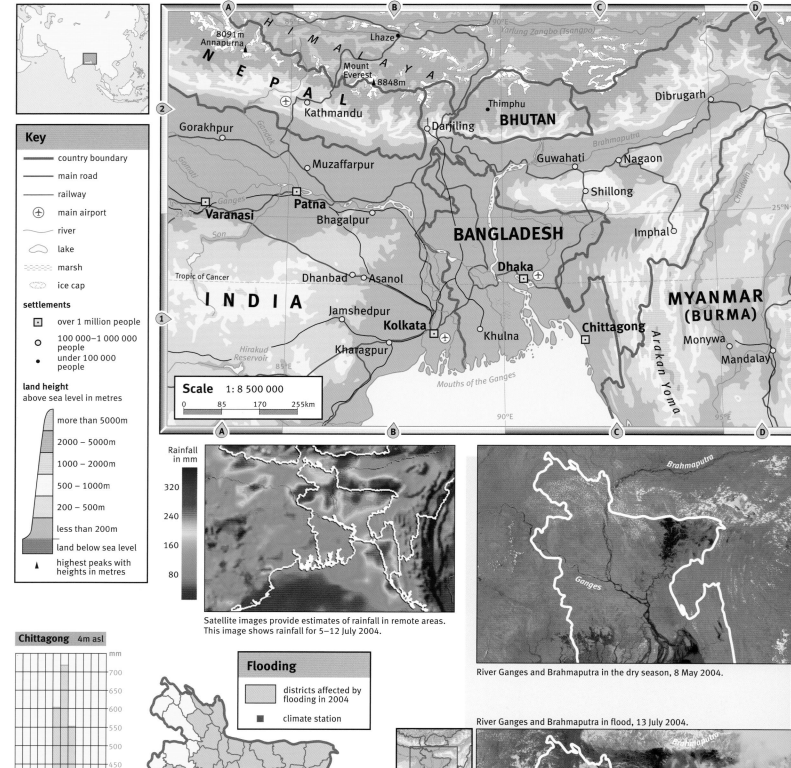

Key

———	country boundary
———	main road
———	railway
⊕	main airport
∿	river
⬭	lake
▦	marsh
⬯	ice cap

settlements

⊡	over 1 million people
○	100 000 – 1 000 000 people
•	under 100 000 people

land height
above sea level in metres

- more than 5000m
- 2000 – 5000m
- 1000 – 2000m
- 500 – 1000m
- 200 – 500m
- less than 200m
- land below sea level

▲ highest peaks with heights in metres

Scale 1: 8 500 000

0   85   170   255km

Rainfall
in mm

320
240
160
80

Satellite images provide estimates of rainfall in remote areas.
This image shows rainfall for 5–12 July 2004.

River Ganges and Brahmaputra in the dry season, 8 May 2004.

River Ganges and Brahmaputra in flood, 13 July 2004.

satellite image area

- water
- clouds
- vegetation

Chittagong 4m asl

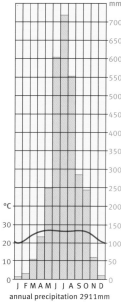

mm

700
650
600
550
500
450
400
350
300
250
200
150
100
50

°C
30
20
10
0

J F M A M J J A S O N D

annual precipitation 2911mm

Flooding

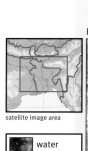

▦	districts affected by flooding in 2004
■	climate station

Chittagong

Zenithal Equal Area Projection
© Oxford University Press

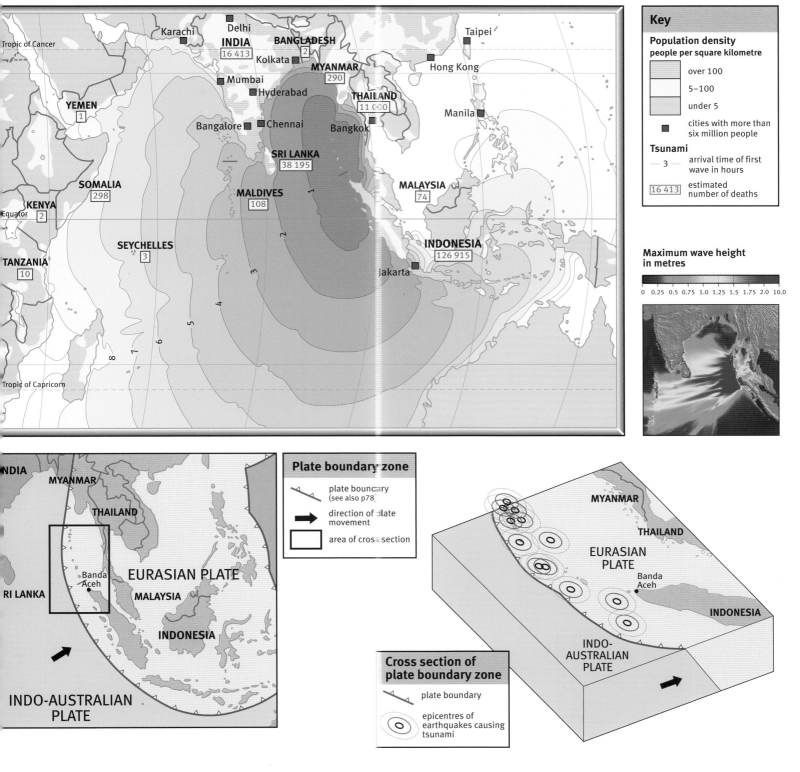

Key

Population density
people per square kilometre
- over 100
- 5–100
- under 5
- cities with more than six million people

Tsunami
- 3 arrival time of first wave in hours
- 16 413 estimated number of deaths

Maximum wave height in metres

0 0.25 0.5 0.75 1.0 1.25 1.5 1.75 2.0 10.0

Plate boundary zone
- plate boundary (see also p78)
- direction of plate movement
- area of cross section

Cross section of plate boundary zone
- plate boundary
- epicentres of earthquakes causing tsunami

EURASIAN PLATE

INDO-AUSTRALIAN PLATE

Banda Aceh **before** the tsunami

Banda Aceh **after** the tsunami

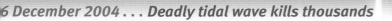

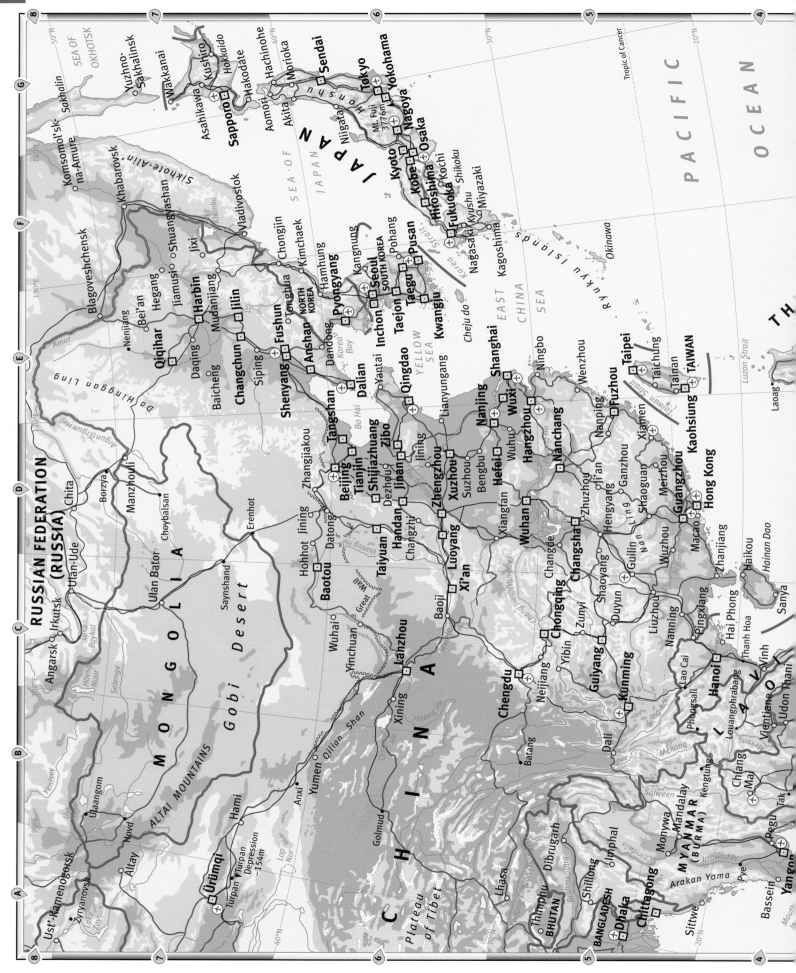

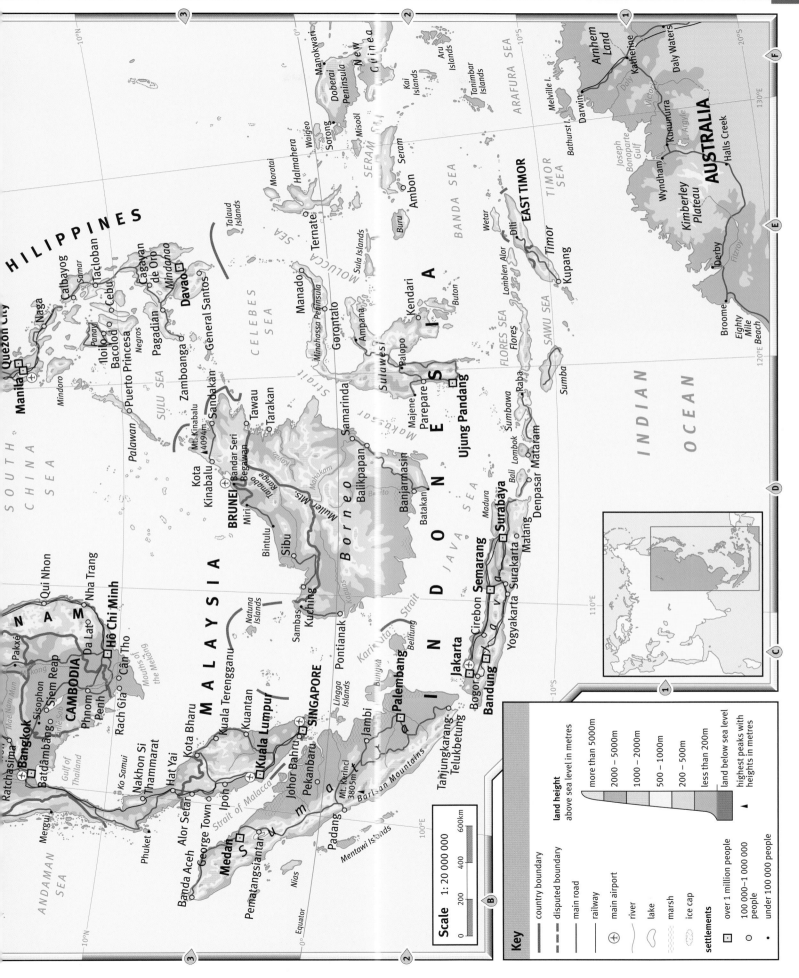

PHILIPPINES

Quezon City
Manila
Naga
Calbayog
Samar
Tacloban
Panay
Iloilo
Cebu
Bacolod
Negros
Puerto Princesa
Mindoro
Palawan
Cagayan de Oro
Mindanao
Davao
Pagadian
General Santos
Zamboanga
Sandakan
Tawau
Tarakan
Mt. Kinabalu 4094m
Kota Kinabalu
Bandar Seri Begawan
BRUNEI
Miri
Bintulu
Sibu
Kuching
Sambas
Pontianak
Talaud Islands

SOUTH CHINA SEA
SULU SEA
CELEBES SEA

MALAYSIA

Natuna Islands

INDONESIA

Borneo
Samarinda
Balikpapan
Banjarmasin
Batakan
Mahakam
Barito
Kapuas
Müller Mts.
Tanabo Range
Kayan

VIETNAM
Qui Nhon
Nha Trang
Da Lat
Hô Chi Minh
Rach Gia
Can Tho
Mouths of the Mekong

CAMBODIA
Phnom Penh
Siem Reap
Sisophon
Battambang
Tonle Sap
Bangkok
Ratchasima
Mae Nam Mun
Mekong

Gulf of Thailand

Mergui
Nakhon Si Thammarat
Ko Samui
Hat Yai
Phuket
Kota Bharu
Kuala Terengganu
Kuantan
Alor Setar
George Town
Ipoh
Kuala Lumpur
Johor Bahru
SINGAPORE
Pekanbaru
Medan
Banda Aceh
Pematangsiantar
Padang
Mt. Kerinci 3805m
Barisan Mountains
Jambi
Palembang
Lingga Islands
Bangka
Belitung
Tanjungkarang-Telukbetung

ANDAMAN SEA

Nias
Mentawai Islands

Karimata Strait

Sumatra

MANOKWARI
New Guinea
Doberai Peninsula
Sorong
Waigeo
Misoöl
Kai Islands
Aru Islands
Tanimbar Islands
ARAFURA SEA

Morotai
Halmahera
Ternate
Manado
Gorontalo
Minahasa Peninsula
Ampana
Buru
Seram
SERAM SEA
Ambon
MOLUCCA SEA
Sula Islands

Sulawesi
Palopo
Parepare
Majene
Kendari
Buton
Ujung Pandang
BANDA SEA
Wetar
Dili
EAST TIMOR
Alor
Lomblen
Timor
Kupang
SAWU SEA

Makassar Strait

FLORES SEA
Flores
Sumba
Sumbawa
Raba
Lombok
Bali
Denpasar
Mataram
Madura
Surabaya
Malang
Surakarta
Semarang
Cirebon
Yogyakarta
Jakarta
Bandung
Bogor

JAVA SEA
Sunda Strait

Arnhem Land
Melville I.
Bathurst I.
Darwin
Katherine
Daly Waters
Victoria
Daly
Kununurra
L. Argyle
AUSTRALIA
Wyndham
Kimberley Plateau
Halls Creek
Derby
Fitzroy
Broome
Eighty Mile Beach
Joseph Bonaparte Gulf

TIMOR SEA

INDIAN OCEAN

Scale 1: 20 000 000
0 200 400 600km

Key

settlements		land height above sea level in metres
country boundary		more than 5000m
disputed boundary		2000 – 5000m
main road		1000 – 2000m
railway		500 – 1000m
main airport		200 – 500m
river		less than 200m
lake		land below sea level
marsh		highest peaks with heights in metres
ice cap		

settlements
☐ over 1 million people
☐ 100 000–1 000 000 people
○ under 100 000 people

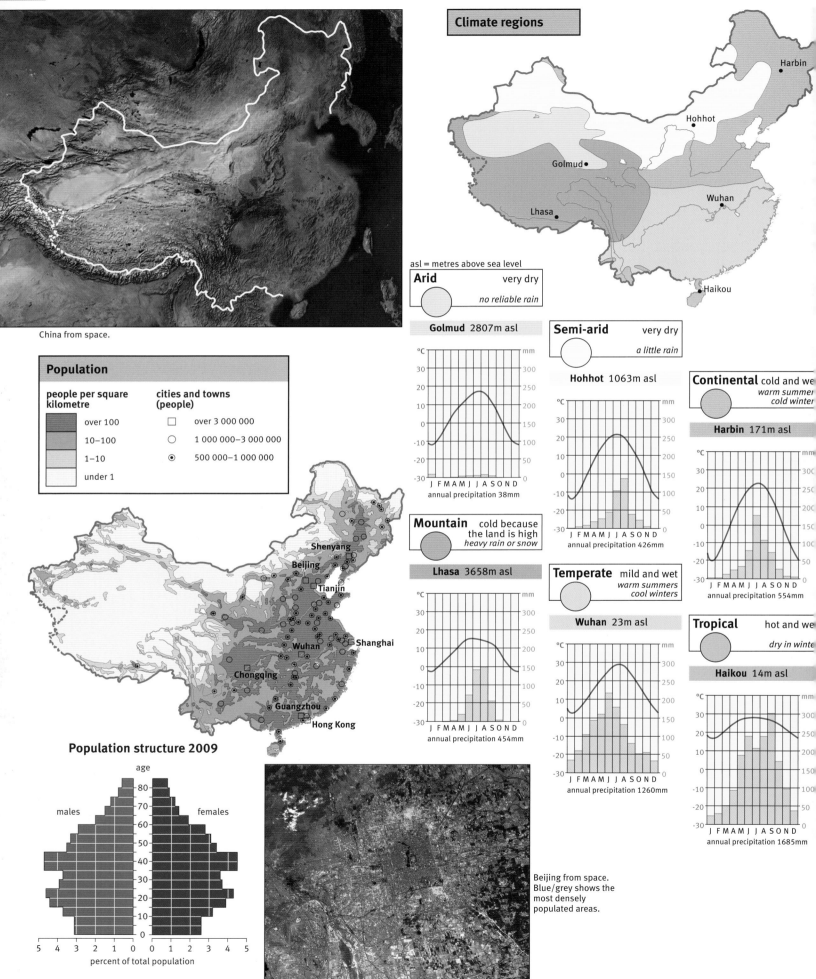

China from space.

Climate regions

asl = metres above sea level

Harbin
Hohhot
Golmud
Wuhan
Lhasa
Haikou

Arid — very dry
no reliable rain

Semi-arid — very dry
a little rain

Continental cold and we
warm summer
cold winter

Mountain cold because the land is high
heavy rain or snow

Temperate mild and wet
warm summers
cool winters

Tropical hot and we
dry in winte

Golmud 2807m asl
annual precipitation 38mm

Hohhot 1063m asl
annual precipitation 426mm

Harbin 171m asl
annual precipitation 554mm

Lhasa 3658m asl
annual precipitation 454mm

Wuhan 23m asl
annual precipitation 1260mm

Haikou 14m asl
annual precipitation 1685mm

Population

people per square kilometre
- over 100
- 10–100
- 1–10
- under 1

cities and towns (people)
- □ over 3 000 000
- ○ 1 000 000–3 000 000
- ◉ 500 000–1 000 000

Shenyang
Beijing
Tianjin
Wuhan
Shanghai
Chongqing
Guangzhou
Hong Kong

Population structure 2009

age
80
70
60
50
40
30
20
10
0

males   females

5 4 3 2 1 0   0 1 2 3 4 5
percent of total population

Beijing from space.
Blue/grey shows the
most densely
populated areas.

Farming

- arable
- livestock and grassland
- forest
- non agricultural land
- rice

Gansu

Xinjiang

Yunnan

Yunnan

Xinjiang

Gansu

Yunnan

Industry

- very large industrial centres
- large industrial centres

Daqing
Harbin
Jilin
Fushun
Shenyang
Anshan
Beijing
Dalian
Baotou
Dagang Tianjin
Taiyuan
Lanzhou
Xi'an
Nanjing
Wuhan Shanghai
Chengdu
Guangzhou

Shihezi, Xinjiang

Chengdu

Shanghai

Water resources

Drainage basins

- Pacific Ocean
- inland
- Indian Ocean
- Arctic Ocean
- irrigated land
- river embankment
- major HEP station

Tarim He
Qinghai Hu
Huang He
Lancang Jiang
Yarlung Zangbo Jiang
Nu Jiang
Jinsha Jiang
Three Gorges Dam
Gezhouba Dam
Chang Jiang
Dongting Hu
Poyang Hu
Xi Jiang

Three Gorges Dam and Gezhouba Dam

Key

▬▬▬	country boundary
▪ ▪ ▪	disputed boundary
▬▬	main road
──	railway
⊕	main airport
~	river
◠	lake
≈≈≈	marsh

settlements

⊡	over 1 million people
○	100 000–1 000 000 people
•	under 100 000 people

land height
above sea level in metres

more than 5000m
2000 – 5000m
1000 – 2000m
500 – 1000m
200 – 500m
less than 200m
land below sea level

▲ highest peaks with heights in metres

Scale 1: 7 000 000
One centimetre on the map represents 70 kilometres on the ground.

0   70   140   210km

RUSSIAN FEDERATION (RUSSIA)

Sikhote Alin

Iman

Ussuri

Dal'negorsk

Nakhodka

SOUTH KOREA

Pohang

Taegu

Pusan

Korea Strait

Tsushima

Iki

Sasebo

Nagasaki

Kita-Kyūshu

Shimonoseki

Fukuoka

Kurume

Kumamoto

▲Kuju-san 1788m

▲1739m

Kyūshū

Miyazaki

Kagoshima

Yaku-shima

Osumi-kaikyo

Tanega-shima

SEA OF OKHOTSK

Rebun-tō
Rishiri-tō

Wakkanai

Monbetsu

Asahikawa

Asahi-dake ▲2290m

Kitami

Hokkaidō

Nemuro

Kushiro

Kunashir

Administered by Russia. Claimed by Japan.

Ishikari-wan

Otaru

Yūbari

Obihiro

Sapporo

Tomakomai

Muroran

Samani

Erimo-misaki

Mori

Okushiri-tō

Hakodate

Tsugaru-kaikyo

SEA OF JAPAN

Aomori

Hachinohe

Hirosaki

Ōdate

Noshiro

Morioka

Miyako

Akita

Kamaishi

Sakata

Ishinomaki

Yamagata

Sendai

Niigata

Sadoga-shima

Fukushima

Aizu-wakamatsu

Kōriyama

Agano

Nagaoka

Iwaki

Suzu-misaki

Nagano

Honshū

Kashiwazaki

Iōetsu

Hitachi

JAPAN

Ueda

Utsunomiya

Mito

Takaoka

Kanazawa

Toyama

▲3180m

Matsumoto

Ōyama

Tsuchiura

Komatsu

Urawa

Chiba

Fukui

Tōkyō

Kawasaki

Oki-shotō

Matsue

Tottori

Maizuru

Wakasa-wan

Biwa-ko

Gifu

Nagoya

Fuji-san ▲3776m

Yokohama

Numazu

Chūgoku-sanchi

Okayama

Kyōto

Ogaki

Toyota

Shizuoka

Ō-shima

Kōbe

Ōsaka

Tsu

Suzuka

Hamamatsu

Sakai

Ise

Hiroshima

Takamatsu

Seto-naikai

Tokushima

Wakayama

Kii-suidō

Izu-shotō

Matsuyama

Kōchi

Shikoku

Shiono-misaki

PACIFIC OCEAN

Ashizuri-misaki

140°E

135°E

140°E

145°E

40°N

35°N

Zenithal Equidistant Projection
© Oxford University Press

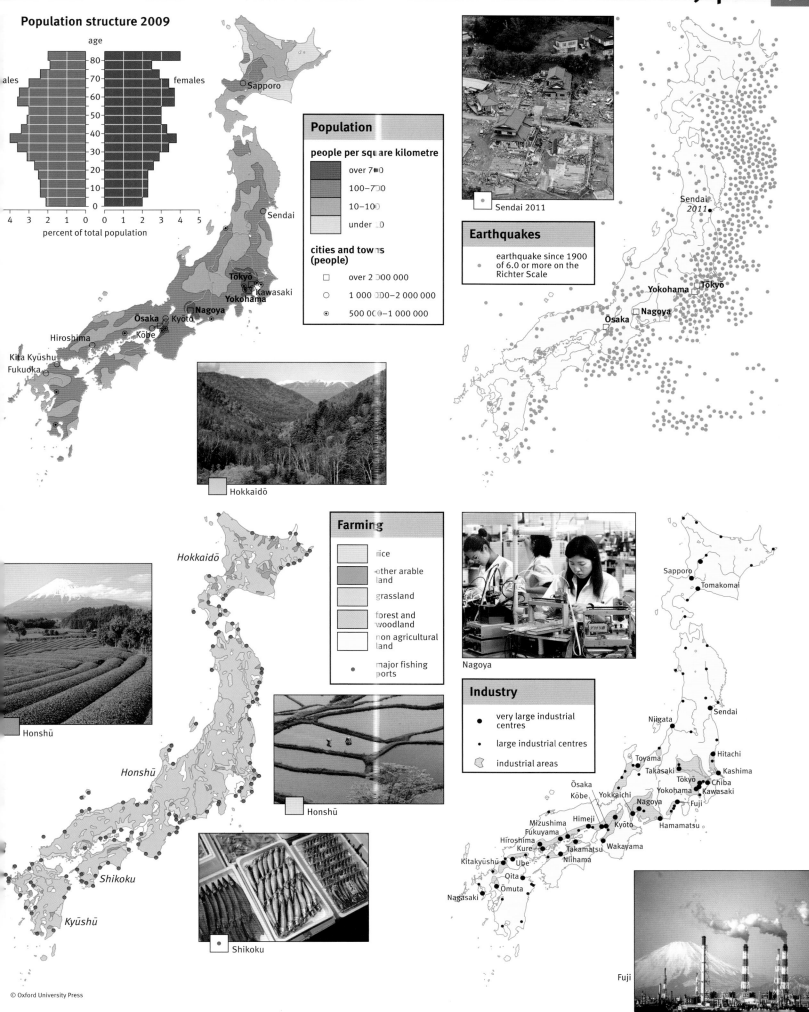

Population structure 2009

age

males / females

80, 70, 60, 50, 40, 30, 20, 10, 0

5 4 3 2 1 0 0 1 2 3 4 5
percent of total population

Population

people per square kilometre
- over 700
- 100–700
- 10–100
- under 10

cities and towns (people)
- ☐ over 2 000 000
- ○ 1 000 000–2 000 000
- ◉ 500 000–1 000 000

Sapporo

Sendai

Tōkyō
Kawasaki
Yokohama
Nagoya
Ōsaka Kyōto
Hiroshima Kōbe
Kita Kyūshū
Fukuoka

Hokkaidō

Sendai 2011

Earthquakes

- earthquake since 1900 of 6.0 or more on the Richter Scale

Sendai 2011

Yokohama Tōkyō
Ōsaka Nagoya

Farming

- rice
- other arable land
- grassland
- forest and woodland
- non agricultural land
- • major fishing ports

Hokkaidō

Honshū

Honshū

Honshū

Shikoku

Kyūshū

Shikoku

Nagoya

Industry

- ● very large industrial centres
- • large industrial centres
- ▨ industrial areas

Sapporo
Tomakomai

Niigata
Sendai

Hitachi
Toyama
Takasaki Kashima
Ōsaka Tōkyō
Kōbe Yokkaichi Chiba
Nagoya Yokohama
Mizushima Kawasaki
Himeji Fuji
Fukuyama Kyōto Hamamatsu
Hiroshima Wakayama
Kure Takamatsu
Kitakyūshū Niihama
Ube
Ōita
Nagasaki Ōmuta

Fuji

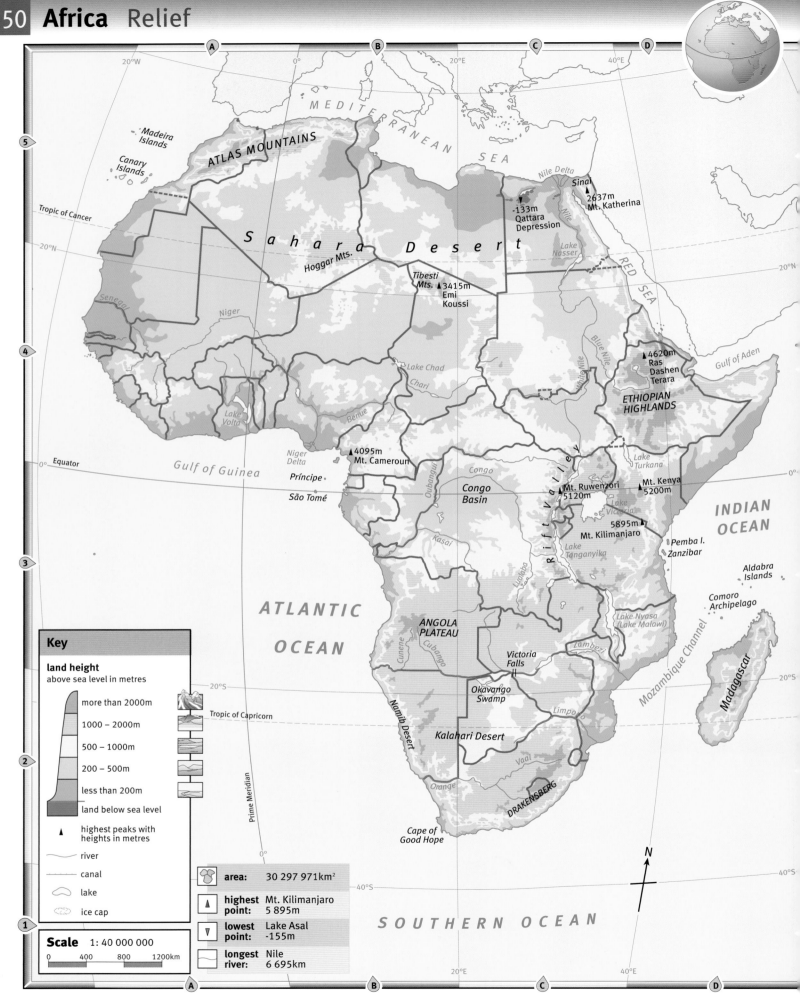

A | B | C | D

MEDITERRANEAN SEA

Madeira Islands

Canary Islands

ATLAS MOUNTAINS

Tropic of Cancer

20°N

S a h a r a   D e s e r t

Hoggar Mts.

Senegal

Niger

Tibesti Mts. ▲3415m Emi Koussi

Lake Chad

Chari

Benue

Lake Volta

Niger Delta

▲4095m Mt. Cameroun

Gulf of Guinea

Príncipe

São Tomé

Equator 0°

Oubangui

Congo

Congo Basin

Kasai

Nile Delta

Sinai
▲2637m Mt. Katherina

▼-133m Qattara Depression

Nile

Lake Nasser

RED SEA

White Nile

Blue Nile

▲4620m Ras Dashen Terara

ETHIOPIAN HIGHLANDS

Gulf of Aden

Lake Turkana

Rift Valley

Mt. Ruwenzori ▲5120m

Mt. Kenya ▲5200m

Lake Victoria

5895m▲ Mt. Kilimanjaro

Pemba I.

Zanzibar

INDIAN OCEAN

Lake Tanganyika

Aldabra Islands

Comoro Archipelago

Luapula

ATLANTIC OCEAN

ANGOLA PLATEAU

Cunene

Cubango

Lake Nyasa (Lake Malawi)

Zambezi

Victoria Falls

Mozambique Channel

Madagascar

Okavango Swamp

20°S

Tropic of Capricorn

Namib Desert

Kalahari Desert

Limpopo

Vaal

Prime Meridian

0°

Orange

DRAKENSBERG

Cape of Good Hope

N

40°S

SOUTHERN OCEAN

20°W   0°   20°E   40°E

20°N

20°S

40°S

Key

land height
above sea level in metres

- more than 2000m
- 1000 – 2000m
- 500 – 1000m
- 200 – 500m
- less than 200m
- land below sea level

▲ highest peaks with heights in metres

～ river

⊶ canal

◯ lake

⬭ ice cap

Scale 1: 40 000 000

0   400   800   1200km

	area:	30 297 971km²
highest point:	Mt. Kilimanjaro	5 895m
lowest point:	Lake Asal	-155m
longest river:	Nile	6 695km

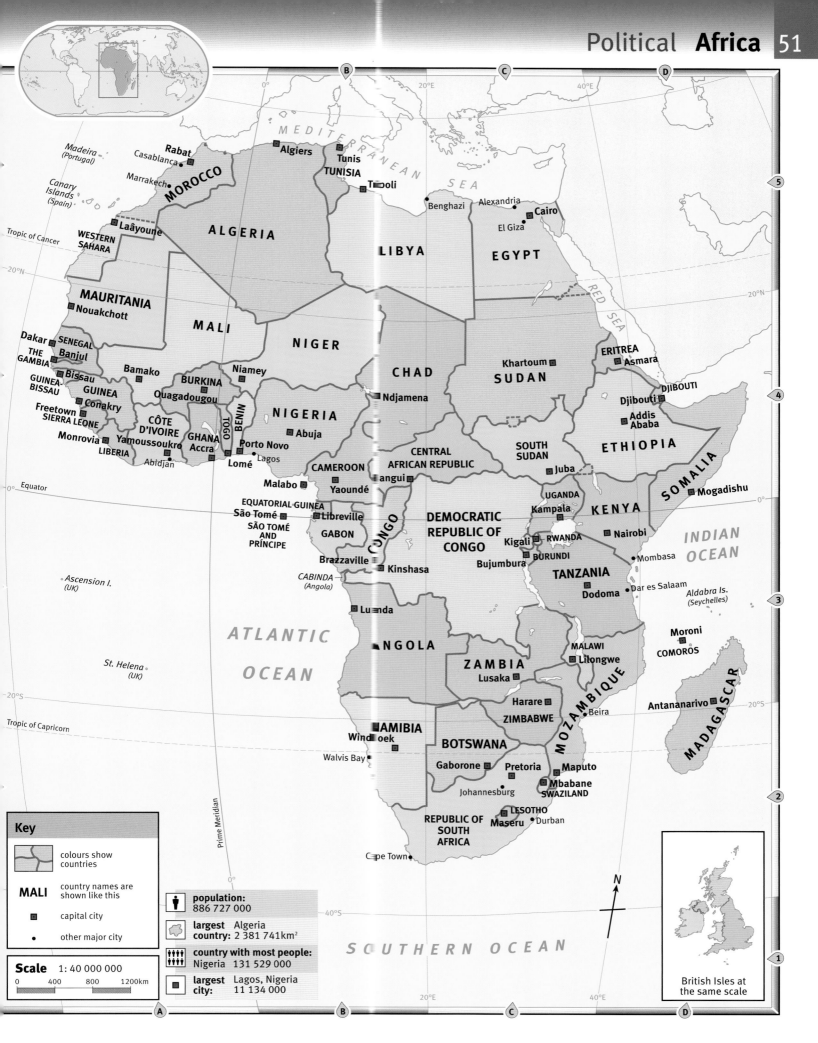

MEDITERRANEAN SEA

Madeira (Portugal)

Rabat
Casablanca
Marrakech
MOROCCO

Canary Islands (Spain)

Tropic of Cancer

Laâyoune
WESTERN SAHARA

Algiers
Tunis
TUNISIA
Tripoli

ALGERIA

LIBYA

Benghazi   Alexandria
Cairo
El Giza
EGYPT

RED SEA

20°N   20°N

MAURITANIA
Nouakchott

MALI

NIGER

CHAD

SUDAN
Khartoum

ERITREA
Asmara

Dakar
SENEGAL
Banjul
THE GAMBIA
Bissau
GUINEA-BISSAU
GUINEA
Conakry
Freetown
SIERRA LEONE
Monrovia
LIBERIA

Bamako

BURKINA
Ouagadougou

Niamey

Ndjamena

Djibouti
DJIBOUTI
Djibouti

CÔTE D'IVOIRE
GHANA
Yamoussoukro
Accra
Abidjan
TOGO
BENIN
Lomé
Porto Novo

NIGERIA
Abuja
Lagos

CENTRAL AFRICAN REPUBLIC

SOUTH SUDAN
Juba

Addis Ababa
ETHIOPIA

0°   Equator

CAMEROON
Bangui
Malabo
Yaoundé
EQUATORIAL GUINEA
São Tomé
Libreville
SÃO TOMÉ AND PRÍNCIPE
GABON

DEMOCRATIC REPUBLIC OF CONGO

CONGO
Brazzaville
Kinshasa

UGANDA
Kampala
Kigali
RWANDA
Bujumbura
BURUNDI

KENYA
Nairobi
Mombasa

SOMALIA
Mogadishu

0°

INDIAN OCEAN

Ascension I. (UK)

CABINDA (Angola)

Luanda

TANZANIA
Dodoma
Dar es Salaam

Aldabra Is. (Seychelles)

3

ATLANTIC OCEAN

St. Helena (UK)

ANGOLA

ZAMBIA
Lusaka

MALAWI
Lilongwe

Moroni
COMOROS

MADAGASCAR

20°S   20°S

Tropic of Capricorn

NAMIBIA
Windhoek
Walvis Bay

Harare
ZIMBABWE

BOTSWANA
Gaborone

MOZAMBIQUE
Beira

Antananarivo

Maputo
SWAZILAND
Mbabane

Pretoria
Johannesburg

2

LESOTHO
Maseru   Durban

REPUBLIC OF SOUTH AFRICA

Cape Town

Prime Meridian

0°

N

SOUTHERN OCEAN

40°S

Key

colours show countries

MALI   country names are shown like this

☐ capital city

• other major city

Scale 1: 40 000 000

0   400   800   1200km

👤 population: 886 727 000

largest country: Algeria 2 381 741km²

👪 country with most people: Nigeria 131 529 000

■ largest city: Lagos, Nigeria 11 134 000

British Isles at the same scale

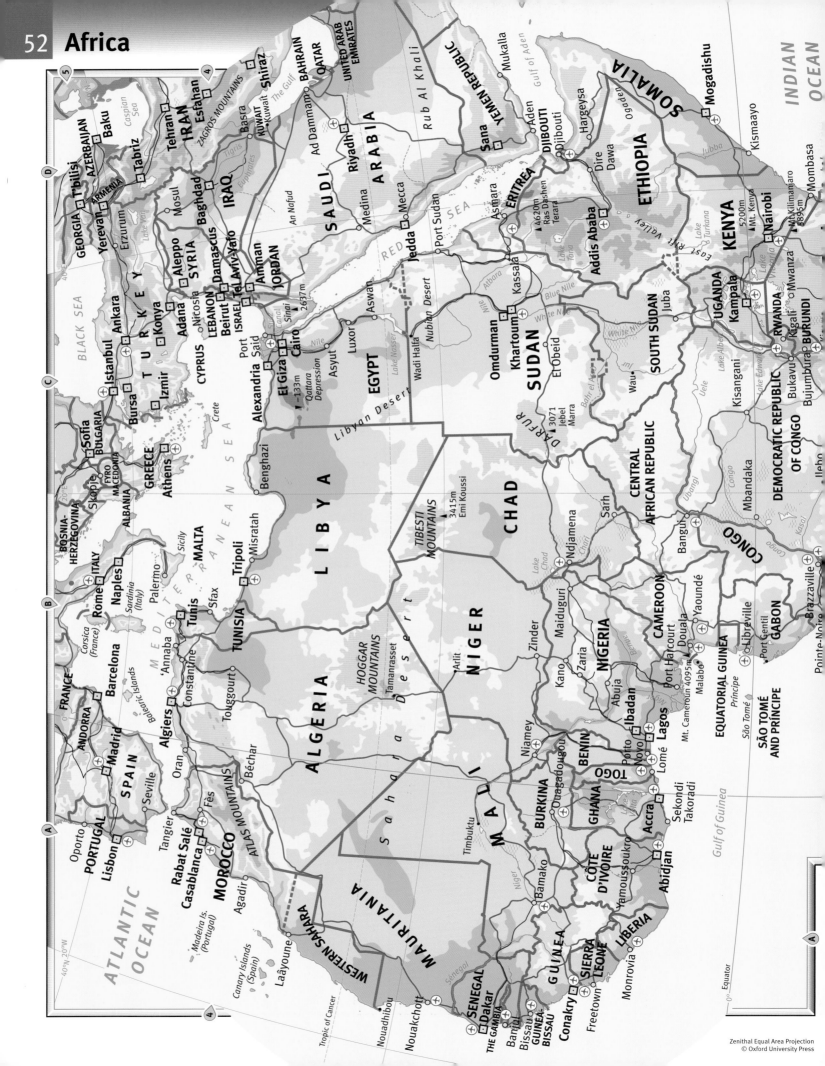

INDIAN OCEAN

SOMALIA ■ Mogadishu

Mukalla

Gulf of Aden

Aden

Hargeysa

Kismaayo

ETHIOPIA

Dire Dawa

▲4620m Ras Dashen Terara

Mt. Kenya 5200m

KENYA

■ Nairobi

Mt.Kilimanjaro 5895m

Mombasa

ERITREA

Asmara

Kassala

Djibouti

DJIBOUTI

Addis Ababa

Lake Turkana

UGANDA

Kampala

Mwanza

RWANDA

Kigali

Bukavu

BURUNDI

Bujumbura

Lake Victoria

Lake Albert

Lake Edward

YEMEN REPUBLIC

Sana

SAUDI ARABIA

Medina

Mecca

Riyadh

Ad Dammam

QATAR

BAHRAIN

UNITED ARAB EMIRATES

Rub Al Khali

The Gulf

KUWAIT

Kuwait

Basra

Baghdad

IRAQ

Mosul

Euphrates

Tigris

IRAN

Tehran

Esfahan

Shiraz

Tabriz

AZERBAIJAN

Baku

Caspian Sea

ARMENIA

Yerevan

GEORGIA

T'bilisi

Erzurum

Lake Van

ZAGROS MOUNTAINS

An Nafud

Jedda

RED SEA

Port Sudan

Aswan

Wadi Halfa

Lake Nasser

Nubian Desert

Omdurman

Khartoum

El Obeid

SUDAN

Atbara

Blue Nile

White Nile

SOUTH SUDAN

Juba

Wau

Bahr el Arab

DARFUR

▲3071 Jebel Marra

CENTRAL AFRICAN REPUBLIC

Bangui

Kisangani

Mbandaka

DEMOCRATIC REPUBLIC OF CONGO

Congo

Uele

Ubangi

Kasai

CONGO

Brazzaville

Pointe-Noire

Libreville

Port Gentil

GABON

Yaoundé

Douala

CAMEROON

Mt. Cameroun 4095m ▲

Malabo

EQUATORIAL GUINEA

Príncipe

São Tomé

SÃO TOMÉ AND PRÍNCIPE

Benue

Ndjamena

Lake Chad

Chari

Sarh

CHAD

▲3415m Emi Koussi

TIBESTI MOUNTAINS

Maiduguri

Zinder

Kano

Zaria

NIGERIA

Abuja

Ibadan

Lagos

Port Harcourt

NIGER

Arlit

Zinder

Niamey

BENIN

Porto Novo

TOGO

Lomé

Lake Volta

GHANA

Accra

Sekondi Takoradi

Kumasi

Ouagadougou

BURKINA

CÔTE D'IVOIRE

Yamoussoukro

Abidjan

MALI

Timbuktu

Bamako

Niger

SENEGAL

Dakar

Sénégal

THE GAMBIA

Banjul

GUINEA BISSAU

Bissau

GUINEA

Conakry

SIERRA LEONE

Freetown

LIBERIA

Monrovia

MAURITANIA

Nouakchott

Nouadhibou

WESTERN SAHARA

Laâyoune

Tropic of Cancer

Equator

Gulf of Guinea

ALGERIA

Béchar

HOGGAR MOUNTAINS

Tamanrasset

Sahara Desert

LIBYA

Tripoli

Misrath

Benghazi

Sfax

TUNISIA

Tunis

'Annaba

Constantine

Touggourt

MOROCCO

Rabat Salé

Casablanca

Tangier

Fès

Agadir

ATLAS MOUNTAINS

Algiers

Oran

EGYPT

Cairo

El Giza ▼ -133m

Qattara Depression

Alexandria

Port Said

Suez Canal

Sinai 2637m

Luxor

Asyut

Libyan Desert

Nile

JORDAN

Amman

Tel Aviv-Yafo

ISRAEL

Beirut

LEBANON

Damascus

SYRIA

Aleppo

Adana

CYPRUS

Nicosia

TURKEY

Ankara

Konya

Izmir

Bursa

Istanbul

GREECE

Athens

Crete

MALTA

Palermo

Sicily

Catania

ITALY

Naples

Rome

Sardinia (Italy)

Corsica (France)

ALBANIA

FYRO MACEDONIA

Skopje

BULGARIA

Sofia

BOSNIA-HERZEGOVINA

BLACK SEA

MEDITERRANEAN SEA

FRANCE

Barcelona

ANDORRA

Madrid

SPAIN

Seville

PORTUGAL

Lisbon

Oporto

Balearic Islands

Madeira Is. (Portugal)

Canary Islands (Spain)

ATLANTIC OCEAN

40°N 20°W

20°E

40°E

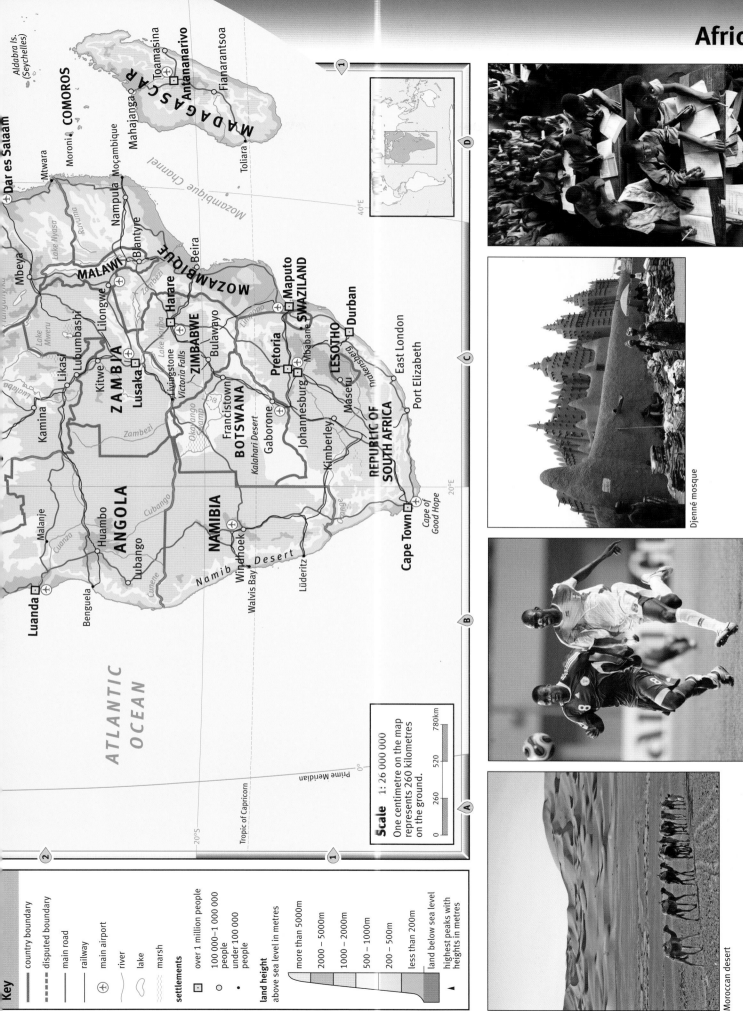

ATLANTIC OCEAN

MADAGASCAR

Aldabra Is.
(Seychelles)

COMOROS
Moroni

Mtwara

Dar es Salaam

Antananarivo
Toamasina
Mahajanga
Fianarantsoa
Toliara

Mozambique Channel

Nampula
Moçambique

Beira

Blantyre

MALAWI

MOZAMBIQUE

Ruvuma

Lake Nyasa

Mbeya

Lake Mweru

Likasi
Lubumbashi

Kamina

Kitwe

ZAMBIA

Lusaka

Harare

ZIMBABWE

Bulawayo

Livingstone
Victoria Falls

Lake Kariba

Zambezi

Maputo
SWAZILAND
Mbabane

Pretoria

Johannesburg

LESOTHO
Maseru

Durban

Drakensberg

East London

Port Elizabeth

REPUBLIC OF
SOUTH AFRICA

Kimberley

Gaborone

BOTSWANA

Francistown

Kalahari Desert

Okavango Swamp

Luanda

ANGOLA

Malanje

Benguela

Huambo

Lubango

Cuanza

Cubango

Cunene

Cuito

NAMIBIA

Windhoek

Walvis Bay

Lüderitz

Namib Desert

Orange

Cape Town

Cape of
Good Hope

Tropic of Capricorn

Prime Meridian

20°S

0°

20°E

40°E

Dar es Salaam

Mweru

Lualaba

Zambezi

Limpopo

Scale 1: 26 000 000
One centimetre on the map represents 260 kilometres on the ground.

0   260   520   780km

Key

country boundary
- - - - disputed boundary
main road
railway
✈ main airport
river
lake
marsh

settlements
■ over 1 million people
○ 100 000–1 000 000 people
• under 100 000 people

land height
above sea level in metres

more than 5000m
2000 – 5000m
1000 – 2000m
500 – 1000m
200 – 500m
less than 200m
land below sea level

▲ highest peaks with heights in metres

Classroom in Togo

Djenné mosque

African Cup of Nations

Moroccan desert

Key

—	country boundary
- - -	disputed boundary
—	regional boundary
—	main road
—	railway
⊕	main airport
∿	river
∿	seasonal river
⌒	lake
⣿	marsh

settlements

⊡	over 1 million people
○	100 000–1 000 000 people
•	under 100 000 people

land height
above sea level in metres

	more than 5000m
	2000 – 5000m
	1000 – 2000m
	500 – 1000m
	200 – 500m
	less than 200m
	land below sea level
▲	highest peaks with heights in metres

Scale 1: 7 000 000

0   70   140   210km

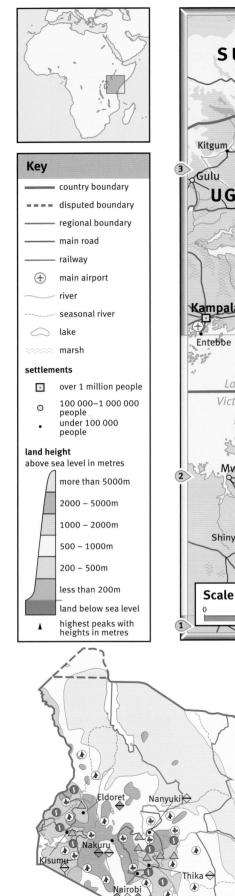

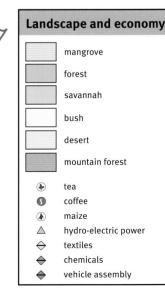

Landscape and economy

	mangrove
	forest
	savannah
	bush
	desert
	mountain forest
♨	tea
❶	coffee
⚶	maize
△	hydro-electric power
◇	textiles
◈	chemicals
◆	vehicle assembly

mangrove

forest

savannah

bush

desert

mountain fores

Zenithal Equal Area Projection
© Oxford University Press

Climate regions

as = metres above sea level

Tropical	hot with some seasonal rain *drier north*
Tropical	hot and wet *wetter, cooler highlands*
Tropical	hot and wet *hotter, humid coast*

Wajir 244m asl

mm

J F M A M J J A S O N D

annual precipitation 264mm

Eldoret 2120m asl

°C / mm

J F M A M J J A S O N D

annual precipitation 1223mm

Mombasa 57m asl

°C / mm

J F M A M J J A S O N D

annual precipitation 1144mm

• Wajir

• Eldoret

• Mombasa

over 100 people per square kilometre

under 10 people per square kilometre

Population structure 2009

age

males / females

80
70
60
50
40
30
20
10
0

9 8 7 6 5 4 3 2 1 0   0 1 2 3 4 5 6 7 8 9

percent of total population

Population

people per square kilometre

over 100

10–100

under 10

cities and towns (people)

○ over 1 000 000

◉ 100 000–1 000 000

• 25 000–100 000

Eldoret
Kisumu
Nakuru
Meru
Nairobi
Machakos
Mombasa

Tourism can have an impact on local landscapes and people.

Tourism

National Parks and wildlife reserves

○ coastal resorts

✳ sites of natural beauty

cultural heritage sites

archaeological sites

Lake Turkana

Marsabit

Kisumu
Mount Kenya National Park
Nakuru
✳ 5200m
Mount Kenya
Meru National Park
Aberdare National Park
Lake Naivasha
Masai Mara National Res.
Nairobi
Amboseli National Park
Tsavo National Park
Gedi Ruins
Malindi
Watamu
Kilifi
Mombasa
Lamu

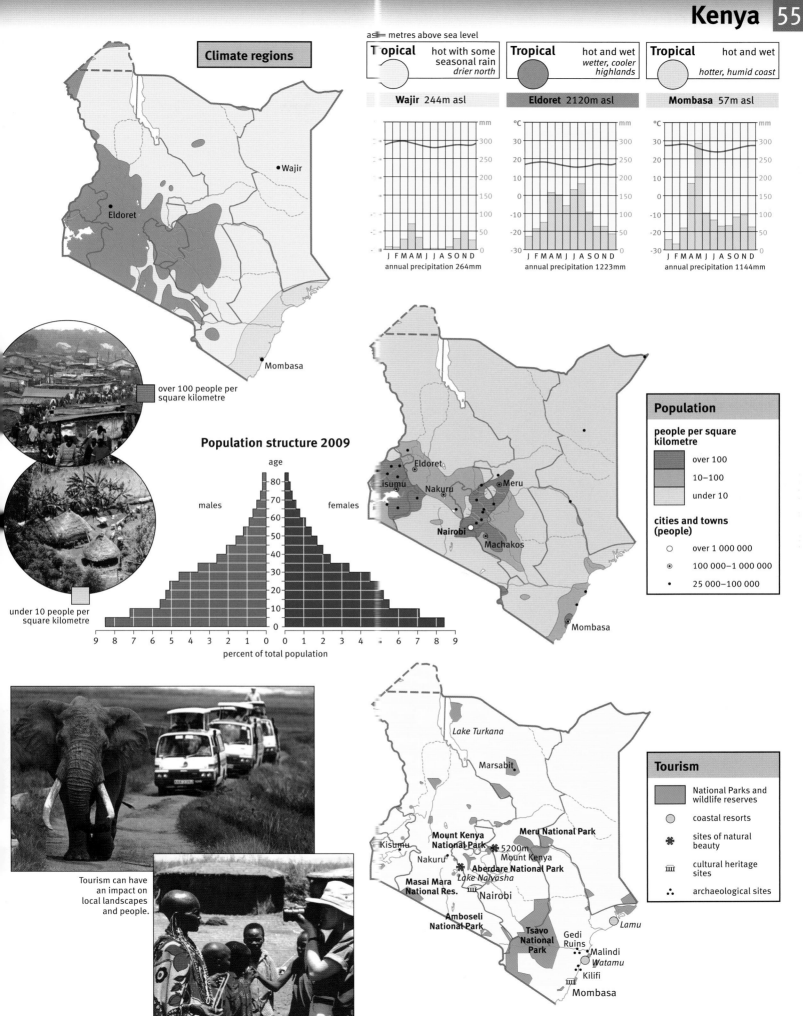

BERING SEA

Aleutian Islands

St. Lawrence Island

ARCTIC OCEAN

BEAUFORT SEA

North Pole

Ⓐ
Ⓑ
Ⓒ
Ⓓ
Ⓔ Ⓕ Ⓖ
Ⓗ
Ⓙ

Ellesmere Island

Queen Elizabeth Islands

Banks Island

Parry Islands

Devon Island

Victoria Island

GREENLAND SEA

Greenland

Mt. Forel 3360m

Denmark Strait

Yukon

Arctic Circle

Mt. McKinley 6194m

Mt. Logan 5951m

Gulf of Alaska

Queen Charlotte Islands

Vancouver Island

Coast Mountains

Mackenzie

Great Bear Lake

Great Slave Lake

Liard

Peace

Saskatchewan

Columbia

Snake

Great Basin

Sierra Nevada

4418m Mt. Whitney

Death Valley -86m

Great Salt Lake

Colorado

Colorado Plateau

R O C K Y   M O U N T A I N S

G r e a t   P l a i n s

Missouri

Canadian Shield

Hudson Bay

Hudson Strait

Baffin Island

Baffin Bay

Davis Strait

Cape Farewell

Lake Winnipeg

Lake Superior

The Great Lakes

Lake Michigan

Lake Huron

Lake Erie

Lake Ontario

St. Lawrence

Hudson

Gulf of St. Lawrence

Newfoundland

Cape Cod

Arkansas

Ohio

Tennessee

Mississippi

APPALACHIAN MTS.

Rio Grande

Gulf of California

Sierra Madre Occidental

Sierra Madre Oriental

5452m Popocatepetl

5699m Citlaltépetl

Mississippi Delta

Gulf of Mexico

Florida

Yucatan Peninsula

Greater Antilles

Hispaniola

West Indies

Leeward Is.

CARIBBEAN SEA

Lesser Antilles

Windward Is.

Trinidad

Lake Nicaragua

Panama Isthmus

PACIFIC OCEAN

ATLANTIC OCEAN

Tropic of Cancer

Equator

Key

land height
above sea level in metres

- more than 2000m
- 1000 – 2000m
- 500 – 1000m
- 200 – 500m
- less than 200m
- land below sea level

▲ highest peaks with heights in metres

~~ river

canal

lake

ice cap

Scale 1: 40 000 000

0   400   800   1200km

	area:	22 656 216km²
▲	highest point:	Mt. McKinley 6 194m
▼	lowest point:	Death Valley -86m
	longest river:	Mississippi-Missouri 5 969km

Oblique Mercator Projection
© Oxford University Press

ARCTIC OCEAN

60°N   80°N   80°N   0°

A
B
C
D   E   F   G
J
H

Arctic Circle

USA
ALASKA
Anchorage

GREENLAND
(Denmark)

20°W

YUKON
TERRITORY

NORTHWEST TERRITORIES

NUNAVUT

Nuuk

60°N

40°W

BRITISH COLUMBIA

ALBERTA

C A N A D A

Vancouver
Seattle
Portland
WASHINGTON

Edmonton

Calgary

SASKATCHEWAN

MANITOBA

ONTARIO

QUÉBEC

Newfoundland and Labrador

PACIFIC

OREGON

MONTANA

Winnipeg

St-Pierre & Miquelon
(France)

OCEAN

140°W

San Francisco
Sacramento
NEVADA

IDAHO

WYOMING

Salt Lake City

UTAH

UNITED STATES OF AMERICA

NORTH DAKOTA

SOUTH DAKOTA

NEBRASKA

COLORADO

Minneapolis

MINNESOTA

WISCONSIN

MICHIGAN

Chicago
ILLINOIS

IOWA

Detroit

Toronto

Québec

Ottawa

Montréal
MAINE

NEW BRUNSWICK

NOVA SCOTIA
Halifax

NEW YORK

VT.
N.H.
MA.
Boston

Tropic of Cancer

Los Angeles
San Diego
CALIFORNIA

ARIZONA
Phoenix

NEW MEXICO

Denver

KANSAS

Kansas City
MISSOURI
St Louis

OKLAHOMA

INDIANA
OHIO

Pittsburgh
PENNSYLVANIA

Washington D.C.
W.V.
KENTUCKY

VIRGINIA

New York
N.J.
Philadelphia
MD.
DE.

CT. R.I.

20°N

TEXAS

ARKANSAS

TENNESSEE

NORTH CAROLINA

Dallas

MS.

ALABAMA

GEORGIA

SOUTH CAROLINA

Atlanta

Bermuda
(UK)

CT.	CONNECTICUT
DE.	DELAWARE
MA.	MASSACHUSETTS
MD.	MARYLAND
MS.	MISSISSIPPI
N.H.	NEW HAMPSHIRE
N.J.	NEW JERSEY
R.I.	RHODE ISLAND
VT.	VERMONT
W.V.	WEST VIRGINIA

Houston
LOUISIANA
New Orleans

Monterrey

Gulf of Mexico

FLORIDA
Miami

THE BAHAMAS
Nassau

ATLANTIC

OCEAN

Guadalajara

MEXICO

Mexico City

Puebla

Havana

CUBA

Kingston

JAMAICA

DOMINICAN REPUBLIC

PUERTO RICO
(USA)

San Juan

ST. KITTS AND NEVIS

20°N

Belmopan
GUATEMALA
BELIZE
Guatemala City
HONDURAS
San Salvador
Tegucigalpa
EL SALVADOR
NICARAGUA
Managua

Port-au-Prince
HAITI

Santo Domingo

ANTIGUA & BARBUDA
DOMINICA
ST. VINCENT & THE GRENADINES
ST. LUCIA
BARBADOS
GRENADA
Port of Spain
TRINIDAD & TOBAGO

CARIBBEAN SEA

San José
COSTA RICA

Panama City
PANAMA

British Isles at the same scale

Key

colours show countries

CUBA country names are shown like this

◼ capital city

• other major city

Scale 1 : 40 000 000
0 400 800 1200km

👤 **population:**
511 166 000

🗺 **largest** Canada
country: 9 970 601km²

👥 **country with most people:**
USA 298 213 000

◼ **largest** Mexico City, Mexico
city: 18 934 000

Equator

100°W   80°W   60°W

D   E   F   G

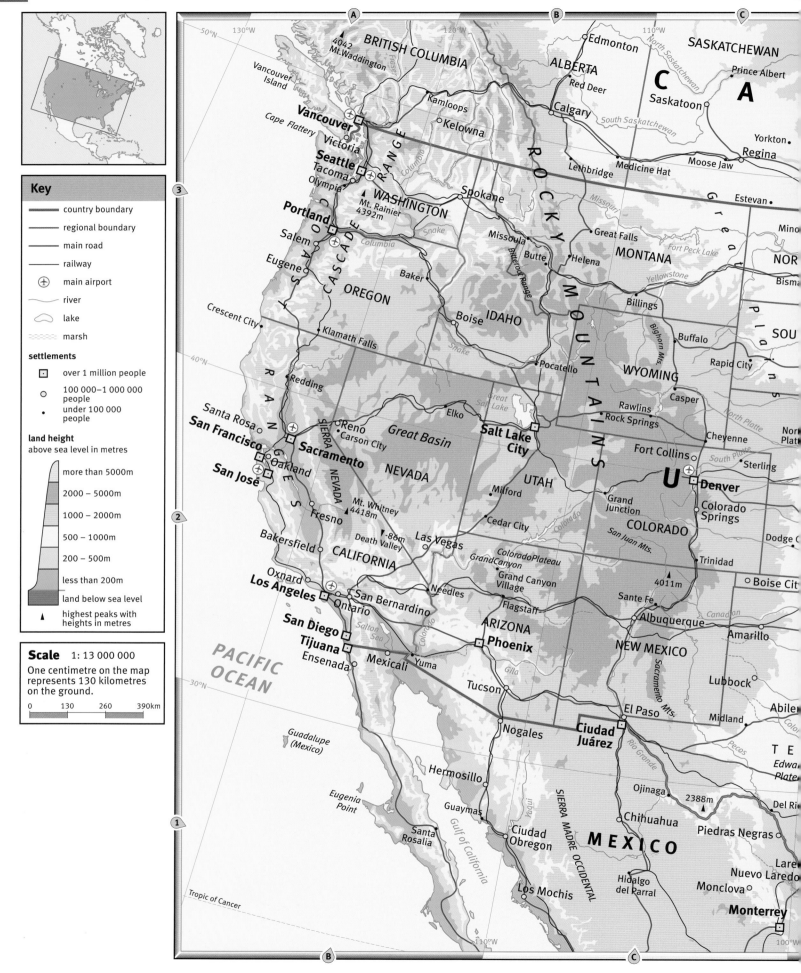

Key

- —— country boundary
- —— regional boundary
- —— main road
- —— railway
- ⊕ main airport
- river
- lake
- marsh

settlements

- ⊡ over 1 million people
- ○ 100 000 – 1 000 000 people
- • under 100 000 people

land height
above sea level in metres

- more than 5000m
- 2000 – 5000m
- 1000 – 2000m
- 500 – 1000m
- 200 – 500m
- less than 200m
- land below sea level
- ▲ highest peaks with heights in metres

Scale 1: 13 000 000

One centimetre on the map represents 130 kilometres on the ground.

0   130   260   390km

PACIFIC OCEAN

Tropic of Cancer

Conical Orthomorphic Projection
© Oxford University Press

Norway House
Lake Winnipeg
MANITOBA
nitoba
Portage La Prairie
Brandon
Winnipeg
Lake of the Woods
Upper Red Lake
Lower Red Lake
Grand Forks
KOTA
Bemidji
Fargo
MINNESOTA
Duluth
KOTA
rre
Mitchell
Sioux Falls
Sioux City
BRASKA
Lincoln
Omaha
S
KANSAS
Salina
Topeka
Wichita
Mahoma City
Tulsa
Fort Smith
OKLAHOMA
hita Falls
t Worth
Dallas
Texarkana
Shreveport
S
Austin
San Antonio
Houston
Galveston
Corpus Christi
Reynosa
Matamoros

CANADA
ONTARIO
Lake Winnipeg
Attawapiskat
ames Bay
Akimiski Isla
QUÉBEC
Waskaganish
Waskaganish
Moosonee
Hearst
Cochrane
Rouyn-Noranda
Timmins
Val-d'Or
Longlac
Réservoir Gouin
Lac Mistassini
Saquenay
Rivière-du-Loup
Québec
Sept-Îles
Île d'Anticosti
Gaspé
Baie Comeau
NEW BRUNSWICK
Fredericton
MAINE
Presque Isle
Sherbrooke
Saint John
Bangor
Bay of Fundy
Yarmouth
Thunder Bay
Lake Nipigon
Lake Superior
Michipicoten
Ironwood
WISCONSIN
Marquette
The Great Lakes
Sault Ste. Marie
Sudbury
North Bay
Ottawa
Montréal
VERMONT
NEW HAMPSHIRE
Augusta
Portland
Concord
Kingston
NEW YORK
Lake Ontario
Rochester
Syracuse
Albany
MASSACHUSETTS
Boston
Cape Cod
Providence
RHODE ISLAND
CONNECTICUT
Hartford
St. Paul
Minneapolis
Green Bay
Traverse City
MICHIGAN
Lake Michigan
Lake Huron
Grand Rapids
London
Toronto
St. Catharines
Buffalo
Lake Erie
Madison
Milwaukee
IOWA
Cedar Rapids
Des Moines
Chicago
Iowa City
Lansing
Detroit
Toledo
Fort Wayne
Cleveland
Akron
Pittsburgh
PENNSYLVANIA
Harrisburg
Scranton
Newark
New York
Trenton
Philadelphia
NEW JERSEY
Albert Lea
ILLINOIS
Bloomington
Springfield
A
INDIANA
Indianapolis
Columbus
OHIO
Cincinnati
WEST VIRGINIA
Charleston
Baltimore
Dover
DELAWARE
Washington
D.C.
MARYLAND
Chesapeake Bay
Kansas City
Topeka
Jefferson City
MISSOURI
St. Louis
Springfield
Ozark Plateau
Missouri
Louisville
Frankfort
Lexington
KENTUCKY
Bowling Green
Nashville
Richmond
VIRGINIA
Norfolk
Greensboro
Raleigh
Cape Hatteras
Little Rock
White
Arkansas
ARKANSAS
Memphis
TENNESSEE
Chattanooga
Knoxville
Greenville
APPALACHIAN MTS.
Charlotte
NORTH CAROLINA
Wilmington
Columbia
SOUTH CAROLINA
Charleston
ATLANTIC OCEAN
Birmingham
MISSISSIPPI
Meridian
Jackson
ALABAMA
Montgomery
Columbus
GEORGIA
Atlanta
Macon
Savannah
LOUISIANA
Baton Rouge
Lafayette
New Orleans
Mobile
Tallahassee
Jacksonville
Daytona Beach
Cape Canaveral
Orlando
FLORIDA
Tampa
St. Petersburg
Lake Okeechobee
West Palm Beach
Naples
Miami
Mississippi Delta
Gulf of Mexico
Florida Keys
Straits of Florida
Andros
Freeport
Grand Bahama
Great Abaco
THE BAHAMAS
Nassau
New Providence Island
Eleuthera
Cat Island
Tropic of Cancer
Long Island

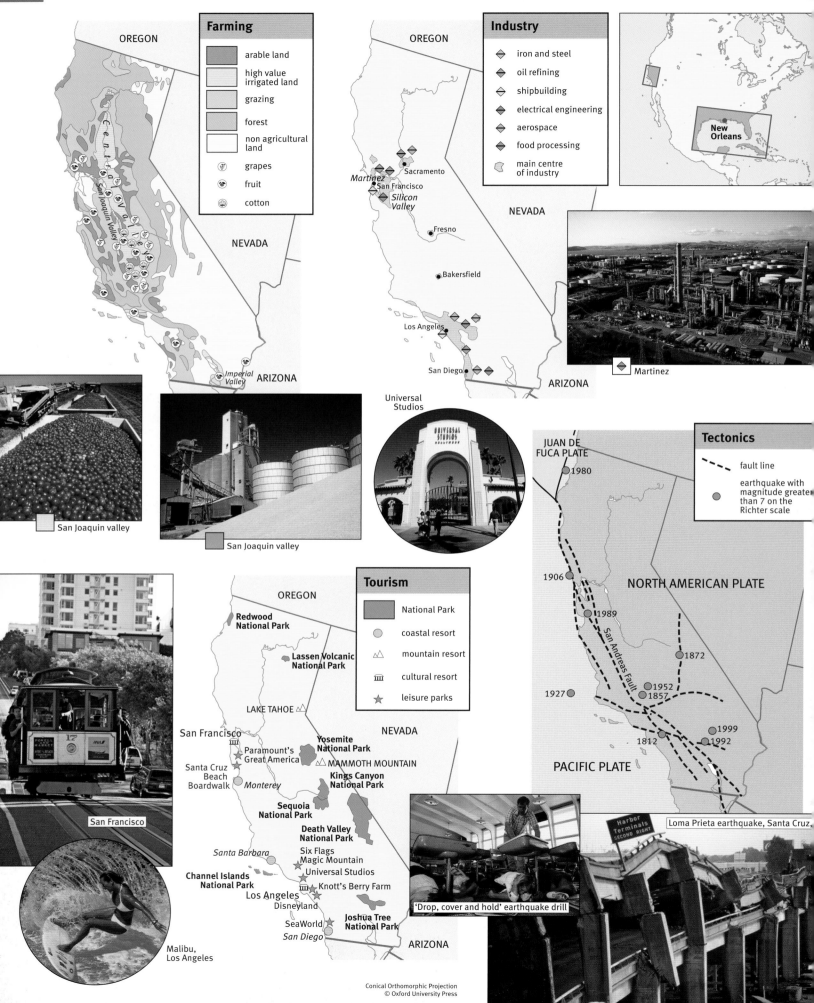

Farming

	arable land
	high value irrigated land
	grazing
	forest
	non agricultural land

- grapes
- fruit
- cotton

OREGON

Central Valley

San Joaquin Valley

NEVADA

Imperial Valley

ARIZONA

San Joaquin valley

San Joaquin valley

Industry

- iron and steel
- oil refining
- shipbuilding
- electrical engineering
- aerospace
- food processing
- main centre of industry

OREGON

Martinez
Sacramento
San Francisco
Silicon Valley

NEVADA

Fresno

Bakersfield

Los Angeles

San Diego

ARIZONA

Martinez

New Orleans

Universal Studios

Tectonics

- - - fault line
- earthquake with magnitude greater than 7 on the Richter scale

JUAN DE FUCA PLATE

1980

NORTH AMERICAN PLATE

1906

1989

1872

San Andreas Fault

1927

1952
1857

1812

1999
1992

PACIFIC PLATE

San Francisco

Tourism

	National Park
○	coastal resort
△△	mountain resort
🏛	cultural resort
★	leisure parks

OREGON

Redwood National Park

Lassen Volcanic National Park

LAKE TAHOE △△

NEVADA

San Francisco
Paramount's Great America
Santa Cruz Beach Boardwalk
Monterey

Yosemite National Park
△△ MAMMOTH MOUNTAIN

Kings Canyon National Park

Sequoia National Park

Death Valley National Park

Santa Barbara
Six Flags Magic Mountain
Universal Studios
Channel Islands National Park
Knott's Berry Farm
Los Angeles
Disneyland

SeaWorld
Joshua Tree National Park
San Diego

ARIZONA

'Drop, cover and hold' earthquake drill

Loma Prieta earthquake, Santa Cruz,

Harbor Terminals SECOND RIGHT

Malibu, Los Angeles

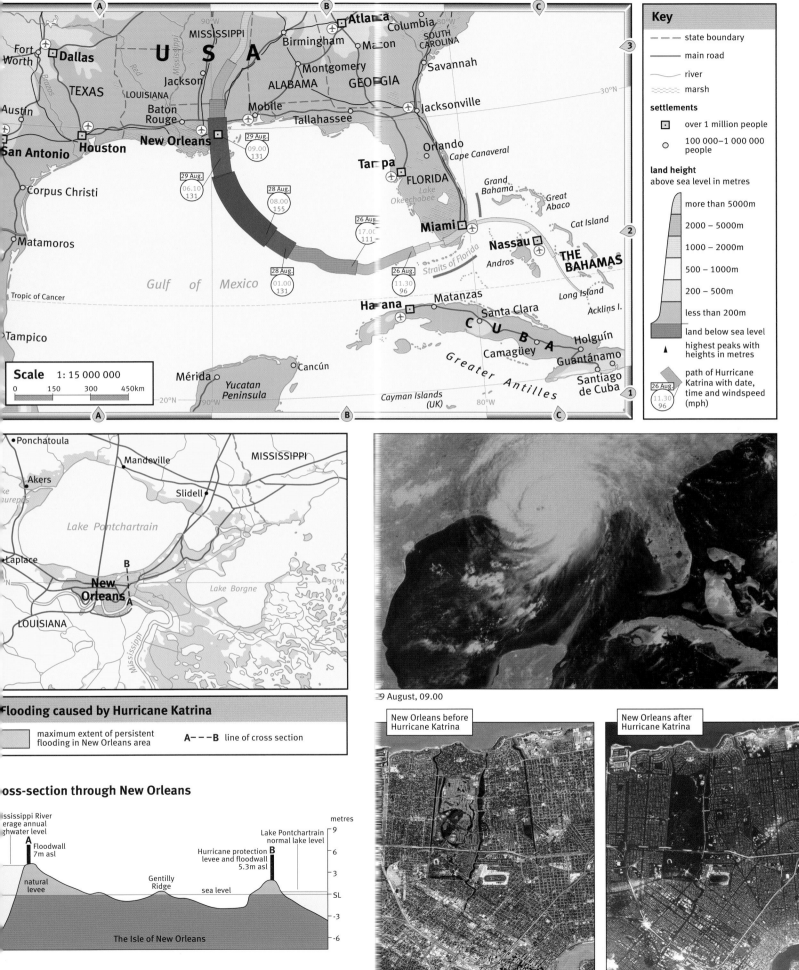

Key

- – – – state boundary
- ——— main road
- river
- marsh

settlements
- ▣ over 1 million people
- ○ 100 000–1 000 000 people

land height
above sea level in metres

- more than 5000m
- 2000 – 5000m
- 1000 – 2000m
- 500 – 1000m
- 200 – 500m
- less than 200m
- land below sea level
- ▲ highest peaks with heights in metres
- path of Hurricane Katrina with date, time and windspeed (mph)

26 Aug.
11.30
96

Scale 1: 15 000 000
0   150   300   450km

USA
MISSISSIPPI
Fort Worth   Dallas
TEXAS
Austin
San Antonio   Houston
LOUISIANA
Jackson
Baton Rouge
New Orleans
Corpus Christi
Matamoros
Tampico
Tropic of Cancer
Mérida
Yucatan Peninsula
Cancún
Gulf of Mexico

Birmingham
Montgomery
ALABAMA
Mobile
Tallahassee

Atlanta
Columbia
SOUTH CAROLINA
Macon
GEORGIA
Savannah
Jacksonville
30°N
Orlando   Cape Canaveral
FLORIDA
Tampa
Lake Okeechobee
Miami

Grand Bahama
Great Abaco
Cat Island
THE BAHAMAS
Nassau
Andros
Long Island
Acklins I.
Straits of Florida

Havana
Matanzas
Santa Clara
CUBA
Camagüey
Holguín
Guantánamo
Santiago de Cuba
Greater Antilles
Cayman Islands (UK)
80°W
90°W
20°N

29 Aug. 09.00 131
29 Aug. 06.10 131
28 Aug. 08.00 155
26 Aug. 17.00 111
28 Aug. 01.00 131
26 Aug. 11.30 96

Zenithal Equidistant Projection
© Oxford University Press

Ponchatoula
Mandeville
MISSISSIPPI
Akers
Slidell
Lake Pontchartrain
Laplace
New Orleans
LOUISIANA
Lake Borgne
Mississippi
30°N
B
A

Flooding caused by Hurricane Katrina

maximum extent of persistent flooding in New Orleans area

A – – – B line of cross section

Cross-section through New Orleans

Mississippi River average annual highwater level
A
Floodwall 7m asl
natural levee
Gentilly Ridge
sea level
Hurricane protection levee and floodwall 5.3m asl
B
Lake Pontchartrain normal lake level
metres
9
6
3
SL
-3
-6
The Isle of New Orleans

29 August, 09.00

New Orleans before Hurricane Katrina

New Orleans after Hurricane Katrina

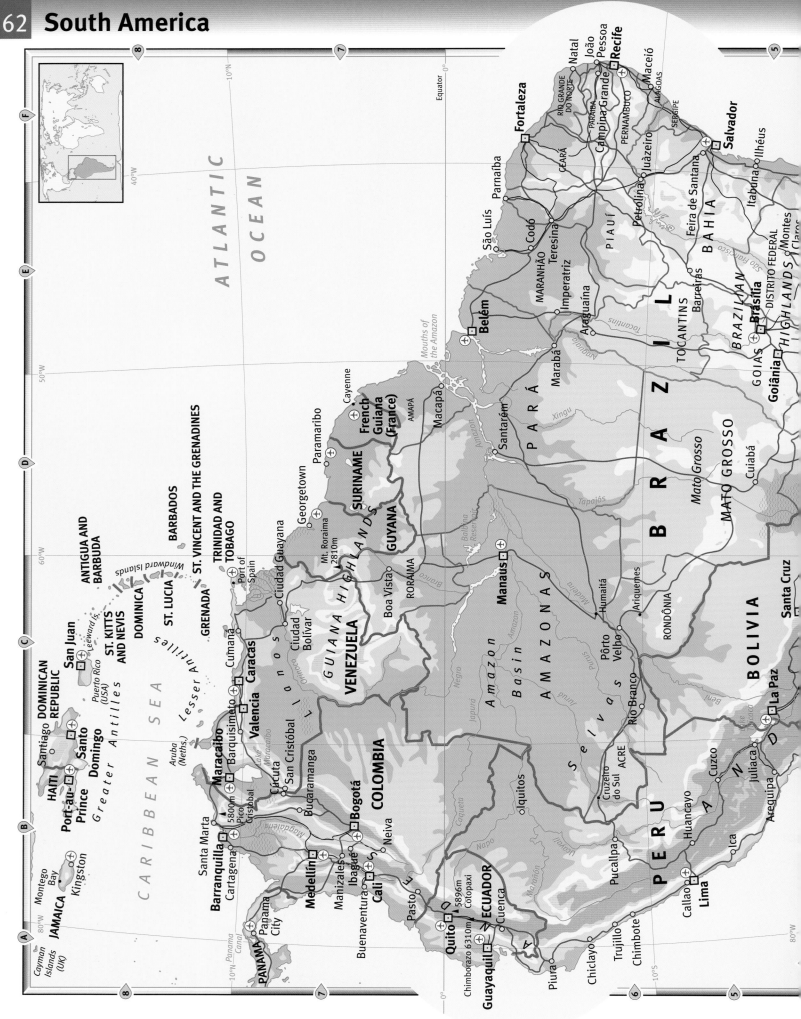

ATLANTIC

OCEAN

Equator 0°

Cayman Islands (UK)

JAMAICA
Montego Bay
Kingston

CARIBBEAN SEA

HAITI
Port-au-Prince

DOMINICAN REPUBLIC
Santiago
Santo Domingo
San Juan
Puerto Rico (USA)

Greater Antilles

Leeward Is.

ST. KITTS AND NEVIS
ANTIGUA AND BARBUDA

DOMINICA

ST. LUCIA
Windward Islands
BARBADOS

ST. VINCENT AND THE GRENADINES

GRENADA

TRINIDAD AND TOBAGO

Lesser Antilles

Aruba (Neths.)

Netherlands Antilles

PANAMA
Panama City
Panama Canal

COLOMBIA
Barranquilla
Cartagena
Santa Marta
Pico Cristóbal 5800m
Cúcuta
San Cristóbal
Bucaramanga
Medellín
Manizales
Ibagué
Buenaventura
Cali
Neiva
Pasto
Caquetá
Magdalena

ECUADOR
Quito
Chimborazo 6310m
Cotopaxi 5896m
Guayaquil
Cuenca

PERU
Piura
Chiclayo
Trujillo
Chimbote
Callao
Lima
Ica
Arequipa
Juliaca
Cuzco
Huancayo
Pucallpa
Iquitos
Cruzeiro do Sul

Maracaibo
Barquisimeto
Valencia
Caracas
Cumaná
Ciudad Bolívar
Ciudad Guayana
Port of Spain

VENEZUELA
Lake Maracaibo
Orinoco
Llanos

GUIANA HIGHLANDS
Mt. Roraima 2810m

Georgetown
Paramaribo
Cayenne

GUYANA
SURINAME
French Guiana (France)

Boa Vista
RORAIMA
Branco

Macapá
AMAPÁ
Mouths of the Amazon

Belém
PARÁ
Santarém
Marabá
Araguaína
Imperatriz
Tocantins
Xingu
Tapajós

Manaus
AMAZONAS
Amazon Basin
Selvas
Negro
Japurá
Napo
Marañón
Ucayali
Huallaga
Madeira
Purus
Balbina Reservoir
Humaitá
Ariquemes
Pôrto Velho
Rio Branco
ACRE
RONDÔNIA

BOLIVIA
La Paz
Santa Cruz
Beni

BRAZIL
São Luís
Parnaíba
Codó
Teresina
MARANHÃO
PIAUÍ
CEARÁ
Fortaleza
Parnaíba
RIO GRANDE DO NORTE
Natal
João Pessoa
Campina Grande
PARAÍBA
PERNAMBUCO
Recife
Maceió
ALAGOAS
SERGIPE
Petrolina
Juàzeiro
Feira de Santana
Salvador
BAHIA
Itabuna
Ilhéus
São Francisco
Montes Claros
BRAZILIAN HIGHLANDS
Barreiras
TOCANTINS
DISTRITO FEDERAL
Brasília
GOIÁS
Goiânia
MATO GROSSO
Mato Grosso
Cuiabá

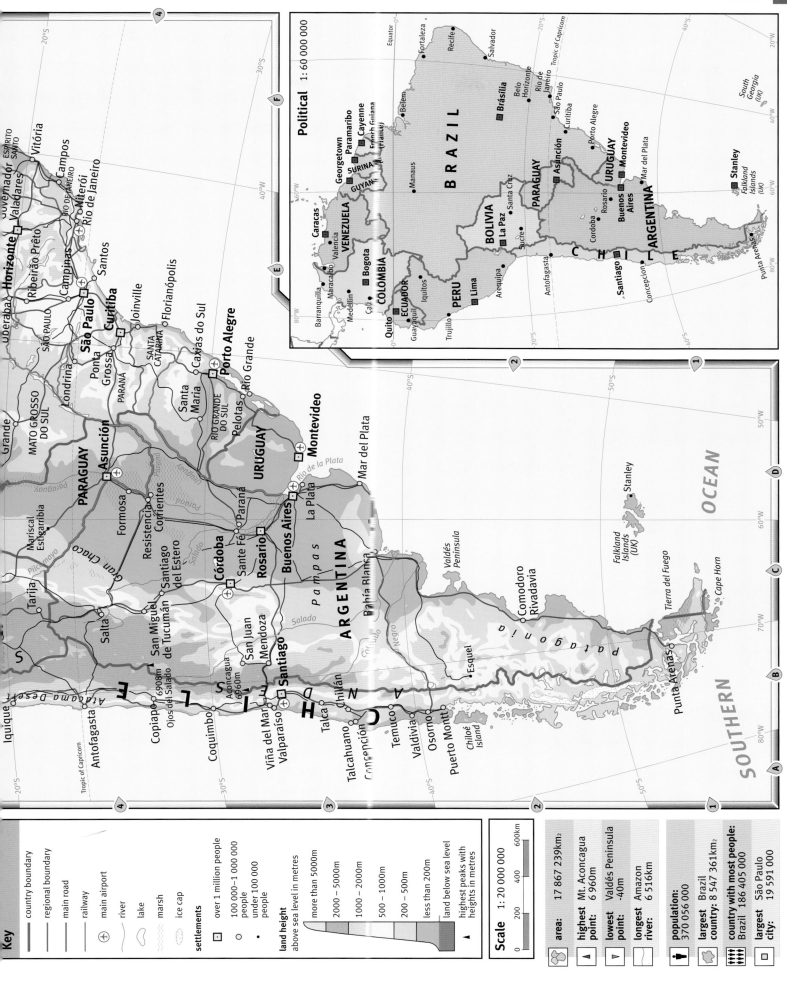

Key

- country boundary
- regional boundary
- main road
- railway
- ⊕ main airport
- river
- lake
- marsh
- ice cap

settlements
- ☐ over 1 million people
- ○ 100 000–1 000 000 people
- • under 100 000 people

land height
above sea level in metres
- more than 5000m
- 2000 – 5000m
- 1000 – 2000m
- 500 – 1000m
- 200 – 500m
- less than 200m
- land below sea level

▲ highest peaks with heights in metres

Scale 1: 20 000 000

0 200 400 600km

Political 1 : 60 000 000

area: 17 867 239km²

highest point: Mt. Aconcagua 6 960m

lowest point: Valdés Peninsula -40m

longest river: Amazon 6 516km

population: 370 056 000

largest country: Brazil 8 547 361km²

country with most people: Brazil 186 405 000

largest city: São Paulo 19 591 000

© Oxford University Press

asl = metres above sea level

Equatorial warm and wet
rain all year or as monsoon

Tropical hot and wet
dry in winter

Temperate mild and wet
warm summers cool winters

Climate regions

Rio Branco 143m asl

°C / mm

annual precipitation 1938mm

Manaus 44m asl

°C / mm

annual precipitation 2088mm

Porto Alegre 3m asl

°C / mm

annual precipitation 1333mm

Manaus

Rio Branco

Porto Alegre

over 100 people per square kilometre

Population

people per square kilometre

over 100

10–100

1–10

under 1

cities and towns (people)

☐ over 3 000 000

○ 1 000 000–3 000 000

⊙ 500 000–1 000 000

under 1 person per square kilometre

Belém

Manaus

Fortaleza

Recife

Salvador

Goiânia

Brásília

Belo Horizonte

Campinas

São Paulo

Rio de Janeiro

Guarulhos

Curitiba

Porto Alegre

Population structure 2009

age

males

females

80
70
60
50
40
30
20
10
0

5 4 3 2 1 0 0 1 2 3 4 5

percent of total population

literacy and life expectancy are lowest in the north east

Quality of life

Literacy
percentage of people over 15 years able to read and write

over 85%

75–85%

65–75%

under 65%

Life expectancy
average number of years a person can expect to live

○ over 70

● under 65

Transverse Mercator Projection
© Oxford University Press

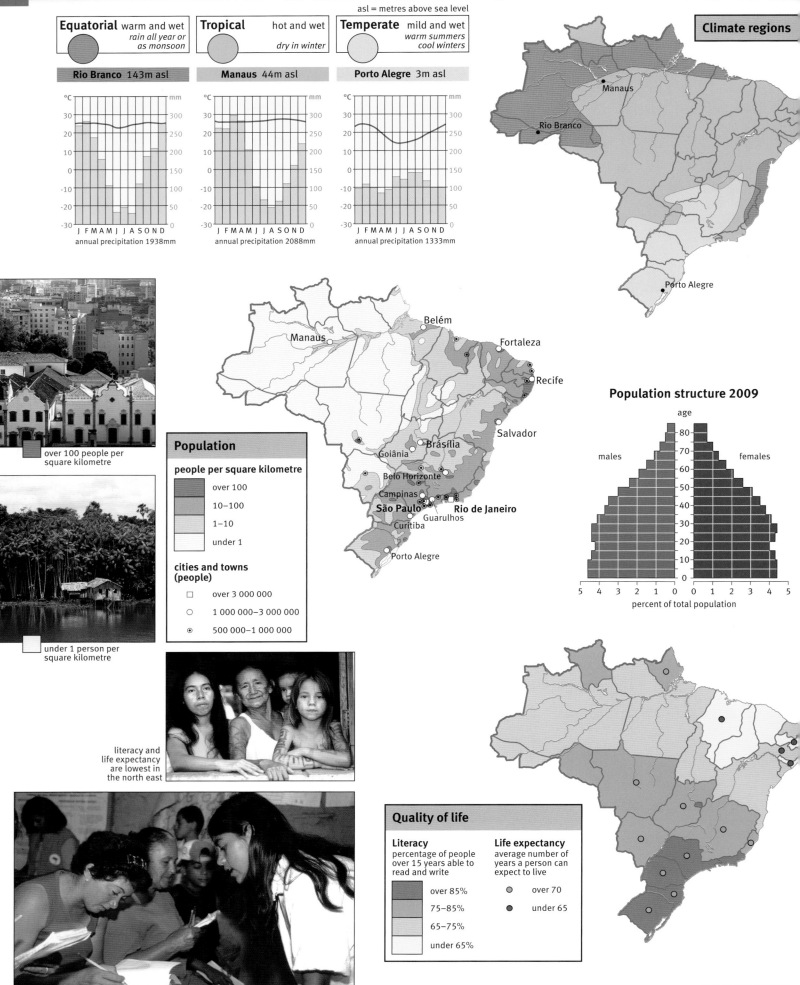

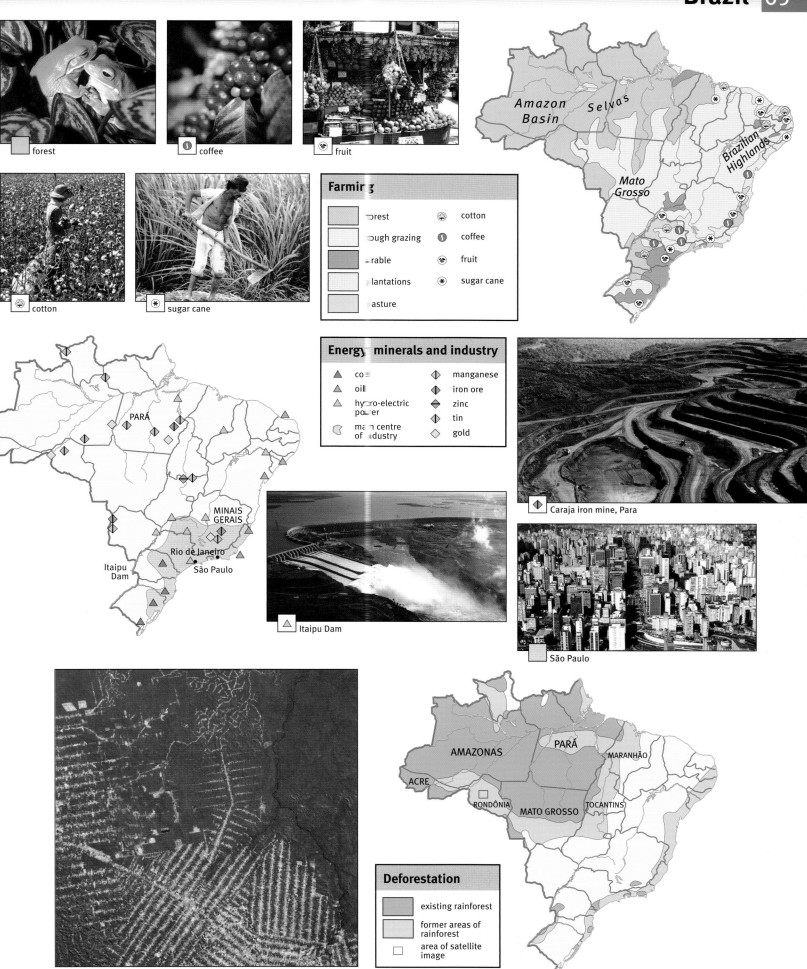

forest

coffee

fruit

cotton

sugar cane

Amazon Basin

Selvas

Mato Grosso

Brazilian Highlands

Farming

	forest	cotton	
	rough grazing	coffee	
	arable	fruit	
	plantations	sugar cane	
	pasture		

Energy, minerals and industry

	coal	manganese	
	oil	iron ore	
	hydro-electric power	zinc	
	main centre of industry	tin	
		gold	

PARÁ

MINAIS GERAIS

Rio de Janeiro

Itaipu Dam

São Paulo

Caraja iron mine, Para

Itaipu Dam

São Paulo

Satellite image of Rondônia.
Light areas show 'fishbone' pattern of deforestation.

AMAZONAS

PARÁ

MARANHÃO

ACRE

RONDÔNIA

MATO GROSSO

TOCANTINS

Deforestation

	existing rainforest
	former areas of rainforest
	area of satellite image

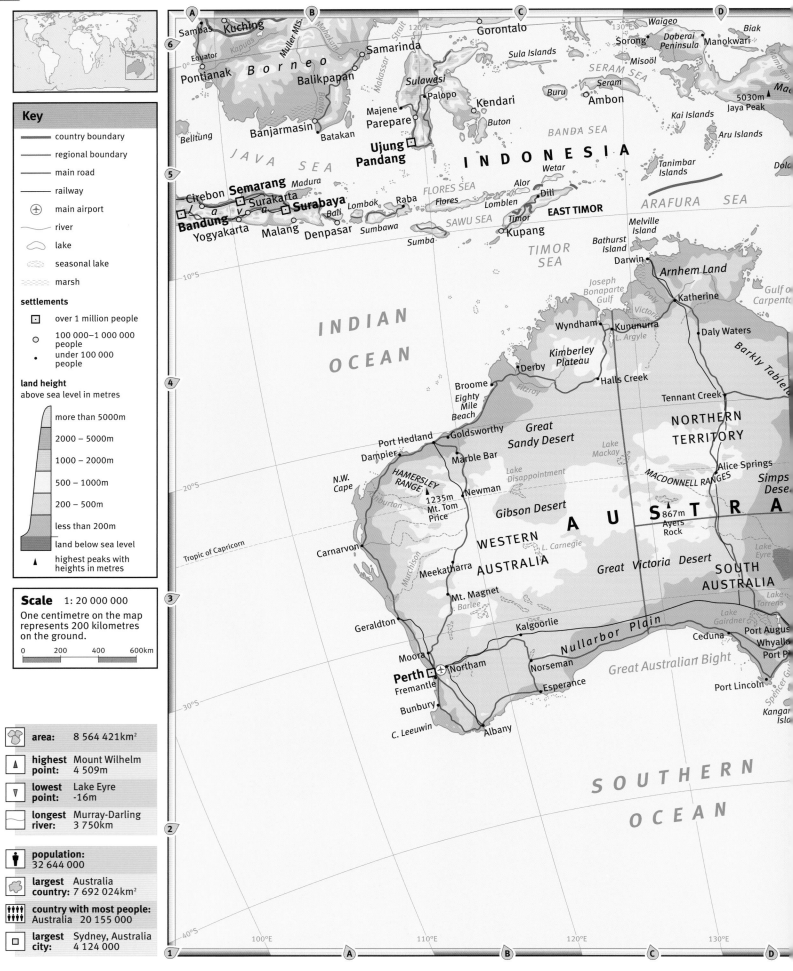

Key

━━━	country boundary
───	regional boundary
───	main road
───	railway
⊕	main airport
∿	river
⌒	lake
≋	seasonal lake
≈≈	marsh

settlements

⊡	over 1 million people
○	100 000–1 000 000 people
•	under 100 000 people

land height
above sea level in metres

- more than 5000m
- 2000 – 5000m
- 1000 – 2000m
- 500 – 1000m
- 200 – 500m
- less than 200m
- land below sea level
- ▲ highest peaks with heights in metres

Scale   1: 20 000 000

One centimetre on the map represents 200 kilometres on the ground.

0	200	400	600km

🗺	**area:**	8 564 421km²
▲	**highest point:**	Mount Wilhelm 4 509m
▼	**lowest point:**	Lake Eyre -16m
∿	**longest river:**	Murray-Darling 3 750km
🧍	**population:**	32 644 000
	largest country:	Australia 7 692 024km²
	country with most people:	Australia 20 155 000
⊡	**largest city:**	Sydney, Australia 4 124 000

Zenithal Equidistant Projection
© Oxford University Press

Jayapura

Admiralty Is.

BISMARCK SEA

New Ireland

Rabaul

New Britain

Wewak

Madang

4509m
Mt. Wilhelm

Lae

Kerema

PAPUA NEW GUINEA

New Guinea

ountains

Sepik

Gulf of Papua

Owen Stanley Range

Port Moresby

Torres Strait

Cape York

SOLOMON SEA

Bougainville Island

Choiseul

Santa Isabel

SOLOMON

ISLANDS

New Georgia Is.

Woodlark I.

D'Entrecasteaux Islands

Honiara

Guadalcanal

Malaita

San Cristobal

Rennell

Cape York Peninsula

GREAT

Cape Melville

BARRIER

Cooktown

Cairns

CORAL SEA

Santa Cruz Islands

Espiritu Santo

Banks Islands

VANUATU

Malakula

Vila · Éfaté

Erromango

Mitchell

Reef

DIVIDING

Townsville

Charters Towers

Mackay

Îles Chesterfield

Îs. Loyauté

Vanua Levu

Viti Levu

Suva

FIJI

Kadavu

Cloncurry

Hughenden

QUEENSLAND

RANGE

Emerald

Rockhampton

New Caledonia (Fr.)

Nouméa

NAURU

Tarawa

Gilbert Islands

Equator

KIRIBATI

TUVALU

Funafuti

Longreach

Barcaldine

GREY RANGE

Charleville

Roma

Toowoomba

Dalby

Bundaberg

Maryborough

Gympie

Brisbane

Gold Coast

Lismore

Tropic of Capricorn

Cunnamula

Bourke

Moree

Grafton

Tamworth

Port Macquarie

Norfolk I. (Aust.)

I

A

NEW SOUTH WALES

Darling

Broken Hill

Dubbo

Orange

Newcastle

Lord Howe I. (Aust.)

Kermadec Is. (NZ)

Adelaide

Mildura

Lachlan

Murrumbidgee

ACT

Albury

Bendigo

VICTORIA

Ballarat

Mount ...bier

Murray

SNOWY MTS.

Canberra

GREAT

2230m
Mt. Kosciuszko

Sydney

Wollongong

Melbourne

Geelong

Cape Howe

TASMAN

SEA

North Cape

Warrnambool

Bass Strait

Devonport

Launceston

TASMANIA

Hobart

S.E. Cape

Auckland

Hamilton

New Plymouth

Rotorua

North Island

Napier

Greymouth

Nelson

Palmerston North

Wellington

Cook Strait

Mt. Cook
3764

Southern Alps

South Island

Christchurch

NEW ZEALAND

Cape Prov...nce

...wart I.

Invercargill

Dunedin

Chatham Is. (NZ)

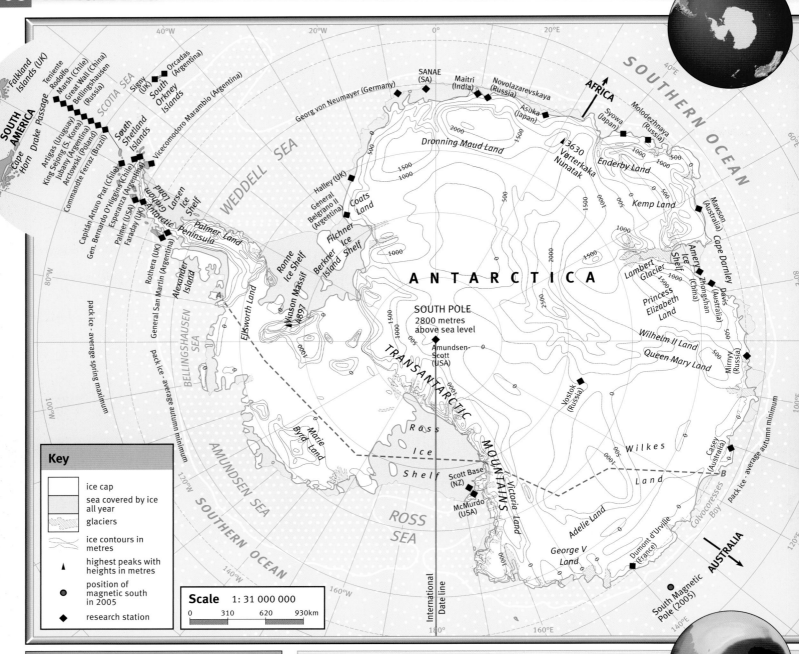

Falkland Islands (UK)
SOUTH AMERICA
Cape Horn
Drake Passage
Teniente Rodolfo Marsh (Chile)
Great Wall (China)
Bellingshausen (Russia)
Artigas (Uruguay)
King Sejong (S. Korea)
Jubany (Argentina)
Arctowski (Poland)
Commandte Ferraz (Brazil)
Capitán Arturo Prat (Chile)
Gen. Bernardo O'Higgins (Chile)
Esperanza (Argentina)
Palmer (USA)
Faraday (UK)
Rothera (UK)
General San Martin (Argentina)
Alexander Island
Ellsworth Land
BELLINGSHAUSEN SEA
pack ice - average spring maximum
pack ice - average autumn minimum
AMUNDSEN SEA
SOUTHERN OCEAN
Marie Byrd Land
Larsen Ice Shelf
Palmer Land
Antarctic Peninsula
Ronne Ice Shelf
Wilson Massif 4897
Berkner Island
Filchner Ice Shelf
Coats Land
General Belgrano II (Argentina)
Halley (UK)
Vicecomodoro Marambio (Argentina)
South Shetland Islands
South Orkney Islands
Signy (UK)
Orcadas (Argentina)
SCOTIA SEA
WEDDELL SEA
SANAE (SA)
Maitri (India)
Novolazarevskaya (Russia)
Georg von Neumayer (Germany)
Dronning Maud Land
Asuka (Japan)
AFRICA
Syowa (Japan)
Molodezhnaya (Russia)
SOUTHERN OCEAN
Vørterkaka Nunatak 3630
Enderby Land
Kemp Land
Mawson (Australia)
Cape Darnley
Amery Ice Shelf
Zhongshan (China)
Davis (Australia)
Lambert Glacier
Princess Elizabeth Land
Wilhelm II Land
Queen Mary Land
Mirny (Russia)
Casey (Australia)
Colvocoresses Bay
pack ice - average autumn minimum
AUSTRALIA
South Magnetic Pole (2005)
Dumont d'Urville (France)
Adelie Land
George V Land
Victoria Land
ROSS SEA
Ross Ice Shelf
McMurdo (USA)
Scott Base (NZ)
TRANSANTARCTIC MOUNTAINS
Amundsen-Scott (USA)
SOUTH POLE 2800 metres above sea level
ANTARCTICA
Vostok (Russia)
Wilkes Land
International Date Line

Key

	ice cap
	sea covered by ice all year
	glaciers
	ice contours in metres
▲	highest peaks with heights in metres
⦿	position of magnetic south in 2005
◆	research station

Scale 1: 31 000 000
0   310   620   930km

McMurdo Research Station

The Antarctic ozone 'hole'

Ozone in the stratosphere absorbs harmful ultra-violet rays. Pollutants in the air destroy ozone, making the ozone layer thinner. Strong winds and intense cold of the Antarctic winter concentrate the effects of pollutants so that ozone is thinnest over Antarctica in spring (September and October).

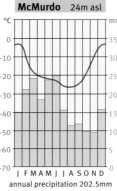

thinnest ozone
thickest ozone

17 September 2001

Warming of the Antarctic peninsula

The Larsen ice shelf was a 220m thick layer of ice floating on the sea.
In 2002 about 3,250 km² of ice broke up into the ocean.

17 February 2002
5 March 2002

McMurdo 24m asl
°C / mm
J F M A M J J A S O N D
annual precipitation 202.5mm

Vostok 0m asl
°C / mm
J F M A M J J A S O N D
annual precipitation 4.5mm

Satellite image of Antarctica using a mosaic of Advanced Very High Resolution Radiometer (AVHRR) images.

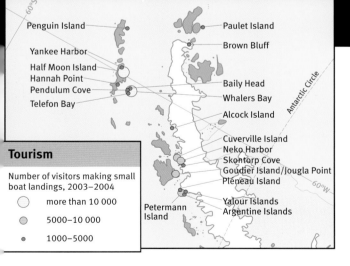
Antarctic tourism

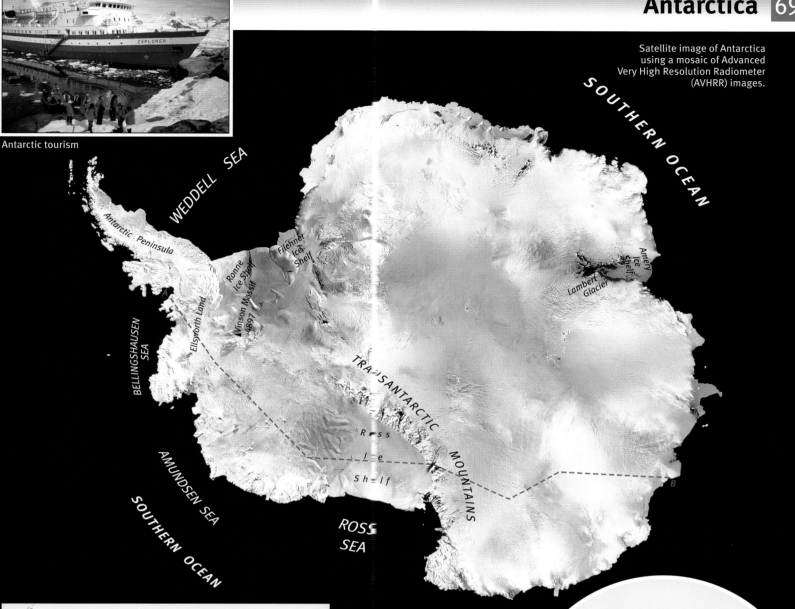

SOUTHERN OCEAN

WEDDELL SEA

Antarctic Peninsula

Filchner Ice Shelf

Ronne Ice Shelf

Amery Ice Shelf

Lambert Glacier

Ellsworth Land

▲Vinson Massif 4897

BELLINGSHAUSEN SEA

TRANSANTARCTIC MOUNTAINS

Ross Ice Shelf

AMUNDSEN SEA

SOUTHERN OCEAN

ROSS SEA

Tourism

Penguin Island
Yankee Harbor
Half Moon Island
Hannah Point
Pendulum Cove
Telefon Bay
Paulet Island
Brown Bluff
Baily Head
Whalers Bay
Alcock Island
Cuverville Island
Neko Harbor
Skontorp Cove
Goudier Island/Jougla Point
Pleneau Island
Yalour Islands
Argentine Islands
Petermann Island

Antarctic Circle
60°W

Number of visitors making small boat landings, 2003–2004
- more than 10 000
- 5000–10 000
- 1000–5000

Antarctica tourist landings

number of tourists in thousands: 1993–94 ≈ 8, 2003–04 ≈ 20
Antarctic summer seasons

Natural resources

The Antarctic Treaty has banned mining in Antarctica

- silver
- gold
- coal
- cobalt
- copper
- chromium
- iron
- molybdenum
- manganese
- nickel
- oil
- lead
- titanium
- uranium
- zinc

British Antarctic Survey www.antarctica.ac.uk

Cross section through Antarctica

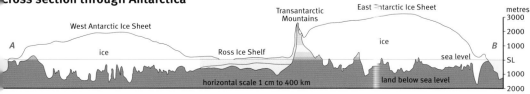

West Antarctic Ice Sheet, Transantarctic Mountains, East Antarctic Ice Sheet
A — ice — Ross Ice Shelf — ice — B
metres 3000, 2000, 1000, SL, 1000, 2000
sea level
horizontal scale 1 cm to 400 km
land below sea level

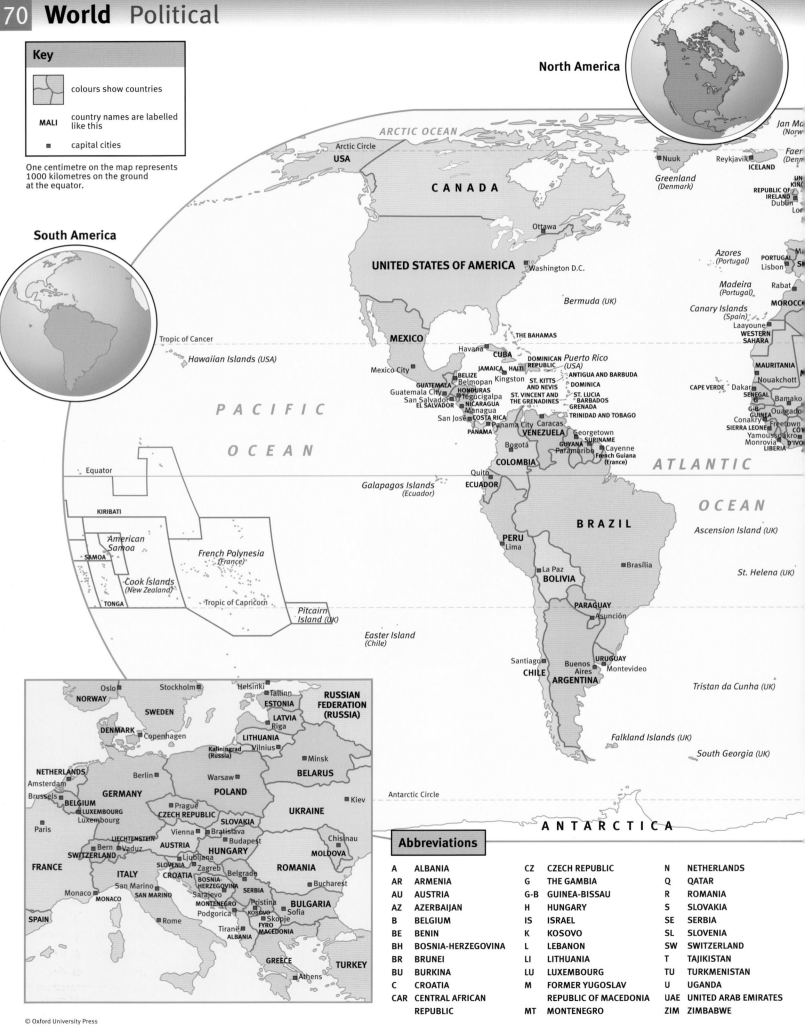

Key

- colours show countries
- MALI   country names are labelled like this
- ■   capital cities

One centimetre on the map represents 1000 kilometres on the ground at the equator.

North America

South America

ARCTIC OCEAN

Arctic Circle

USA

Jan Ma (Norw

Nuuk   Reykjavik   **ICELAND**

Faer (Denm

CANADA

Greenland (Denmark)

UN KING

REPUBLIC OF IRELAND Dublin

Ottawa

Lor

Azores (Portugal)

PORTUGAL   **Ma**

UNITED STATES OF AMERICA   ■ Washington D.C.

Lisbon

Bermuda (UK)

Madeira (Portugal)

Rabat

MOROCC

Tropic of Cancer

Canary Islands (Spain)

Laayoune

WESTERN SAHARA

MEXICO

THE BAHAMAS

Havana   **CUBA**

DOMINICAN *Puerto Rico*

MAURITANIA

Hawaiian Islands (USA)

REPUBLIC *(USA)*

ANTIGUA AND BARBUDA

Nouakchott

Mexico City

JAMAICA   **HAITI**

DOMINICA

CAPE VERDE Dakar

BELIZE

Kingston

ST. KITTS

SENEGAL

PACIFIC

GUATEMALA Belmopan

AND NEVIS

G

Guatemala City

HONDURAS

ST. LUCIA

G-B GUINEA Bamako

San Salvador Tegucigalpa

BARBADOS

Conakry   Ouagad

ST. VINCENT AND

SIERRA LEONE Freetown

EL SALVADOR **NICARAGUA**

THE GRENADINES **GRENADA**

Yamoussoukro

Managua

TRINIDAD AND TOBAGO

Monrovia

D'I

OCEAN

San José **COSTA RICA**

Caracas

LIBERIA

PANAMA Panama City

Georgetown

Bogotá

VENEZUELA **SURINAME**

GUYANA Paramaribo

Cayenne

ATLANTIC

COLOMBIA

French Guiana (France)

Equator

Quito

OCEAN

ECUADOR

Galapagos Islands (Ecuador)

KIRIBATI

B R A Z I L

Ascension Island (UK)

American Samoa

PERU

Lima

French Polynesia (France)

SAMOA

La Paz ■ Brasília

St. Helena (UK)

Cook Islands (New Zealand)

BOLIVIA

TONGA

Tropic of Capricorn

PARAGUAY

Asunción

Pitcairn Island (UK)

Easter Island (Chile)

Tristan da Cunha (UK)

Santiago

Buenos Aires

URUGUAY

Montevideo

CHILE

ARGENTINA

Falkland Islands (UK)

South Georgia (UK)

Antarctic Circle

A N T A R C T I C A

Oslo   Stockholm   Helsinki

NORWAY

SWEDEN

Tallinn

ESTONIA

RUSSIAN FEDERATION (RUSSIA)

LATVIA

Riga

DENMARK

Copenhagen

LITHUANIA

Vilnius

NETHERLANDS

Kaliningrad (Russia)

■ Minsk

Amsterdam

Berlin

BELARUS

Brussels

GERMANY

Warsaw

POLAND

■ Kiev

BELGIUM

LUXEMBOURG

Prague

Luxembourg

CZECH REPUBLIC

UKRAINE

Paris

SLOVAKIA

LIECHTENSTEIN

Vienna

Bratislava

Chisinau

AUSTRIA

Budapest

MOLDOVA

Bern

SWITZERLAND

Vaduz

HUNGARY

FRANCE

SLOVENIA

Ljubljana

Zagreb

ROMANIA

ITALY

CROATIA

Belgrade

Bucharest

San Marino

BOSNIA-

Monaco

SAN MARINO

HERZEGOVINA

SERBIA

MONACO

Sarajevo

BULGARIA

Rome

Pristina

SPAIN

MONTENEGRO

Sofia

Podgorica

Skopje

FYRO

Tiranë

MACEDONIA

ALBANIA

GREECE

TURKEY

Athens

Abbreviations

A	ALBANIA	CZ	CZECH REPUBLIC	N	NETHERLANDS
AR	ARMENIA	G	THE GAMBIA	Q	QATAR
AU	AUSTRIA	G-B	GUINEA-BISSAU	R	ROMANIA
AZ	AZERBAIJAN	H	HUNGARY	S	SLOVAKIA
B	BELGIUM	IS	ISRAEL	SE	SERBIA
BE	BENIN	K	KOSOVO	SL	SLOVENIA
BH	BOSNIA-HERZEGOVINA	L	LEBANON	SW	SWITZERLAND
BR	BRUNEI	LI	LITHUANIA	T	TAJIKISTAN
BU	BURKINA	LU	LUXEMBOURG	TU	TURKMENISTAN
C	CROATIA	M	FORMER YUGOSLAV	U	UGANDA
CAR	CENTRAL AFRICAN		REPUBLIC OF MACEDONIA	UAE	UNITED ARAB EMIRATES
	REPUBLIC	MT	MONTENEGRO	ZIM	ZIMBABWE

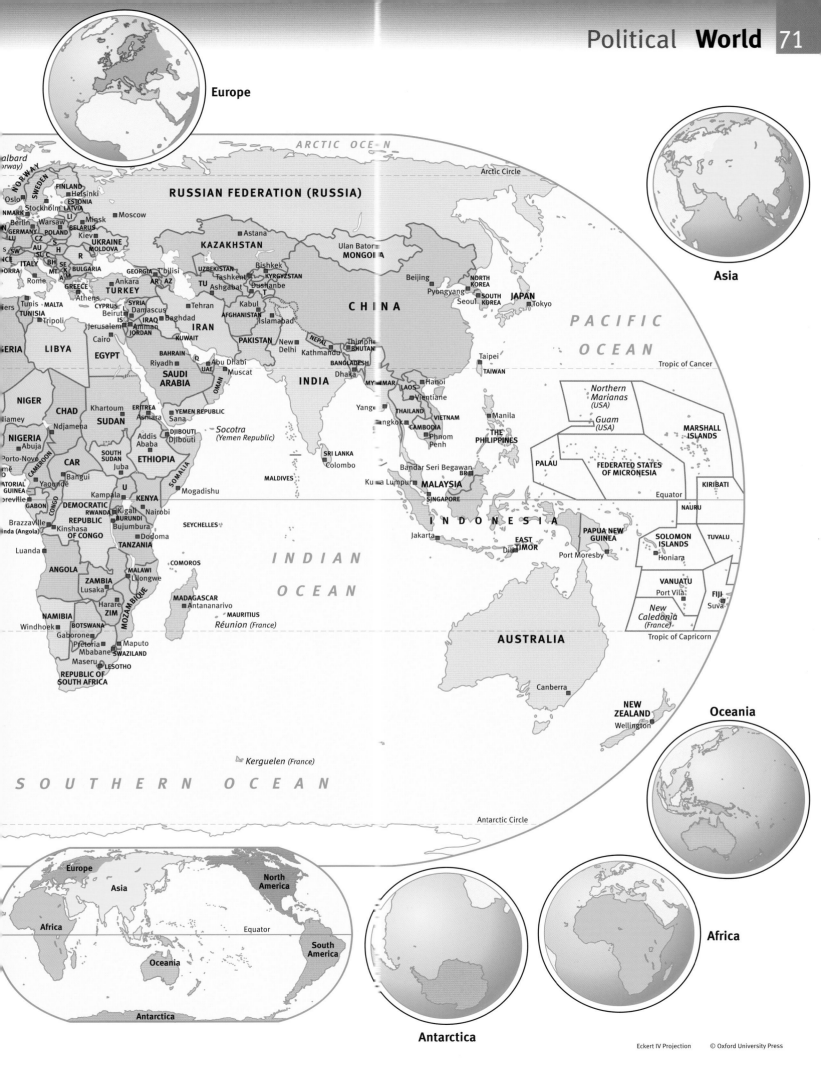

Europe

Asia

ARCTIC OCEAN

Arctic Circle

Svalbard (Norway)

NORWAY
SWEDEN
FINLAND
Helsinki
Oslo
Stockholm
ESTONIA
LATVIA
NMARK
Berlin
Warsaw
LI
Minsk
Moscow
GERMANY
POLAND
BELARUS
Kiev
LU
CZ
UKRAINE
SW
AU
S
H
MOLDOVA
Astana
NCE
ITALY
BH
SE
R
K
BULGARIA
RRA
Rome
MT
AM
GEORGIA
T'bilisi
UZBEKISTAN
Tashkent
Bishkek
KAZAKHSTAN
Ulan Bator
MONGOLIA
GREECE
TURKEY
Ankara
AR
AZ
TU
Ashgabat
Dushanbe
KYRGYZSTAN
Beijing
NORTH
KOREA
Tunis
MALTA
Athens
CYPRUS
SYRIA
Damascus
Tehran
Kabul
T
Pyongyang
SOUTH
KOREA
JAPAN
TUNISIA
Beirut
IS
IRAQ
Baghdad
AFGHANISTAN
Islamabad
CHINA
Seoul
Tokyo
Tripoli
Jerusalem
Amman
JORDAN
IRAN
New
Delhi
NEPAL
Thimph
BHUTAN
Taipei
ERIA
LIBYA
Cairo
KUWAIT
PAKISTAN
Kathmandu
TAIWAN

PACIFIC

OCEAN

Tropic of Cancer

BAHRAIN
Riyadh
Q
Abu Dhabi
UAE
Muscat
OMAN
INDIA
Dhaka
BANGLADESH
MY
MAR
LAOS
Hanoi
SAUDI
ARABIA

NIGER
CHAD
Khartoum
ERITREA
Asmara
YEMEN REPUBLIC
Sana
*Socotra
(Yemen Republic)*
Yang
THAILAND
Vientiane
Northern
Marianas
(USA)
MARSHALL
ISLANDS
NIGERIA
Abuja
SUDAN
Ndjamena
DJIBOUTI
Djibouti
ngkok
VIETNAM
CAMBODIA
Manila
Guam
(USA)
Porto-Novo
CAR
SOUTH
SUDAN
Addis
Ababa
ETHIOPIA
Juba
Phnom
Penh
THE
PHILIPPINES
FEDERATED STATES
OF MICRONESIA
ATORIAL
GUINEA
Yaoundé
Bangui
CAMEROON
SRI LANKA
Colombo
Bandar Seri Begawan
BR
PALAU
KIRIBATI
breville
GABON
U
Kampala
KENYA
SOMALIA
Mogadishu
MALDIVES
Ku a Lumpur
MALAYSIA
Equator
NAURU
CONGO
DEMOCRATIC
REPUBLIC
OF CONGO
RWANDA
Kigali
BURUNDI
Bujumbura
Nairobi
SINGAPORE
da (Angola)
Brazzaville
Kinshasa
SEYCHELLES
Dodoma
INDONESIA
Jakarta
EAST
TIMOR
Dili
PAPUA NEW
GUINEA
Port Moresby
SOLOMON
ISLANDS
Honiara
TUVALU
Luanda
TANZANIA
COMOROS
ANGOLA
MALAWI
Lilongwe
MADAGASCAR
Antananarivo
VANUATU
Port Vila
FIJI
Suva
ZAMBIA
Lusaka
INDIAN
MAURITIUS
Réunion (France)
New
Caledonia
(France)
Tropic of Capricorn
NAMIBIA
Harare
ZIM
MOZAMBIQUE
OCEAN
Windhoek
BOTSWANA
Gaborone
Pretoria
Maputo
Mbabane
SWAZILAND
Maseru
LESOTHO
REPUBLIC OF
SOUTH AFRICA

AUSTRALIA

Canberra

NEW
ZEALAND
Wellington

Oceania

Kerguelen (France)

SOUTHERN OCEAN

Antarctic Circle

Europe
Asia
North
America
Africa
Equator
Oceania
South
America
Antarctica

Africa

Antarctica

Eckert IV Projection   © Oxford University Press

Equatorial scale 1: 100 000 000

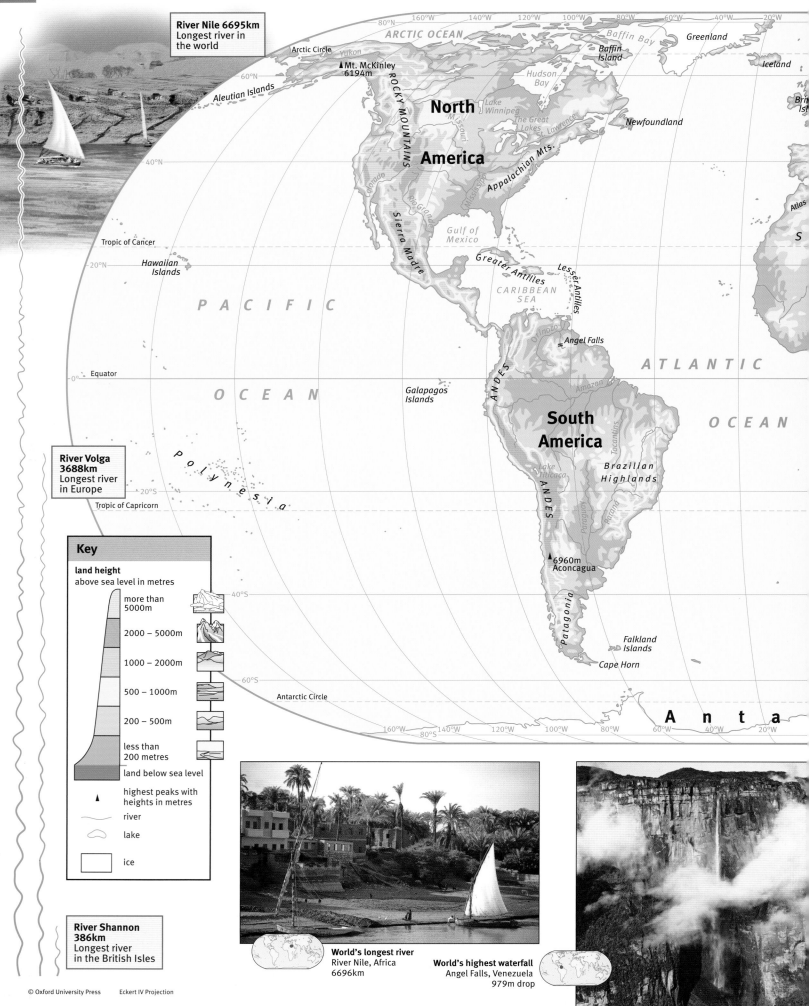

River Nile 6695km
Longest river in the world

ARCTIC OCEAN

Arctic Circle

Yukon

Mt. McKinley
6194m

Aleutian Islands

ROCKY MOUNTAINS

North
America

Baffin Bay

Greenland

Baffin Island

Iceland

Hudson Bay

Lake Winnipeg

The Great Lakes

Newfoundland

St. Lawrence

Missouri

Colorado

Rio Grande

Mississippi

Appalachian Mts.

Atlas

Tropic of Cancer

Hawaiian Islands

Sierra Madre

Gulf of Mexico

Greater Antilles

Lesser Antilles

CARIBBEAN SEA

PACIFIC

OCEAN

Galapagos Islands

Orinoco

Angel Falls

ATLANTIC

Equator

ANDES

Amazon

OCEAN

South
America

Tocantins

Brazilian Highlands

Polynesia

River Volga 3688km
Longest river in Europe

Lake Titicaca

ANDES

Paraguay

Paraná

Tropic of Capricorn

6960m
Aconcagua

Key

land height
above sea level in metres

more than 5000m

2000 – 5000m

1000 – 2000m

500 – 1000m

200 – 500m

less than 200 metres

land below sea level

▲ highest peaks with heights in metres

river

lake

ice

Patagonia

Falkland Islands

Cape Horn

Antarctic Circle

Anta

River Shannon 386km
Longest river in the British Isles

World's longest river
River Nile, Africa
6696km

World's highest waterfall
Angel Falls, Venezuela
979m drop

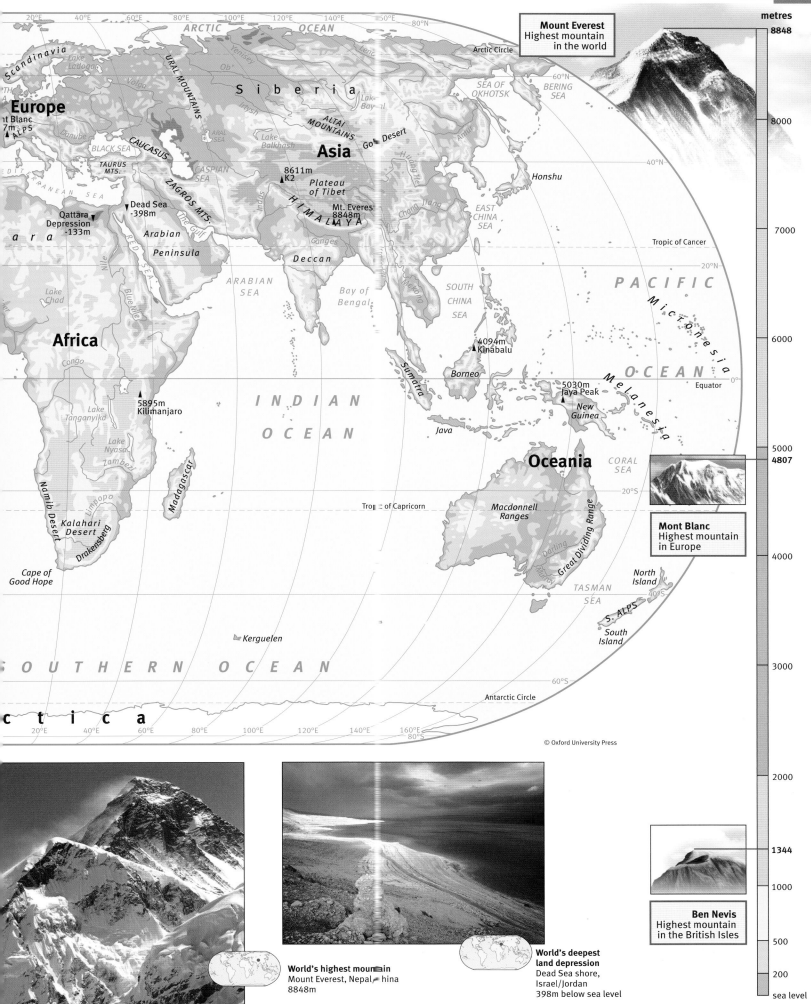

metres
8848

8000

Mount Everest
Highest mountain
in the world

20°E 40°E 60°E 80°E 100°E 120°E 140°E 50°E 80°N

ARCTIC OCEAN
Arctic Circle

Scandinavia
Lake Ladoga
URAL MOUNTAINS
Yenisey
Ob'
Lena
SEA OF OKHOTSK
60°N
BERING SEA

S i b e r i a
Lak Bay al

ALTAI MOUNTAINS
Go Desert

Europe
t Blanc
7m ALPS

Danube
Volga
BLACK SEA
CAUCASUS
TAURUS MTS.
CASPIAN SEA
ARAL SEA
Lake Balkhash
Irtysh

Asia

8611m
K2
Plateau of Tibet
Amur
Honshu
40°N

ZAGROS MTS.
Dead Sea -398m
The Gulf
Indus
HIMALAYA
Mt. Everes 8848m

Huang He
Chang Jiang
EAST CHINA SEA

7000

Qattara Depression -133m
a r a
Nile
RED SEA
Blue Nile
Arabian Peninsula
Ganges
Deccan

Tropic of Cancer

Africa
Congo
Lake Chad
ARABIAN SEA
Bay of Bengal
Mekong
SOUTH CHINA SEA

P A C I F I C
20°N

Lake Tanganyika
5895m
Kilimanjaro
I N D I A N
Sumatra
4094m
Kinabalu
Borneo

M i c r o n e s i a

6000

Lake Nyasa
Zambezi
O C E A N
Java
5030m
Jaya Peak
New Guinea

O C E A N
M e l a n e s i a
Equator
0°

5000
4807

Namib Desert
Madagascar
Kalahari Desert
Drakensberg
Limpopo

Oceania
CORAL SEA
Macdonnell Ranges
Great Dividing Range

Mont Blanc
Highest mountain
in Europe

20°S

Cape of Good Hope
Tropic of Capricorn
Darling
Murray
TASMAN SEA
North Island
S. ALPS
40°S
South Island

4000

Kerguelen
S O U T H E R N   O C E A N

3000

Antarctic Circle

c t i c a
20°E 40°E 60°E 80°E 100°E 120°E 140°E 160°E 80°S
60°S

© Oxford University Press

2000

World's highest mountain
Mount Everest, Nepal hina
8848m

World's deepest land depression
Dead Sea shore,
Israel/Jordan
398m below sea level

1344

1000

Ben Nevis
Highest mountain
in the British Isles

500

200

sea level

Equatorial scale 1: 240 000 000

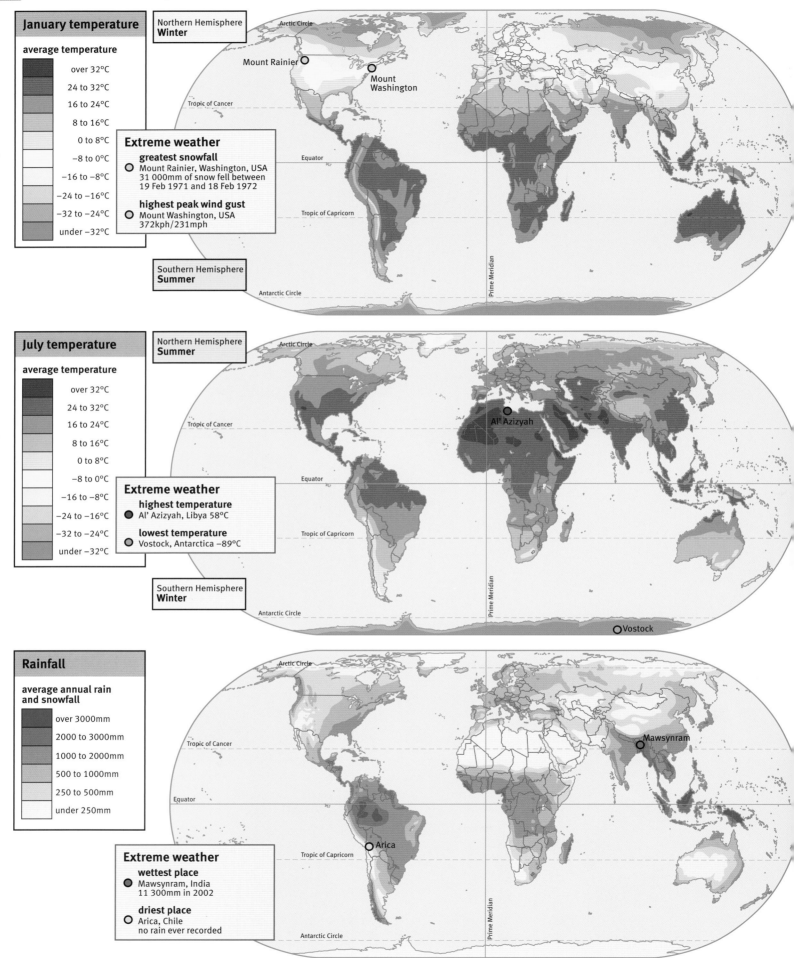

January temperature

average temperature

	over 32°C
	24 to 32°C
	16 to 24°C
	8 to 16°C
	0 to 8°C
	−8 to 0°C
	−16 to −8°C
	−24 to −16°C
	−32 to −24°C
	under −32°C

Northern Hemisphere **Winter**

Extreme weather

greatest snowfall
◯ Mount Rainier, Washington, USA
31 000mm of snow fell between
19 Feb 1971 and 18 Feb 1972

highest peak wind gust
◯ Mount Washington, USA
372kph/231mph

Southern Hemisphere **Summer**

Mount Rainier ◯
Mount Washington ◯

Arctic Circle
Tropic of Cancer
Equator
Tropic of Capricorn
Antarctic Circle
Prime Meridian

July temperature

average temperature

	over 32°C
	24 to 32°C
	16 to 24°C
	8 to 16°C
	0 to 8°C
	−8 to 0°C
	−16 to −8°C
	−24 to −16°C
	−32 to −24°C
	under −32°C

Northern Hemisphere **Summer**

Extreme weather

highest temperature
● Al' Azizyah, Libya 58°C

lowest temperature
◯ Vostock, Antarctica −89°C

Southern Hemisphere **Winter**

Al' Azizyah ◯
Vostock ◯

Arctic Circle
Tropic of Cancer
Equator
Tropic of Capricorn
Antarctic Circle
Prime Meridian

Rainfall

average annual rain
and snowfall

	over 3000mm
	2000 to 3000mm
	1000 to 2000mm
	500 to 1000mm
	250 to 500mm
	under 250mm

Extreme weather

wettest place
● Mawsynram, India
11 300mm in 2002

driest place
◯ Arica, Chile
no rain ever recorded

Mawsynram ◯
Arica ◯

Arctic Circle
Tropic of Cancer
Equator
Tropic of Capricorn
Antarctic Circle
Prime Meridian

Eckert IV Projection
© Oxford University Press

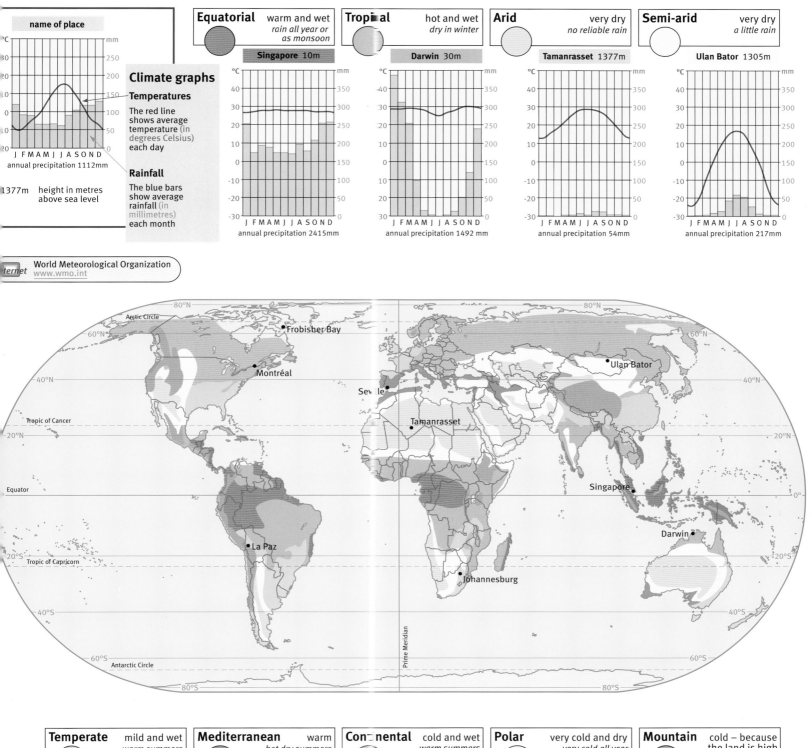

name of place

Climate graphs

Temperatures

The red line shows average temperature (in degrees Celsius) each day

annual precipitation 1112mm

1377m   height in metres above sea level

Rainfall

The blue bars show average rainfall (in millimetres) each month

Equatorial   warm and wet
rain all year or as monsoon

Singapore 10m
annual precipitation 2415mm

Tropical   hot and wet
dry in winter

Darwin 30m
annual precipitation 1492 mm

Arid   very dry
no reliable rain

Tamanrasset 1377m
annual precipitation 54mm

Semi-arid   very dry
a little rain

Ulan Bator 1305m
annual precipitation 217mm

World Meteorological Organization
www.wmo.int

Temperate   mild and wet
warm summers
cool winters

Johannesburg 1665m
annual precipitation 710mm

Mediterranean   warm
hot dry summers
warm wet winters

Seville 8m
annual precipitation 534mm

Continental   cold and wet
warm summers
cold winters

Montréal 57m
annual precipitation 1047mm

Polar   very cold and dry
very cold all year
especially winters

Frobisher Bay 21m
annual precipitation 427mm

Mountain   cold – because
the land is high
heavy rain or snow

La Paz 3632m
annual precipitation 610mm

tropical forest

deciduous forest

coniferous forest

ARCTIC OCEAN

Arctic Circle

Yukon

North America

Great Plains

Prairie

St. Lawrence

Mississippi

Rio Grande

Tropic of Cancer

CARIBBEAN SEA

PACIFIC OCEAN

ATLANTIC OCEAN

Orinoco

Equator

Amazon

Amazon Basin

South America

Tropic of Capricorn

Paraguay

Paraná

Pampas

Patagonia

Antarctic Circle

Key

	coniferous forest trees have leaves all year
	deciduous forest trees drop their leaves in winter
	tropical forest tall trees growing close together
	savannah tall grass parkland and scattered trees
	temperate grassland prairies, steppes, pampas and veld
	semi desert short grass and small dry bushes
	desert sand and stones with few plants
	tundra moss and bog with some short trees
	ice no plants
	mountains thin soils and steep slopes

desert

semi desert

savannah

temperate grassland

ARCTIC OCEAN

Arctic Circle

Yenisey

S i b e r i a

60°N

Volga

The Steppes

Europe

Asia

Ural

40°N

MEDITERRANEAN SEA

Indus

Himalaya

Chang Jiang

Huang He

Amur

PACIFIC

Nile

Arabian
Desert

Ganges

Mekong

Tropic of Cancer

a r a

20°N

OCEAN

h e l

Africa

OCEAN

Congo

Equator

Congo
Basin

0°

INDIAN

Zambezi

OCEAN

Oceania

20°S

Veld

Great
Sandy Desert

Tropic of Capricorn

Kalahari
Desert

Great
Victoria Desert

Darling

40°S

Equatorial scale 1: 100 000 000
© Oxford University Press

S O U T H E R N   O C E A N

60°S

Antarctic Circle

20°E   40°E   60°E   80°E   100°E   120°E   140°E   60°E   80°S

tundra

mountains

ice

Inside the Earth

continental crust
33 km deep

oceanic crust
10 km deep

mantle
3000 km deep

molten core
5000 km deep

solid core
6385 km deep

EURASIAN PLATE

HELLENIC
PLATE

AFRICAN PLATE

IRANIAN
PLATE

ARABIAN
PLATE

INDIAN
PLATE

Colliding p
The Alps

The Earth's plates

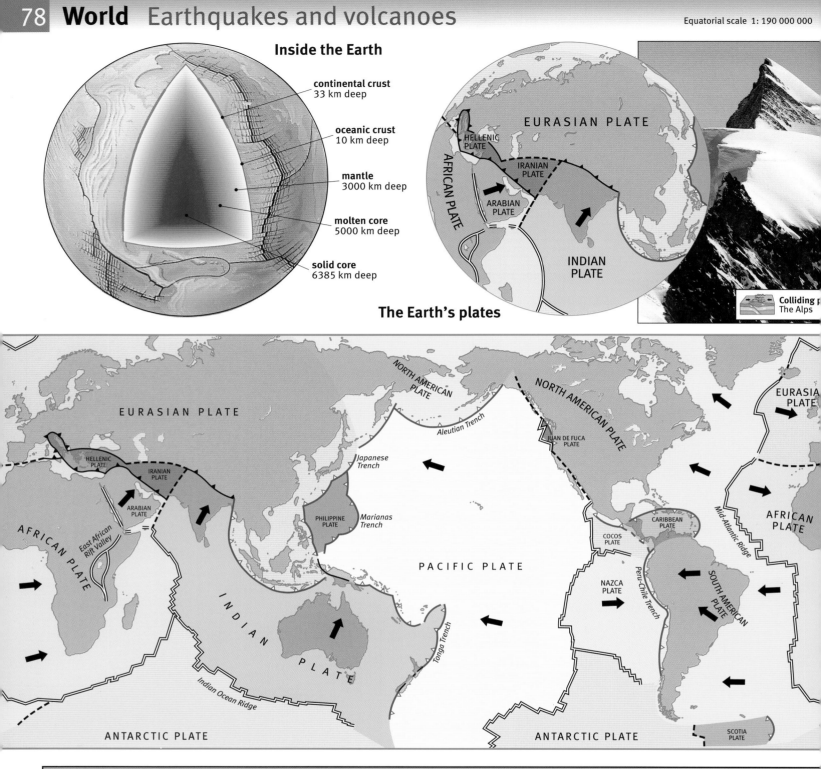

NORTH AMERICAN
PLATE

NORTH AMERICAN PLATE

EURASIA
PLATE

EURASIAN PLATE

HELLENIC
PLATE

IRANIAN
PLATE

ARABIAN
PLATE

Aleutian Trench

JUAN DE FUCA
PLATE

Japanese
Trench

PHILIPPINE
PLATE

Marianas
Trench

AFRICAN
PLATE

East African
Rift Valley

CARIBBEAN
PLATE

COCOS
PLATE

Mid-Atlantic Ridge

AFRICAN
PLATE

PACIFIC PLATE

I N D I A N

P L A T E

NAZCA
PLATE

Peru-Chile Trench

SOUTH AMERICAN
PLATE

Tonga Trench

Indian Ocean Ridge

ANTARCTIC PLATE

ANTARCTIC PLATE

SCOTIA
PLATE

The Earth's plates

plate boundaries

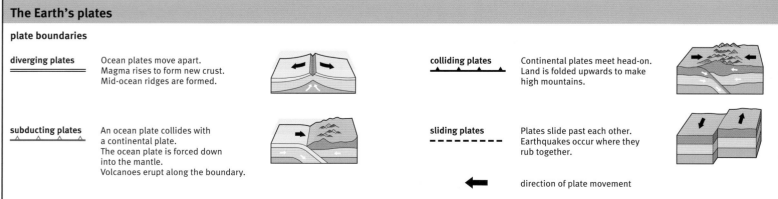

diverging plates

Ocean plates move apart.
Magma rises to form new crust.
Mid-ocean ridges are formed.

colliding plates

Continental plates meet head-on.
Land is folded upwards to make
high mountains.

subducting plates

An ocean plate collides with
a continental plate.
The ocean plate is forced down
into the mantle.
Volcanoes erupt along the boundary.

sliding plates

Plates slide past each other.
Earthquakes occur where they
rub together.

direction of plate movement

Gall Projection
© Oxford University Press

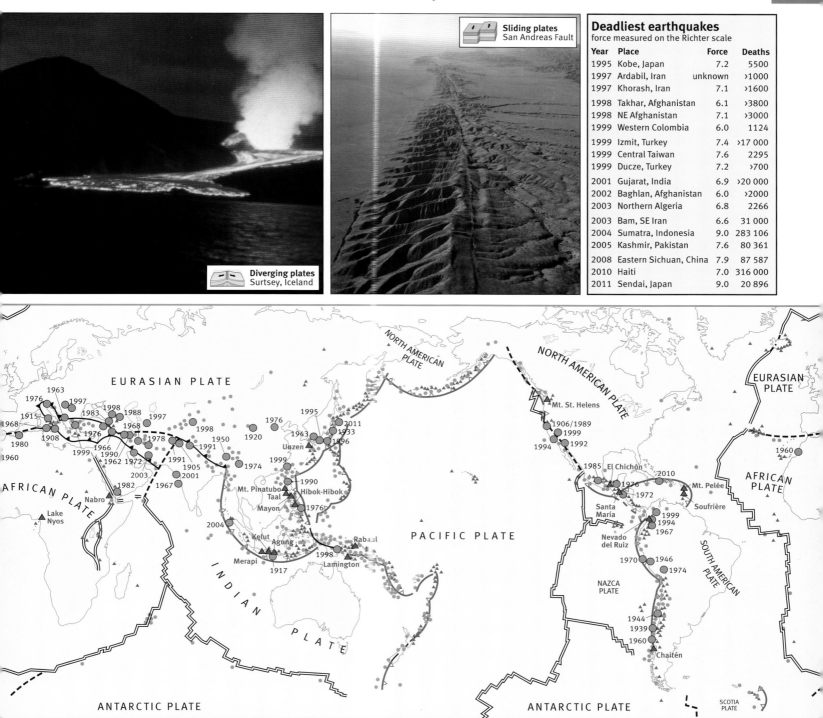

Diverging plates
Surtsey, Iceland

Sliding plates
San Andreas Fault

Subducting plates
Costa Rica

Deadliest earthquakes
force measured on the Richter scale

Year	Place	Force	Deaths
1995	Kobe, Japan	7.2	5500
1997	Ardabil, Iran	unknown	>1000
1997	Khorash, Iran	7.1	>1600
1998	Takhar, Afghanistan	6.1	>3800
1998	NE Afghanistan	7.1	>3000
1999	Western Colombia	6.0	1124
1999	Izmit, Turkey	7.4	>17 000
1999	Central Taiwan	7.6	2295
1999	Ducze, Turkey	7.2	>700
2001	Gujarat, India	6.9	>20 000
2002	Baghlan, Afghanistan	6.0	>2000
2003	Northern Algeria	6.8	2266
2003	Bam, SE Iran	6.6	31 000
2004	Sumatra, Indonesia	9.0	283 106
2005	Kashmir, Pakistan	7.6	80 361
2008	Eastern Sichuan, China	7.9	87 587
2010	Haiti	7.0	316 000
2011	Sendai, Japan	9.0	20 896

Major volcanic eruptions

Year	Volcano	Location
1985	Nevada del Ruiz	Colombia
1989	Redoubt	USA
1991	Unzen	Japan
1991	Pinatubo	Luzon, Philippines
1991	Cerro Hudson	Chile
1992	Spurr	Alaska, USA
1993	Galeras	Colombia
1994	Rabaul	Papua New Guinea
1995	Fogo	Cape Verde Islands
1996	Manam	Papua New Guinea
1997	Soufrière Hills	Montserrat
2001	Mt. Etna	Italy
2002	Nyiragongo	Congo, Dem. Rep.
2008	Chaitén	Chile
2010	Merapi	Indonesia
2011	Nabro	Eritrea

Earthquakes and volcanoes

earthquakes since 1900

- catastrophic earthquakes
- magnitude greater than 7 on the Richter scale

volcanic eruptions since 1900

- ▲ major eruptions
- ▴ active volcanoes

USGS Earthquake Hazards Program
http://earthquake.usgs.gov/

USGS Volcano Hazards Program
http://volcanoes.usgs.gov/

Equatorial scale 1: 105 000 000

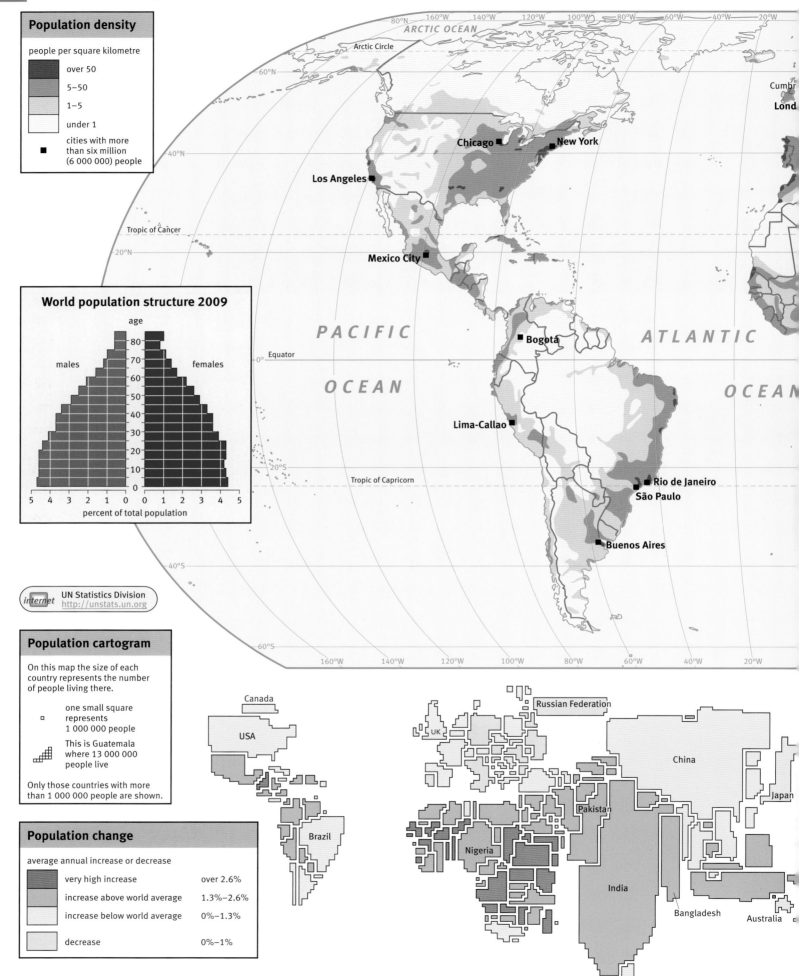

Population density

people per square kilometre

- over 50
- 5–50
- 1–5
- under 1
- ■ cities with more than six million (6 000 000) people

World population structure 2009

age

males   females

80
70
60
50
40
30
20
10
0

5 4 3 2 1 0   0 1 2 3 4 5

percent of total population

internet UN Statistics Division
http://unstats.un.org

Population cartogram

On this map the size of each country represents the number of people living there.

- □ one small square represents 1 000 000 people
- This is Guatemala where 13 000 000 people live

Only those countries with more than 1 000 000 people are shown.

Population change

average annual increase or decrease

- very high increase — over 2.6%
- increase above world average — 1.3%–2.6%
- increase below world average — 0%–1.3%
- decrease — 0%–1%

ARCTIC OCEAN
Arctic Circle
60°N
40°N
Chicago
New York
Los Angeles
Tropic of Cancer
20°N
Mexico City
PACIFIC
OCEAN
Equator 0°
Bogotá
ATLANTIC
OCEAN
Lima-Callao
20°S
Tropic of Capricorn
Rio de Janeiro
São Paulo
Buenos Aires
40°S
60°S

Cumbr
Lond

Canada
Russian Federation
UK
USA
China
Japan
Pakistan
Nigeria
India
Brazil
Bangladesh
Australia

Eckert IV Projection
© Oxford University Press

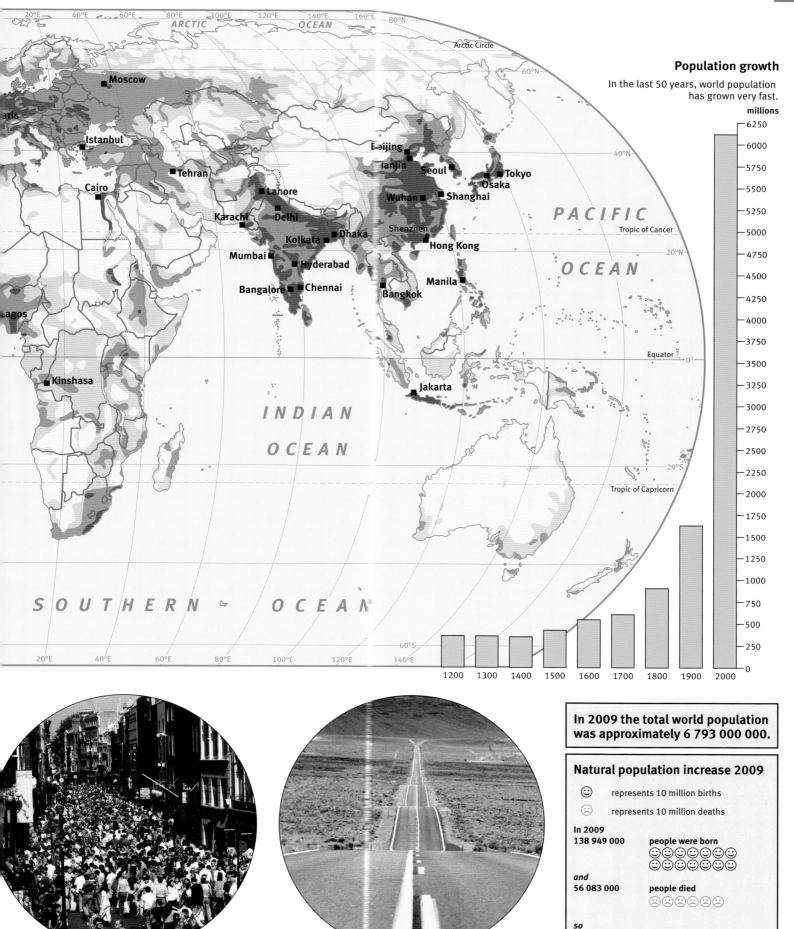

Population growth

In the last 50 years, world population has grown very fast.

millions
- 6250
- 6000
- 5750
- 5500
- 5250
- 5000
- 4750
- 4500
- 4250
- 4000
- 3750
- 3500
- 3250
- 3000
- 2750
- 2500
- 2250
- 2000
- 1750
- 1500
- 1250
- 1000
- 750
- 500
- 250
- 0

1200 1300 1400 1500 1600 1700 1800 1900 2000

ARCTIC OCEAN

Arctic Circle

Moscow

Istanbul

Tehran

Cairo

Paris

Lagos

Kinshasa

Karachi
Lahore
Delhi
Mumbai
Bangalore
Hyderabad
Chennai
Kolkata
Dhaka

Beijing
Tianjin
Seoul
Wuhan
Shanghai
Shenzhen
Hong Kong
Osaka
Tokyo

Bangkok
Manila

Jakarta

PACIFIC OCEAN

Tropic of Cancer

INDIAN OCEAN

Equator

Tropic of Capricorn

SOUTHERN OCEAN

In 2009 the total world population was approximately 6 793 000 000.

Natural population increase 2009

☺ represents 10 million births

☹ represents 10 million deaths

In 2009
138 949 000 people were born
☺☺☺☺☺☺☺
☺☺☺☺☺☺☺

and
56 083 000 people died
☹☹☹☹☹☹

so
82 866 000 people were added to the world's population
☺☺☺☺☺☺☺☺

over 50 people per square kilometre

under 1 person per square kilometre

GDP 2008

GDP per person, adjusted for the local cost of living, in US dollars

- over 10 000
- 2000–10 000
- under 2000
- no data

GDP (Gross Domestic Product) is the value of all the goods and services produced in a country in one year.

Richest: Luxembourg	$64 320	▲
United Kingdom	$36 130	
Poorest: Liberia	$300	▼

Luxembourg

Equator

Liberia

**Many people in rich countries are poor.
Some people in poor countries are rich.**

internet The World Bank
www.worldbank.org

Adult literacy 2010

percentage of people aged 15 and over who can read and write

- over 95%
- 60–95%
- under 60%
- no data

Highest: Georgia	100%	▲
United Kingdom	99%	
Lowest: Burkina	29%	▼

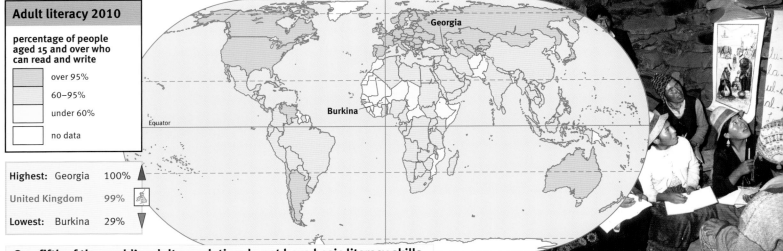

Georgia

Equator

Burkina

One fifth of the world's adult population do not have basic literacy skills.

internet UNESCO Institute for Statistics
www.uis.unesco.org

Life expectancy 2010

average number of years a baby can expect to live

- over 75 years
- 55–75 years
- under 55 years
- no data

Highest: Japan	83 years	▲
United Kingdom	80 years	
Lowest: Zambia	42 years	▼

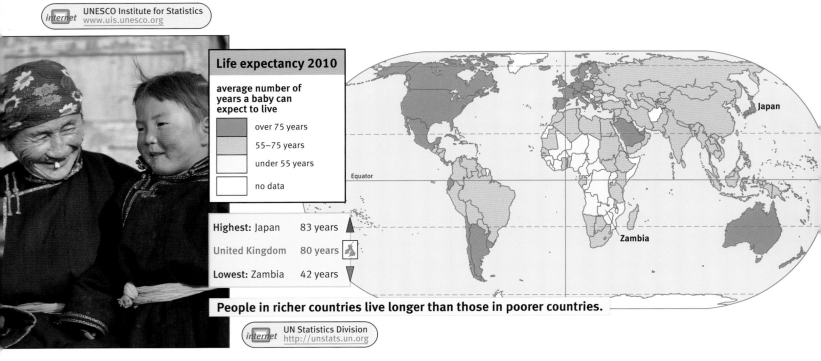

Equator

Japan

Zambia

People in richer countries live longer than those in poorer countries.

internet UN Statistics Division
http://unstats.un.org

Eckert IV Projection
© Oxford University Press

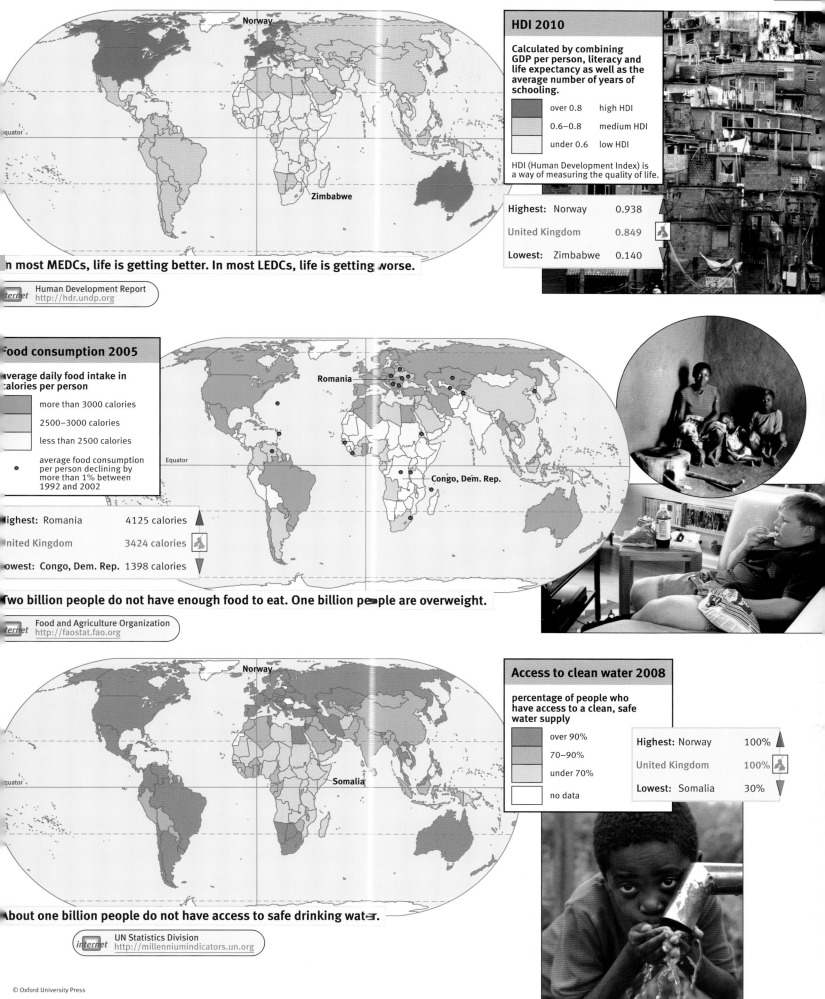

HDI 2010

Calculated by combining GDP per person, literacy and life expectancy as well as the average number of years of schooling.

■	over 0.8	high HDI
▨	0.6–0.8	medium HDI
□	under 0.6	low HDI

HDI (Human Development Index) is a way of measuring the quality of life.

Highest:	Norway	0.938
United Kingdom	0.849	
Lowest:	Zimbabwe	0.140

In most MEDCs, life is getting better. In most LEDCs, life is getting worse.

Human Development Report
http://hdr.undp.org

Food consumption 2005

average daily food intake in calories per person

■	more than 3000 calories
▨	2500–3000 calories
□	less than 2500 calories
•	average food consumption per person declining by more than 1% between 1992 and 2002

Highest:	Romania	4125 calories ▲
United Kingdom	3424 calories	
Lowest:	Congo, Dem. Rep.	1398 calories ▼

Two billion people do not have enough food to eat. One billion people are overweight.

Food and Agriculture Organization
http://faostat.fao.org

Access to clean water 2008

percentage of people who have access to a clean, safe water supply

■	over 90%
▨	70–90%
▨	under 70%
□	no data

Highest:	Norway	100% ▲
United Kingdom	100%	
Lowest:	Somalia	30% ▼

About one billion people do not have access to safe drinking water.

UN Statistics Division
http://millenniumindicators.un.org

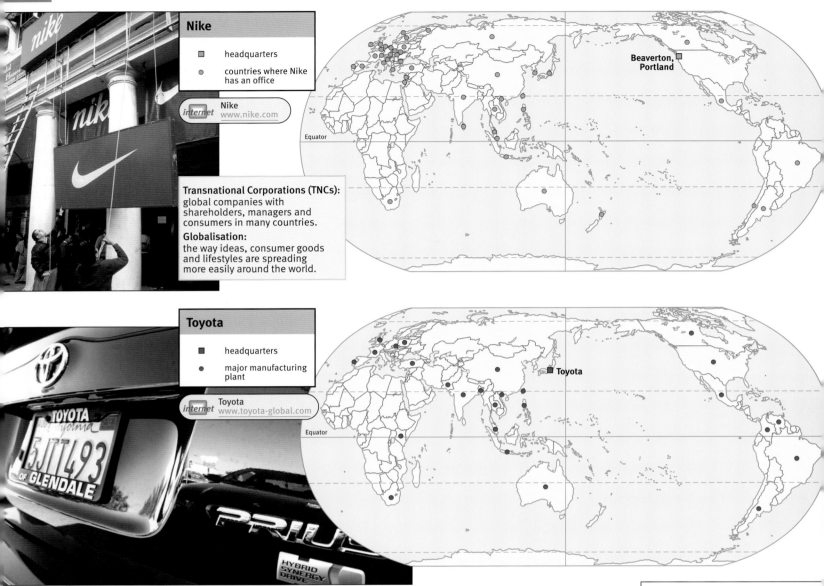

Nike

- ▪ headquarters
- ● countries where Nike has an office

internet Nike
www.nike.com

Beaverton, Portland ▪

Transnational Corporations (TNCs):
global companies with shareholders, managers and consumers in many countries.

Globalisation:
the way ideas, consumer goods and lifestyles are spreading more easily around the world.

Toyota

- ▪ headquarters
- ● major manufacturing plant

internet Toyota
www.toyota-global.com

Toyota ▪

Equator

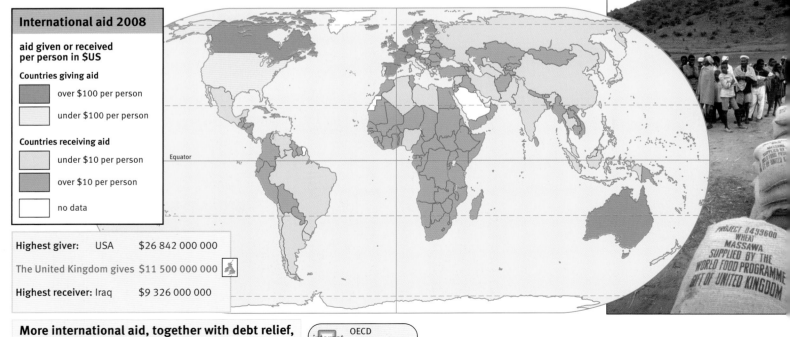

International aid 2008

aid given or received per person in $US

Countries giving aid

- over $100 per person
- under $100 per person

Countries receiving aid

- under $10 per person
- over $10 per person
- no data

Equator

Highest giver:	USA	$26 842 000 000
The United Kingdom gives		$11 500 000 000
Highest receiver:	Iraq	$9 326 000 000

More international aid, together with debt relief, would make poverty history.

internet OECD
www.oecd.org

Eckert IV Projection
© Oxford University Press

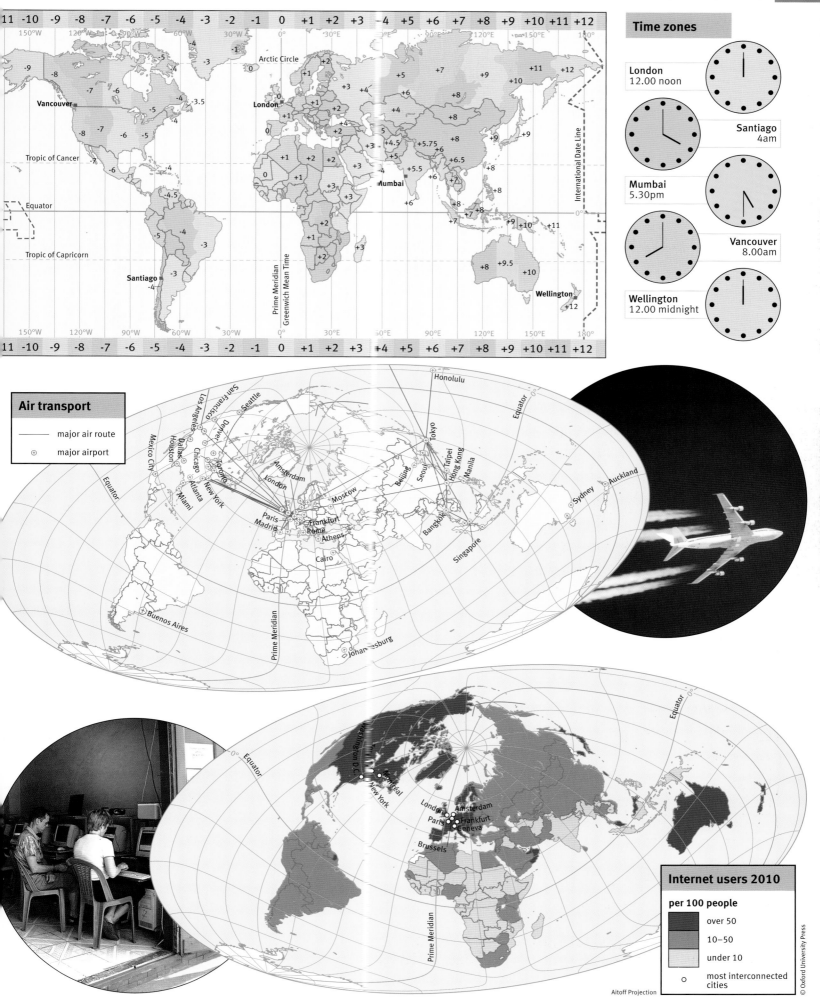

Time zones

London
12.00 noon

Santiago
4am

Mumbai
5.30pm

Vancouver
8.00am

Wellington
12.00 midnight

Air transport

—— major air route

⊕ major airport

Internet users 2010

per 100 people

over 50

10–50

under 10

○ most interconnected cities

Aitoff Projection

© Oxford University Press

Country data files

Country
Area in square kilometres

■ capital city

Maps are shown at the same scale

Population
estimated number of people in 2009

👤 represents 10 million people

Fertility
average number of children per mother

👤 represents one child

Life expectancy
average number of years people can expect to live

🕯 represents 10 years

Work
If there were 100 people in the country this is where they would work

👤 agriculture   👤 industry

👤 services

GDP
GDP per person in US dollars

💰 represents $1000

💰 represents $500

Medical care
number of doctors for every 10 000 people

👤 represents five doctors

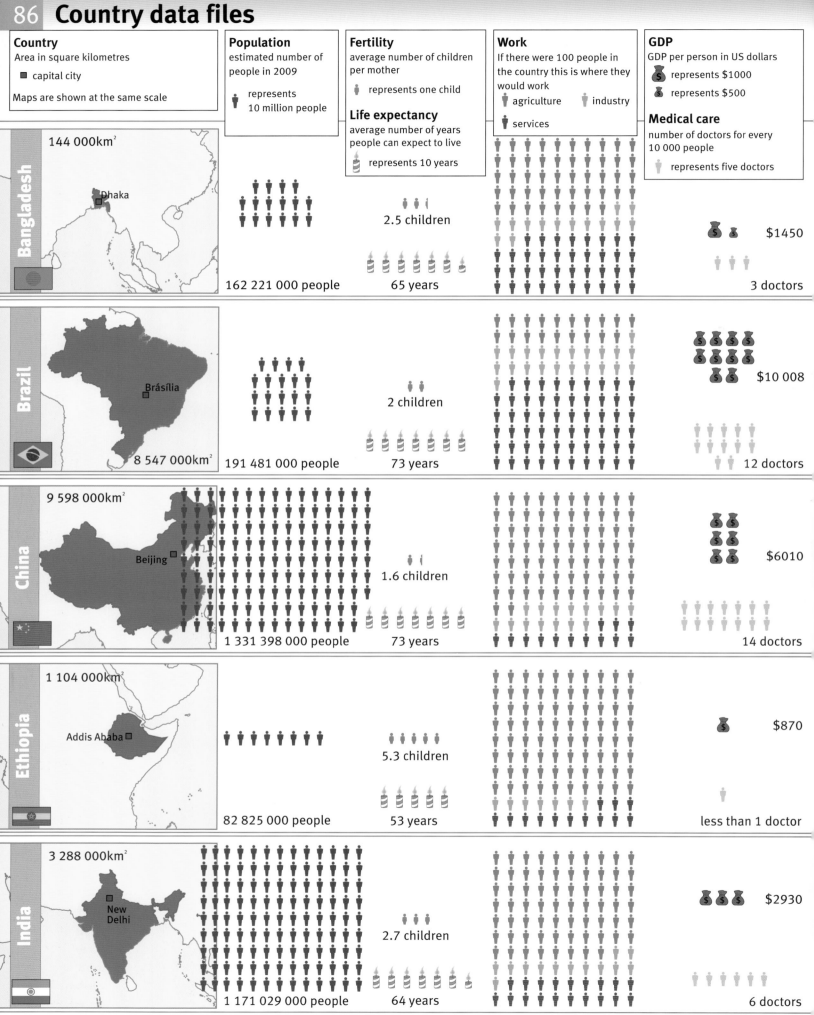

Bangladesh
144 000km²

Dhaka

162 221 000 people

2.5 children

65 years

$1450

3 doctors

Brazil
8 547 000km²

Brásília

191 481 000 people

2 children

73 years

$10 008

12 doctors

China
9 598 000km²

Beijing

1 331 398 000 people

1.6 children

73 years

$6010

14 doctors

Ethiopia
1 104 000km²

Addis Ababa

82 825 000 people

5.3 children

53 years

$870

less than 1 doctor

India
3 288 000km²

New Delhi

1 171 029 000 people

2.7 children

64 years

$2930

6 doctors

© Oxford University Press

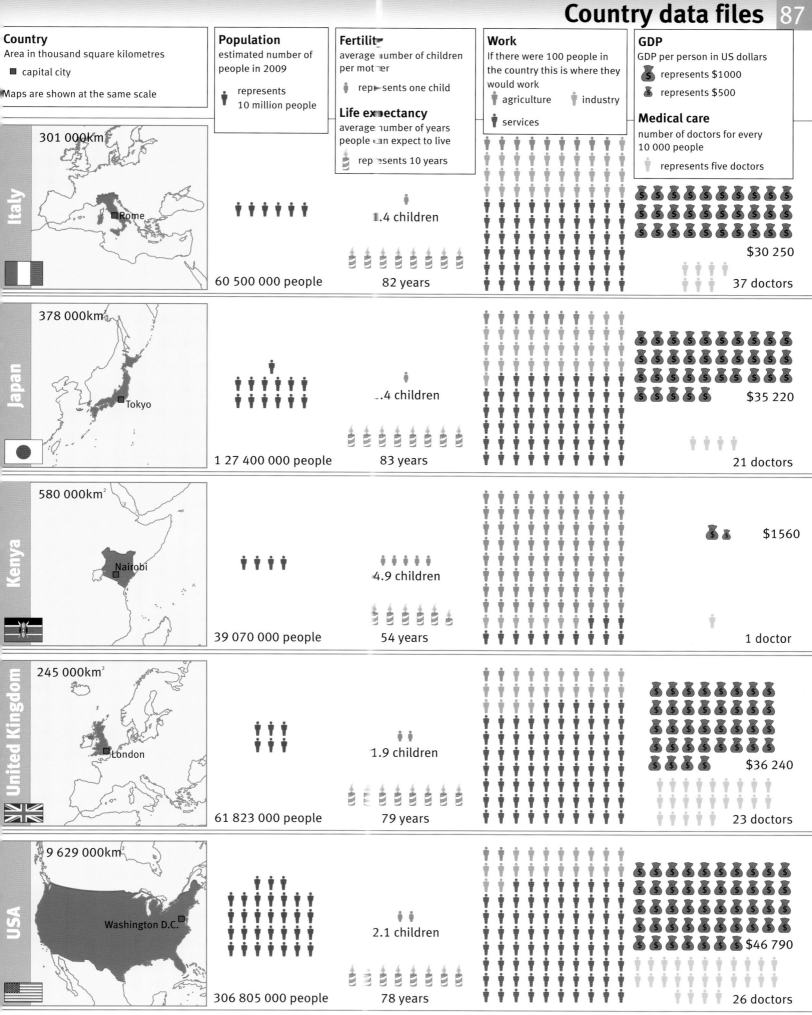

Country
Area in thousand square kilometres

■ capital city

Maps are shown at the same scale

Population
estimated number of people in 2009

👤 represents 10 million people

Fertility
average number of children per mother

👤 represents one child

Life expectancy
average number of years people can expect to live

represents 10 years

Work
If there were 100 people in the country this is where they would work

👤 agriculture 👤 industry

👤 services

GDP
GDP per person in US dollars

💰 represents $1000

💰 represents $500

Medical care
number of doctors for every 10 000 people

👤 represents five doctors

Italy
301 000km² — Rome

60 500 000 people · 1.4 children · 82 years · $30 250 · 37 doctors

Japan
378 000km² — Tokyo

1 27 400 000 people · 2.4 children · 83 years · $35 220 · 21 doctors

Kenya
580 000km² — Nairobi

39 070 000 people · 4.9 children · 54 years · $1560 · 1 doctor

United Kingdom
245 000km² — London

61 823 000 people · 1.9 children · 79 years · $36 240 · 23 doctors

USA
9 629 000km² — Washington D.C.

306 805 000 people · 2.1 children · 78 years · $46 790 · 26 doctors

Country	Land	Population						Employment			Quality of life		2008–2010
							2010						
	Area thousand km²	Total millions	Births per 1000 people	Deaths per 1000 people	Life expectancy years	Population change 2000–2010 per cent	Urban per cent	Primary per cent	Secondary per cent	Tertiary per cent	GDP ($US) per capita explanation: see p82	Health Doctors per 10 000 people	HDI explanation see p83
Afghanistan	652	29.1	39	18	44	28.2	22	ooo	ooo	ooo	ooo	2	0.349
Albania	29	3.2	10	5	75	3.2	49	55	23	22	7950	10	0.719
Algeria	2382	36.0	23	5	72	14.3	63	26	31	43	7940	12	0.677
Andorra	0.5	0.1	10	3	ooo	25.0	90	ooo	ooo	ooo	ooo	35	0.824
Angola	1247	19.0	42	17	47	47.3	57	75	8	17	5020	1	0.403
Antigua and Barbuda	0.4	0.1	14	6	75	42.9	31	ooo			20 570	ooo	ooo
Argentina	2780	40.5	18	8	72	9.5	91	12	32	56	14 020	31	0.775
Armenia	30	3.1	15	10	81	-11.4	64	18	43	39	6310	37	0.695
Australia	7741	22.4	14	6	80	18.5	82	6	26	68	34 040	10	0.937
Austria	84	8.4	9	9	72	2.4	67	8	38	54	37 680	40	0.851
Azerbaijan	87	9.0	17	6	72	16.9	54	31	29	40	7770	40	0.713
Bahamas, The	14	0.3	15	6	74	0.0	83	5	16	79	ooo	ooo	0.784
Bahrain	0.7	1.3	15	2	75	116.7	100	2	30	68	ooo	32	0.801
Bangladesh	144	164.4	22	7	66	27.2	25	65	16	19	1440	3	0.469
Barbados	0.4	0.3	13	8	74	0.0	38	14	30	56	ooo	ooo	0.788
Belarus	208	9.5	12	14	70	-6.9	74	20	40	40	12 150	48	0.732
Belgium	33	10.8	11	9	80	5.9	99	3	28	69	34 760	42	0.867
Belize	23	0.3	27	4	73	50.0	51	33	19	48	6040	8	0.694
Benin	113	9.8	40	10	59	60.7	41	63	8	29	1460	1	0.435
Bhutan	47	0.7	25	8	68	-66.7	32	94	2	4	4880	‹1	ooo
Bolivia	1099	10.4	27	7	66	25.3	65	47	18	35	4140	12	0.643
Bosnia-Herzegovina	51	3.8	9	9	75	-5.0	46	ooo	ooo	ooo	8620	12	0.710
Botswana	582	1.8	30	11	55	12.5	60	46	20	34	13 100	5	0.633
Brazil	8547	193.3	17	6	73	13.6	84	23	23	54	10 070	17	0.699
Brunei	6	0.4	16	3	77	33.3	72	2	24	74	50 200	10	0.805
Bulgaria	111	7.5	11	14	73	-8.5	71	13	48	39	11 950	38	0.743
Burkina	274	16.2	46	12	53	36.1	23	92	2	6	1160	1	0.305
Burundi	28	8.5	36	15	50	26.9	10	92	3	5	380	‹1	0.282
Cambodia	181	15.1	25	8	61	34.8	20	74	8	18	1820	2	0.494
Cameroon	475	20.0	37	14	51	32.5	53	70	9	21	2180	2	0.460
Canada	9971	34.1	11	7	81	9.6	80	3	25	72	36 220	19	0.888
Central African Republic	623	4.8	38	16	49	33.3	38	80	3	17	730	1	0.315
Chad	1284	11.5	46	17	49	49.4	27	83	4	13	1160	‹1	0.295
Chile	757	17.1	15	6	79	12.5	87	19	25	56	13 270	11	0.783
China	9598	1345.6	12	7	74	4.7	47	72	15	13	1272	16	0.663
Colombia	1139	45.5	20	6	74	7.6	75	27	23	50	8510	14	0.689
Comoros	2	0.7	33	7	64	0.0	28	78	9	13	1170	2	0.428
Congo	342	3.9	48	13	53	34.5	60	49	15	36	3090	1	0.489
Congo, Dem. Rep.	2345	67.8	47	17	48	31.1	33	68	13	19	290	1	0.239
Costa Rica	51	4.6	17	4	79	15.0	59	26	27	47	10 950	13	0.725
Côte d'Ivoire	322	22.0	37	14	52	48.6	50	60	10	30	1580	2	0.397
Croatia	57	4.4	10	12	76	-2.2	56	16	34	50	18 420	26	0.767
Cuba	111	11.2	11	8	78	0.0	75	19	30	51	ooo	64	ooo
Cyprus	9	1.1	13	7	79	37.5	62	14	30	56	24 040	24	0.810
Czech Republic	79	10.5	11	10	77	2.9	74	11	45	44	22 790	36	0.841

Country	Land	Population						Employment			Quality of life		
							2010						**2008–2010**
	Area thousand km²	Total millions	Births per 1000	Deaths per 1000	Life expectancy year	Population change 2000–2010 per cent	Urban per cent in 2010	Primary per cent	Secondary per cent	Tertiary per cent	GDP ($US) per capita explanation: see p82	Health Doctors per 10 000 people	HDI explanation: see p83
Denmark	43	5.5	11	10	79	3.8	72	6	28	66	37 280	31	0.866
Djibouti	23	0.9	29	11	55	50.0	76	ooo	ooo	ooo	2330	3	0.402
Dominica	0.8	0.1	15	8	75	42.9	73	ooo	ooo	ooo	8300	ooo	ooo
Dominican Republic	49	9.9	23	6	72	16.5	67	25	29	46	7890	17	0.663
Ecuador	284	14.2	21	5	75	12.7	65	33	19	48	7760	14	0.695
Egypt	1001	80.4	27	6	72	22.4	43	40	22	38	5460	23	0.620
El Salvador	21	6.2	20	7	71	20.4	63	36	21	43	6670	12	0.659
Equatorial Guinea	28	0.7	39	16	49	26.4	39	66	11	23	21 700	3	0.538
Eritrea	118	5.2	37	9	59	21.0	21	80	5	15	630	‹1	ooo
Estonia	45	1.3	12	12	74	-7.9	69	14	41	45	19 280	34	0.812
Ethiopia	1104	85.0	39	12	55	35.8	16	86	2	12	870	‹1	0.328
Fiji	18	0.9	24	7	68	12.5	51	46	15	39	4270	4	0.669
Finland	338	5.4	11	9	80	3.8	65	8	31	61	35 660	34	0.871
France	552	63.0	13	9	81	6.6	77	5	29	66	34 400	37	0.872
French Guiana	91	0.2	28	3	75	0.0	81	ooo	ooo	ooo	ooo	ooo	ooo
Gabon	268	1.5	29	10	60	25.0	84	51	16	33	12 270	3	0.648
Gambia, The	11	1.8	38	12	58	38.5	54	82	8	10	1280	‹1	0.390
Georgia	70	4.6	13	10	74	-8.0	53	26	31	43	4850	42	0.698
Germany	357	81.6	8	10	80	-0.7	73	4	38	58	35 940	35	0.885
Ghana	239	24.0	31	9	61	18.8	48	59	13	28	1430	1	0.467
Greece	132	11.3	11	10	80	6.6	73	23	27	50	28 470	56	0.855
Guatemala	109	14.4	34	6	72	26.3	47	52	17	31	4690	ooo	0.560
Guinea	246	10.8	41	11	57	45.9	28	87	2	11	1190	1	0.340
Guinea-Bissau	36	1.6	43	18	48	33.3	30	85	2	13	530	‹1	0.289
Guyana	215	0.8	23	7	66	-11.1	28	22	25	53	2510	5	0.611
Haiti	28	9.8	28	9	61	19.5	48	68	9	23	1180	ooo	0.404
Honduras	112	7.6	28	5	72	16.9	50	41	20	39	3870	5	0.604
Hungary	93	10.0	10	13	74	0.0	67	15	38	47	17 790	28	0.805
Iceland	103	0.3	15	6	81	0.0	93	ooo	ooo	ooo	25 220	37	0.869
India	3288	1188.8	23	7	64	17.3	29	64	16	20	2960	6	0.519
Indonesia	1905	235.5	20	6	71	11.0	43	55	14	31	3830	1	0.600
Iran	1633	75.1	19	6	71	10.9	69	39	23	38	10.840	10	0.702
Iraq	438	31.5	32	6	67	36.4	67	16	18	66	ooo	6	ooo
Ireland	70	4.5	17	6	79	21.6	60	14	29	57	37 350	32	0.895
Israel	21	7.6	22	5	81	22.6	92	4	29	67	27 450	40	0.872
Italy	301	60.5	10	10	82	5.6	68	9	31	60	30 250	37	0.854
Jamaica	11	2.7	20	7	72	3.8	52	25	23	52	7360	8	0.688
Japan	378	127.4	9	9	83	0.6	86	7	34	59	35 220	21	0.884
Jordan	89	6.5	31	4	73	-3.0	83	15	23	62	5530	26	0.681
Kazakhstan	2717	16.3	23	9	69	0.6	54	22	32	46	9690	38	0.714
Kenya	580	40.0	37	10	57	32.9	18	80	7	13	1580	1	0.470
Kiribati	0.7	0.1	27	9	61	25.0	44	ooo	ooo	ooo	3660	2	ooo
Kuwait	18	3.1	22	2	78	55.0	98	1	25	74	52 610	20	0.771
Kyrgyzstan	199	5.3	24	7	68	12.8	35	32	27	41	2130	24	0.598
Laos	237	6.4	28	7	65	18.5	27	78	6	16	2060	3	0.497

Country data sets

Country	Land	Population						Employment			Quality of life		
	Area thousand km²	Total millions	Births per 1000 people	Deaths per 1000 people	Life expectancy years	Population change 2000–2010 per cent	Urban per cent	Primary per cent	Secondary per cent	Tertiary per cent	GDP ($US) per capita explanation: see p82	Health Doctors per 10 000 people	HDI explanat: see p8
Latvia	65	2.2	10	13	73	-8.3	68	16	40	44	16 740	30	0.769
Lebanon	10	4.3	20	5	72	30.3	87	7	31	62	10 880	30	ooo
Lesotho	30	1.9	28	19	41	-13.6	23	40	28	32	2000	‹1	0.427
Liberia	111	4.1	43	11	56	28.1	58	ooo	ooo	ooo	300	‹1	0.300
Libya	1760	6.5	23	4	74	16.1	77	11	23	66	15 630	12	0.755
Lithuania	65	3.3	11	12	72	-10.8	67	18	41	41	18 210	38	0.783
Luxembourg	3	0.5	11	7	80	25.0	83	ooo	ooo	ooo	64 320	27	0.852
Macedonia, FYRO	26	2.1	12	9	74	5.0	65	21	40	39	9950	25	0.701
Madagascar	587	20.1	37	9	60	26.4	31	78	7	15	1040	2	0.435
Malawi	118	15.4	44	15	49	41.3	14	87	5	8	830	‹1	0.385
Malaysia	330	28.9	21	5	74	30.2	63	27	23	50	13 740	7	0.744
Mali	1240	15.2	46	15	51	35.7	33	86	2	12	1090	1	0.309
Malta	0.3	0.4	10	8	79	0.0	94	ooo	ooo	ooo	22 460	34	0.815
Mauritania	1026	3.4	34	11	57	25.9	40	55	10	35	2000	1	0.433
Mauritius	2	1.3	12	7	73	8.3	42	17	43	40	12 480	11	0.701
Mexico	1958	110.6	19	5	76	11.8	77	28	24	48	14 270	28	0.750
Moldova	34	4.1	11	12	70	-4.7	41	33	30	37	3210	26	0.623
Mongolia	1567	2.8	25	6	67	3.7	61	32	22	46	3480	24	0.622
Montenegro	14	0.6	13	9	74	ooo	64	ooo	ooo	ooo	13 920	18	0.769
Morocco	447	31.9	21	6	71	12.3	57	45	25	30	4330	6	0.567
Mozambique	802	23.4	40	16	48	18.8	31	83	8	9	770	‹1	0.284
Myanmar	677	53.4	20	11	58	17.1	31	73	10	17	1290	4	0.451
Namibia	824	2.2	28	9	61	29.4	35	49	15	36	6270	3	0.606
Nepal	147	28.0	28	8	64	17.2	17	94	0	6	1120	2	0.428
Netherlands	41	16.6	11	8	80	5.1	66	5	26	69	41 670	39	0.890
New Zealand	271	4.4	14	7	80	12.8	86	10	25	65	25 090	20	0.907
Nicaragua	130	6.0	23	4	71	17.6	56	28	26	46	2620	4	0.565
Niger	1267	15.9	52	17	48	48.6	20	90	4	6	680	‹1	0.261
Nigeria	924	158.3	42	17	47	42.0	47	43	7	50	1940	4	0.423
North Korea	121	22.8	15	10	63	-5.0	60	38	32	30	ooo	32	ooo
Norway	324	4.9	13	9	81	8.9	80	6	25	69	58 500	39	0.938
Oman	213	3.1	20	3	72	24.0	72	44	24	32	20 650	16	ooo
Pakistan	796	184.8	30	7	66	18.1	35	52	19	29	2700	8	0.490
Panama	76	3.5	20	5	76	20.7	64	26	16	58	11 650	14	0.755
Papua New Guinea	463	6.8	31	10	59	41.7	13	79	7	14	2000	1	0.431
Paraguay	407	6.5	25	6	72	18.2	58	39	22	39	4820	10	0.755
Peru	1285	29.5	21	6	73	14.8	76	36	18	46	7980	ooo	0.762
Philippines	300	94.0	26	5	72	23.7	63	46	15	39	3900	10	0.758
Poland	323	38.2	11	10	76	-1.5	61	27	36	37	17 310	20	0.858
Portugal	92	10.7	9	10	79	8.1	55	18	34	48	22 080	34	0.904
Qatar	11	1.7	9	1	76	183.3	100	3	32	65	ooo	26	0.803
Romania	238	21.5	10	12	73	-3.6	55	24	47	29	13 500	19	0.767
Russian Federation	17 075	141.9	12	14	68	-3.4	73	14	42	44	15 630	43	0.719
Rwanda	26	10.4	42	14	51	35.1	17	92	3	5	1010	‹1	0.385
St. Lucia	0.6	0.2	14	7	73	0.0	30	ooo	ooo	ooo	9190	ooo	ooo

Country	Land — Area thousand km²	Population — Total millions	Births per 1000	Deaths per 1000	Life expectancy years	Population change 2000–2010 per cent	Urban per cent in 2010	Employment — Primary per cent	Secondary per cent	Tertiary per cent	Quality of life — GDP ($US) per capita explanation: see p82	Health Doctors per 10 000 people	HDI explanation: see p83
Samoa	3	0.2	26	5	73	185.7	22	ooo	ooo	ooo	4340	3	ooo
São Tomé and Príncipe	1	0.2	37	7	66	100.0	58	ooo	ooo	ooo	1780	4	0.488
Saudi Arabia	2150	29.2	28	2	76	35.2	81	19	20	61	22 950	16	0.752
Senegal	197	12.5	39	11	55	31.6	41	77	8	15	1760	1	0.411
Serbia	88	7.3	9	14	74	ooo	58	ooo	ooo	ooo	11 150	20	0.735
Seychelles	0.5	0.1	18	7	73	25.0	53	ooo	ooo	ooo	19 770	12	ooo
Sierra Leone	72	5.8	40	16	47	18.4	36	68	15	17	750	‹1	0.317
Singapore	1	5.1	10	4	81	41.7	100	0	36	64	47 940	14	0.846
Slovakia	49	5.4	11	10	75	0.0	55	12	32	56	21 300	31	0.818
Slovenia	20	2.1	11	9	79	5.0	50	6	46	48	26 910	24	0.828
Solomon Islands	29	0.5	33	8	62	25.0	17	77	7	16	2580	1	0.494
Somalia	638	9.4	46	16	49	-6.9	34	ooo	ooo	ooo	ooo	‹1	ooo
South Africa	1221	49.9	21	12	53	23.5	52	14	32	54	9780	8	0.597
South Korea	99	48.9	9	5	80	4.5	82	18	35	47	28 120	17	0.877
Spain	506	47.1	11	8	81	18.9	77	12	33	55	31 130	41	0.863
Sri Lanka	66	20.7	19	7	74	10.1	15	48	21	31	4480	5	0.658
Sudan	2506	43.2	33	11	58	46.4	38	70	8	22	1930	3	0.379
Suriname	163	0.5	19	7	69	25.0	67	21	18	61	7130	4	0.646
Swaziland	17	1.2	31	16	46	20.0	22	40	22	38	5010	2	0.498
Sweden	450	9.4	12	10	81	5.6	84	ooo	ooo	ooo	38 180	36	0.885
Switzerland	41	7.8	10	8	82	5.4	73	3	35	59	46 460	38	0.874
Syria	185	22.5	28	3	74	39.8	54	33	24	43	4350	6	0.589
Taiwan	36	23.2	8	6	78	ooo	78	ooo	ooo	ooo	ooo	ooo	ooo
Tajikistan	143	7.6	28	4	67	22.6	26	41	23	36	1860	19	0.580
Tanzania	945	45.0	42	12	56	34.3	25	84	5	11	1230	‹1	0.398
Thailand	513	68.1	15	9	69	10.9	31	64	14	22	5990	3	0.654
Togo	57	6.8	33	8	63	47.8	40	66	10	24	820	1	0.428
Tonga	0.8	0.1	29	7	70	0.0	23	ooo	ooo	ooo	3880	3	0.677
Trinidad and Tobago	5	1.3	14	8	69	0.0	12	11	31	58	23 950	14	0.736
Tunisia	164	10.5	18	6	74	9.4	66	28	33	39	7070	13	0.683
Turkey	775	73.6	18	6	72	10.5	76	53	18	29	13 770	16	0.679
Turkmenistan	488	5.2	22	8	65	15.6	47	37	23	40	6210	24	0.669
Uganda	241	33.8	47	13	52	55.0	13	85	5	10	1140	1	0.422
Ukraine	604	45.9	11	15	68	-9.1	69	20	40	40	7210	31	0.710
United Arab Emirates	84	5.4	15	2	77	125.0	83	8	27	65	ooo	15	0.815
United Kingdom	245	62.2	13	9	80	5.8	80	2	29	69	36 130	21	0.849
United States of America	9631	309.6	14	8	78	11.2	79	3	28	69	46 970	27	0.902
Uruguay	177	3.4	14	9	76	3.0	94	14	27	59	12 540	36	0.765
Uzbekistan	447	28.1	23	5	68	15.6	36	34	25	41	2660	26	0.617
Vanuatu	12	0.2	31	6	67	0.0	24	ooo	ooo	ooo	3940	2	ooo
Venezuela	912	28.8	21	5	74	19.0	88	12	27	61	12 380	19	0.696
Vietnam	332	88.9	17	5	74	11.4	28	71	14	15	2700	5	0.572
Yemen	528	23.6	38	8	63	30.4	29	61	17	22	2210	3	0.439
Zambia	753	13.3	45	20	42	44.6	37	75	8	17	1230	1	0.395
Zimbabwe	391	12.6	30	17	43	7.7	37	68	8	24	ooo	2	0.140

name of place · country · grid code · description · page number · latitude · longitude

Snowdon *mt.* UK **14 C5** 53 04N 4 05W

A

Abadan Iran 40 B4 30 20N 48 15E
Aberaeron UK 14 C4 52 49N 44 43W
Aberdare UK 14 D3 51 43N 3 27W
Aberdeen UK 11 F3 57 10N 2 04W
Aberfeldy UK 11 E2 56 37N 3 54W
Abergavenny UK 14 D3 51 50N 3 00W
Abertillery UK 14 D3 51 45N 3 09W
Aberystwyth UK 14 C4 52 25N 4 05W
Abidjan Côte d'Ivoire 52 A3 5 19N 4 01W
Abingdon UK 15 F3 51 41N 1 17W
Aboyne UK 11 F3 57 05N 2 50W
Abu Dhabi UAE 40 C3 24 28N 54 25E
Abuja Nigeria 52 B3 9 10N 7 11E
Accra Ghana 52 A3 5 33N 0 15W
Achill Island RoI 16 A3/B3 53 55N 10 05W
A Coruña Spain 34 B3 43 22N 8 24W
Adana Turkey 35 F2 37 00N 35 19E
Addis Ababa Ethiopia 52 C3 9 03N 38 42E
Adelaide Australia 67 D2 34 55S 138 36E
Aden Yemen Rep. 40 B2 12 50N 45 03E
AFGHANISTAN 40/41 D4/E4
Agra India 41 E3 27 09N 78 00E
Ahmadabad India 41 E3 23 03N 72 40E
Ahvaz Iran 40 B4 31 17N 48 43E
Airdrie UK 11 E1 55 52N 3 59W
Ajaccio Corsica 36 A2 41 55N 8 43E
Akita Japan 48 D2 39 44N 140 05E
Alabama *state* USA 59 E2 32 00N 87 00W
ALBANIA 35 D3/E3
Albany Australia 66 B2 35 00S 117 53E
Ålborg Denmark 32 D2 57 05N 9 50E
Albuquerque USA 58 C2 35 05N 106 38W
Aldeburgh UK 15 J4 52 09N 1 35E
Aldershot UK 15 G3 51 15N 0 47W
Aleppo Syria 40 A4 36 14N 37 10E
Alexandria Egypt 52 C4 31 13N 29 55E
ALGERIA 52 A4/B4
Algiers Algeria 52 B4 36 50N 3 00E
Alicante Spain 34 B2 38 21N 0 29W
Alice Springs Australia 66 D3 23 41S 133 52E
Alloa UK 11 E2 56 07N 3 49W
Almaty Kazakhstan 41 E5 43 19N 76 55E
Alnwick UK 13 H4 55 25N 1 42W
Alps *mts.* Europe 34 C3 46 00N 7 30E
Alton UK 15 G3 51 09N 0 59W
Amazon *r.* Brazil 62 D6 2 30S 65 30W
Amble UK 13 H4 55 20N 1 34W
Ambleside UK 13 G3 54 26N 2 58W
Ambon Indonesia 45 E2 3 41S 128 10E
Amesbury UK 14 F3 51 10N 1 47W
Amlwch UK 14 C5 53 25N 4 20W
Amman Jordan 40 A4 31 04N 46 17E
Ammanford UK 14 D3 51 48N 3 58W
Amritsar India 41 E4 31 35N 74 56E
Amsterdam Netherlands 34 C4 52 22N 4 54E
Ancona Italy 36 B2 43 37N 13 31E
Andaman Islands India 41 G1 12 00N 94 00E
Andes *mts.* South America 62/63 B3/B7 10 00S 77 00W
ANDORRA 34 C3
Andover UK 15 F3 51 13N 1 28W
Anglesey *i.* UK 14 C5 53 18N 4 25W
ANGOLA 53 B2
Ankara Turkey 35 F2 39 55N 32 50E
'Annaba Algeria 52 B4 36 55N 7 47E
An Najaf Iraq 40 B4 31 59N 44 19E
Annan UK 13 F3 54 59N 3 16W
Anshan China 44 E7 41 05N 122 58E
Antananarivo Madagascar 53 D2 18 52S 47 30E
ANTIGUA AND BARBUDA 62 C8
Antofagasta Chile 63 B4 23 40S 70 23W
Antrim UK 16 E4 54 43N 6 13W
Antrim Mountains UK 16 E4/E5 55 00N 6 10W
Antwerp Belgium 34 C4 51 13N 4 25E
Appalachian Mountains USA 59 E2 37 00N 82 00W
Appennines *mts.* Italy 36 A2/C2 44 30N 10 00E
Appleby-in-Westmorland UK 13 G3 53 36N 2 29W
Aral Sea Asia 38 B5/C5 45 00N 60 00E
Aran Islands RoI 17 B3 53 10N 9 50W
Ararat, Mount Turkey 40 B4 39 44N 44 15E
Arbil Iraq 40 B4 36 12N 44 01E
Arbroath UK 11 F2 56 34N 2 35W
Arctic Ocean 72/73
Antarctica 68
Ards Peninsula UK 16 F4 54 25N 5 30W
Arequipa Peru 62 B5 16 25S 71 32W
ARGENTINA 63 C3
Århus Denmark 32 E2 56 15N 10 10E
Arica Chile 62 B5 18 30S 70 20W
Arisaig UK 11 C2 56 51N 5 51W
Arizona *state* USA 58 B2 34 00N 112 00W
Arkansas *r.* USA 59 D2 35 00N 93 00W
Arkansas *state* USA 59 D2 34 00N 93 00W
Arkhangel'sk Russia 40 H3 64 32N 40 40E
Arklow RoI 17 E2 52 48N 6 09W
Armagh UK 16 E4 54 21N 6 39W
ARMENIA 40 B4/B5
Arnold UK 15 F4 53 00N 1 09W
Arran *i.* UK 11 C1 55 35N 5 15W
Arundel UK 15 G2 50 51N 0 34W
Asansol India 42 B1 23 40N 86 59E
Ashbourne UK 14 F5 53 01N 1 43W
Ashford UK 15 H3 51 09N 0 53E
Ashgabat Turkmenistan 40 C4 37 58N 58 24E
Ashington UK 13 H4 55 11N 1 34W
Asmara Eritrea 52 C3 15 20N 38 58E
Astana Kazakhstan 39 C5 51 10N 71 28E
Asunción Paraguay 63 D4 25 15S 57 40W
Aswan Egypt 52 C4 24 05N 32 56E
Atacama Desert Chile 63 B4 22 30S 70 00W
Athens Greece 35 E2 38 00N 23 44E
Athlone RoI 17 D3 53 25N 7 56W
Atlanta USA 59 E2 33 45N 84 23W
Atlantic Ocean 72/73
Atlas Mountains Morocco 52 A4 32 00N 2 00W
At Ta'if Saudi Arabia 40 B3 21 15N 40 21E
Auchterarder UK 11 E2 56 18N 3 43W
Auchtermuchty UK 11 E2 56 17N 3 15W
Auckland New Zealand 67 H2 36 51S 174 46E
Austin USA 59 D2 30 18N 97 47W
AUSTRALIA 66/67
AUSTRIA 34 D3
Aviemore UK 11 E3 57 12N 3 50W
Avignon France 34 C3 43 56N 4 48E
Avon *r.* UK 14 F4 52 15N 1 55W
Axminster UK 14 E2 50 47N 3 00W
Ayers Rock *mt.* Australia 66 D3 25 20S 131 01E
Aylesbury UK 15 G3 51 50N 0 50W
Ayr UK 11 D1 55 28N 4 38W
AZERBAIJAN 40 B4/B5

B

Baffin Bay Canada 56 F4/G4 72 00N 64 00W
Baffin Island Canada 56 F4 70 00N 75 00W
Baghdad Iraq 40 B4 33 20N 44 26E
BAHAMAS, THE 57 F2
BAHRAIN 40 C3
Bakewell UK 14 F5 53 13N 1 40W
Baku Azerbaijan 40 B5 40 22N 49 53E
Bala UK 14 D4 52 54N 3 35W
Balearic Islands Spain 34 C2/C3 40 00N 2 00E
Bali *i.* Indonesia 45 D2 8 30S 115 00E
Balikesir Turkey 35 E2 39 37N 27 51E
Balkhash, Lake Kazakhstan 38 C5 46 00N 75 00E
Ballantrae UK 12 D4 55 06N 5 00W
Ballater UK 11 E3 57 03N 3 03W
Ballybofey RoI 16 D4 54 48N 7 47W
Ballycastle UK 16 E5 55 12N 6 15W
Ballymena UK 16 E4 54 52N 6 17W
Ballymoney UK 16 E5 55 04N 6 31W
Baltimore USA 59 F2 39 18N 76 38W
Bamako Mali 52 A3 12 40N 7 59W
Bamburgh UK 13 H4 55 36N 1 42W
Banbridge UK 16 E4 54 21N 6 16W
Banbury UK 15 F4 52 04N 1 20W
Banchory UK 11 F3 57 30N 2 30W
Banda Aceh Indonesia 45 B3 5 30N 95 20E
Bandar Seri Begawan Brunei 45 D3 4 53N 114 57E
Bandung Indonesia 45 C2 6 57S 107 34E
Bangalore India 41 E2 12 58N 77 35E
Bangkok Thailand 45 C4 13 44N 100 30E
BANGLADESH 42 B1/C2
Bangor UK 16 F4 54 40N 5 40W
Bangor UK 14 C5 53 13N 4 08W
Bangui CAR 52 B3 4 23N 18 37E
Banjarmasin Indonesia 45 D2 3 22S 114 33E
Banjul The Gambia 52 A3 13 28N 16 39W
Baotou China 44 C7 40 38N 109 59E
BARBADOS 62 D8
Barcelona Spain 34 C3 41 25N 2 10E
Bari Italy 36 C2 41 07N 16 52E
Barking UK 15 H3 51 33N 0 06E
Barmouth UK 14 C4 52 43N 4 03W
Barnard Castle UK 13 H3 54 33N 1 55W
Barnet UK 15 G3 51 39N 0 12W
Barnsley UK 13 H2 53 34N 1 28W
Barnstaple UK 14 C3 51 05N 4 04W
Barra *i.* UK 11 A2/A3 57 00N 7 25W
Barranquilla Colombia 62 B8 11 10N 74 50W
Barreiras Brazil 62 E5 12 09S 44 58W
Barrow-in-Furness UK 13 F3 54 07N 3 14W
Barry UK 14 D3 51 24N 3 18W
Barton-upon-Humber UK 13 J2 53 41N 0 27W
Basel Switzerland 34 C3 47 33N 7 36E
Basingstoke UK 15 F3 51 16N 1 05W
Basra Iraq 40 B4 30 30N 47 50E
Bath UK 14 E3 51 23N 2 22W
Bathgate UK 11 E1 55 55N 3 39W
Baton Rouge USA 59 D2 30 30N 91 10W
Baykal, Lake Russia 44 C8 54 00N 109 00E
Bearsden UK 11 D1 55 56N 4 20W
Beccles UK 15 J4 52 28N 1 34E
Bedford UK 15 G4 52 08N 0 29W
Bedworth UK 15 F4 52 29N 1 28W
Beijing China 44 D6 39 55N 116 26E
Beira Mozambique 53 C2 19 49S 34 52E
Beirut Lebanon 40 A4 33 52N 35 30E
BELARUS 33 F2/G2
Belém Brazil 62 E6 1 27S 48 29W
Belfast UK 16 F4 54 35N 5 55W
BELGIUM 34 C4
Belgrade Serbia 35 E3 44 50N 20 30E
Belize Belize 57 E1 17 29N 88 10W
BELIZE 57 E1
Belo Horizonte Brazil 63 E5 19 54S 43 54W
Benbecula *i.* UK 11 A3 57 25N 7 20W
Ben Cruachan *mt.* UK 11 C2 56 26N 5 09W
Benghazi Libya 52 C4 32 07N 20 04E
BENIN 52 B3
Ben Lawers *mt.* UK 11 D2 56 33N 4 15W
Ben Lomond *mt.* UK 11 D2 56 12N 4 38W
Ben More *mt.* UK 11 B2 56 25N 6 02W
Ben More *mt.* UK 11 D2 56 25N 6 02W
Ben Nevis *mt.* UK 11 C2 56 48N 5 00W
Ben Wyvis *mt.* UK 11 D3 57 40N 4 35W
Bérgamo Italy 36 A3 45 42N 9 40E
Bergen Norway 32 D3 60 23N 5 20E
Berlin Germany 34 D4 52 32N 13 25E
Bermuda *i.* Atlantic Ocean 57 F2 32 50N 64 20W
Bern Switzerland 34 C3 46 57N 7 26E
Berwick-upon-Tweed UK 11 H4 55 46N 2 00W
Bethesda UK 14 C5 53 11N 4 03W
Beverley UK 13 J2 53 51N 0 26W
Bexley UK 15 H3 51 27N 0 09E
BHUTAN 42 B2/C2
Bicester UK 15 F3 51 54N 1 09W
Bideford UK 14 C3 51 01N 4 13W
Bideford Bay UK 14 C3 51 05N 4 25W
Biggar UK 11 E1 55 38N 3 32W
Biggleswade UK 15 G4 52 05N 0 17W
Bilbao Spain 34 B3 43 15N 2 56W
Birkenhead UK 13 F2 53 24N 3 02W
Birmingham UK 14 F4 52 30N 1 50W
Birmingham USA 59 E2 33 30N 86 55W
Biscay, Bay of Atlantic Ocean 34 B3 45 30N 2 50W
Bishkek Kyrgyzstan 41 E5 42 53N 74 46E
Bishop Auckland UK 13 H3 54 40N 1 40W
Bishop's Stortford UK 15 H3 51 53N 0 09E
Bissau Guinea-Bissau 52 A3 11 52N 15 39W
Blackburn UK 13 G2 53 45N 2 29W
Black Mountains UK 14 D3/D4 51 55N 3 10W
Blackpool UK 13 F2 53 50N 3 03W
Black Sea Europe 35 E3/F3 43 00N 35 00E
Blaenau Ffestiniog UK 14 D4 52 59N 3 56W
Blairgowrie UK 11 E2 56 36N 3 21W
Blandford Forum UK 14 E2 50 52N 2 11W
Blantyre Malawi 53 C2 15 46S 35 00E
Blyth UK 13 H4 55 07N 1 30W
Boa Vista Brazil 62 C7 3 23S 55 30W
Bodmin UK 14 C2 50 29N 4 43W
Bognor Regis UK 15 G2 50 47N 0 41W
Bogotá Colombia 62 B7 4 38N 74 05W
Boise USA 58 B3 43 38N 116 12W
BOLIVIA 62 C5
Bologna Italy 36 B2 44 30N 11 20E
Bolton UK 13 G2 53 35N 2 26W
Bonar Bridge *tn.* UK 11 D3 57 53N 4 21W
Bonn Germany 34 C4 50 44N 7 06E
Bootle UK 13 F2 53 28N 3 00W
Bordeaux France 34 B3 44 50N 0 34W
Borneo *i.* Indonesia/Malaysia 45 D2/D3 1 00N 113 00E
Bornholm *i.* Denmark 32 E2 55 02N 15 00E
Boscastle UK 14 C2 50 41N 4 42W
BOSNIA-HERZEGOVINA 34/35 D3
Boston UK 15 G4 52 29N 0 01W
Boston USA 59 F3 42 20N 71 05W
BOTSWANA 53 C1
Bournemouth UK 14 F2 50 43N 1 54W
Bracknell UK 15 G3 51 26N 0 46W
Bradford UK 13 H2 53 48N 1 45W
Braemar UK 11 E3 57 01N 3 23W
Brahmaputra *r.* India/Bangladesh 42 C2 27 00N 94 00E
Braintree UK 15 H3 51 53N 0 32E
Brampton UK 13 G3 54 57N 2 43W
Brásilia Brazil 62 E5 15 45S 47 57W
Brasov Romania 35 E3 45 39N 25 35E
Bratislava Slovakia 34 D3 48 10N 17 10E
Bray RoI 17 E3 53 12N 6 06W
BRAZIL 62 B6/F6
Brazilian Highlands Brazil 62 E5 17 00S 44 00W
Brazzaville Congo 52 B2 4 14S 15 14E
Brechin UK 11 F2 56 44N 2 40W
Brecon UK 14 D3 51 57N 3 24W
Brecon Beacons *mts.* UK 14 D3 51 53N 3 30W
Bremen Germany 34 C4 53 05N 8 48E
Brent UK 15 G3 51 34N 0 17W
Brentwood UK 15 H3 51 38N 0 18E
Bréscia Italy 36 B3 45 33N 10 13E
Bressay *i.* UK 10 G6 60 08N 1 05W
Brest France 34 B3 48 23N 4 30W
Brest Belarus 33 F2 52 08N 23 40E
Bridgend UK 14 D3 51 31N 3 35W
Bridgnorth UK 14 E4 52 33N 2 25W
Bridgwater UK 14 E3 51 08N 3 00W
Bridlington UK 13 H3 54 05N 0 12W
Bridport UK 14 E2 50 44N 2 46W
Brigg UK 13 J2 53 34N 0 30W
Brighton UK 15 G2 50 50N 0 10W
Brisbane Australia 67 F3 27 28S 153 03E
Bristol UK 14 E3 51 27N 2 35W
Bristol Channel UK 14 C3/D3 51 20N 3 50W
Brixham UK 14 D2 50 23N 3 30W
Brno Czech Republic 34 D3 49 13N 16 40E
Broadford UK 11 C3 57 14N 5 54W
Brodick UK 11 C1 55 35N 5 09W
Bromley UK 15 H3 51 31N 0 01W
Bromsgrove UK 14 E4 50 20N 2 03W
Bromyard UK 14 E4 52 11N 2 30W
Brora UK 11 E4 58 01N 3 51W
Brough UK 13 G3 54 32N 2 19W
BRUNEI 45 D3
Brussels Belgium 34 C4 50 50N 4 21E
Bucharest Romania 35 E3 44 25N 26 07E
Buckfastleigh UK 14 D2 50 29N 3 46W
Buckhaven UK 11 E2 56 11N 3 03W
Buckingham UK 15 G3 52 00N 1 00W
Budapest Hungary 35 D3 47 30N 19 03E
Bude UK 14 C2 50 50N 4 33W
Bude Bay UK 14 C2 50 50N 4 40W
Buenos Aires Argentina 63 D3 34 40S 58 30W
Buffalo USA 59 F3 42 52N 78 55W
Builth Wells UK 14 D4 52 09N 3 24W
Bujumbura Burundi 52 C2 3 22S 29 19E
Bukhara Uzbekistan 40 D4 39 47N 64 26E
Bulawayo Zimbabwe 53 C1 20 10S 28 43E
BULGARIA 35 E3
Buncrana RoI 16 D5 55 08N 7 27W
Bungay UK 15 J4 52 28N 1 26E
Burgas Bulgaria 35 E3 42 30N 27 29E
BURKINA 52 A3
Burnley UK 13 G2 53 48N 2 14W
Burry Port UK 14 C3 51 42N 4 15W
Bursa Turkey 35 E3 40 12N 29 04E
Burton upon Trent UK 14 F4 52 48N 1 36W
BURUNDI 52 C2
Bury UK 13 G2 53 36N 2 17W
Bury St. Edmunds UK 15 H4 52 15N 0 43E
Bute *i.* UK 11 C1 55 50N 5 05W
Buxton UK 14 F5 53 15N 1 55W

C

Cabinda *province* Angola 52 B2 5 00S 12 00E
Cádiz Spain 34 B2 36 32N 6 18W
Caernarfon UK 14 C5 53 08N 4 16W
Caernarfon Bay UK 14 C5 53 05N 4 30W
Caerphilly UK 14 D3 51 35N 3 14W
Cágliari Italy 36 A1 39 13N 9 08E
Caha Mountains RoI 17 B1 51 40N 9 40W
Cairn Gorm *mt.* UK 11 E3 57 07N 3 40W
Cairngorms *mts.* UK 11 E3 57 10N 3 30W
Cairns Australia 67 E4 16 54S 145 45E
Cairo Egypt 52 C4 30 03N 31 15E
Calais France 34 C4 50 57N 1 52E
Calgary Canada 58 B4 51 05N 114 05W
Cali Colombia 62 B7 3 24N 76 30W
California *state* USA 58 B2 35 00N 119 00W
Callander UK 11 D2 56 15N 4 13W
Calligarry UK 11 C3 57 02N 5 58E
Calne UK 14 E3 51 27N 2 00W
Camberley UK 15 G3 51 21N 0 45W
CAMBODIA 45 C4
Camborne UK 14 B2 50 12N 5 19W
Cambrian Mountains UK 14 D4 52 15N 3 45W
Cambridge UK 15 H4 52 12N 0 07E
CAMEROON 52 B3
Cameroun, Mount Cameroon 52 B3 4 13N 9 10E
Campbeltown UK 11 C1 55 26N 5 36W
Campos Brazil 63 E4 21 46S 41 21W
Campsie Fells *hills* UK 11 D2 56 00N 4 15W
CANADA 57 C3/G3
Canary Islands Spain 52 A4 28 30N 15 10W
Canberra Australia 67 E2 35 17S 149 09E
Cannock UK 14 E4 52 42N 2 01W
Cantabrian Mountains Spain 34 B3 43 00N 5 30W
Canterbury UK 15 J3 51 17N 1 05E
Cape Town RSA 53 B1 33 56S 18 28E
CAPE VERDE 70
Caracas Venezuela 62 C8 10 35N 66 56W
Cardiff UK 14 D3 51 30N 3 13W
Cardigan UK 14 C4 52 06N 4 40W
Caribbean Sea Central America 62 B8/C8 15 00N 75 00W
Carlisle UK 13 G3 54 54N 2 55W
Carmarthen UK 14 C3 51 51N 4 20W
Carn Eige *mt.* UK 11 C3 57 22N 5 07W
Carnforth UK 13 G3 54 08N 2 46W
Carnoustie UK 11 F2 56 30N 2 44W
Carpathians *mts.* Europe 35 E3 49 00N 22 00E
Carrauntoohill *mt.* RoI 17 B1 52 00N 9 45W
Carrickfergus UK 16 F4 54 43N 5 49W
Cartagena Colombia 62 B8 10 24N 75 33W
Cartagena Spain 34 B2 37 36N 0 59W
Casablanca Morocco 52 A4 33 39N 7 35W
Caspian Sea Asia 40 B4/C5 41 00N 50 00E
Castlebar RoI 17 B3 53 52N 9 17W
Castlebay *tn.* UK 11 A2 56 57N 7 28W
Castleblaney RoI 16 E4 54 07N 6 44W
Castle Douglas UK 12 F3 54 57N 3 56W
Castleford UK 13 H2 43 44N 1 21W
Castletown Isle of Man 12 E3 54 04N 4 38W
Catânia Italy 36 C1 37 31N 15 06E
Caucasus *mts.* Asia 40 B5 43 00N 43 00E
Cavan RoI 16 D3 53 58N 7 21W
Cayenne French Guiana 62 D7 4 55N 52 18W
CENTRAL AFRICAN REPUBLIC 52 B3/C3
Ceuta *territory* Spain 34 B2 35 53N 5 19W
CHAD 52 B3/C3
Chad, Lake West Africa 52 B3 13 50N 14 00E
Changchun China 44 E7 43 50N 125 20E
Chang Jiang *r.* China 44 C6/D6 30 00N 116 00E
Changsha China 44 D5 28 10N 113 00E
Channel Islands British Isles 32 C1 49 30N 2 30W
Charlotte USA 59 E2 35 03N 80 50W
Chatham UK 15 H3 51 23N 0 32E
Cheadle UK 13 G2 53 24N 2 13W
Chelmsford UK 15 H3 51 44N 0 28E
Cheltenham UK 14 E3 51 54N 2 04W
Chengdu China 44 C6 30 37N 104 06E
Chennai India 41 F2 13 05N 80 18E
Chepstow UK 14 E3 51 39N 2 41W
Chernivtsi Ukraine 35 E3 48 19N 25 52E
Cheshunt UK 15 G3 51 43N 0 02W
Chester UK 13 G2 53 12N 2 54W